# Fusion Fitness

To my mother with love

# Fusion Fitness

## The All-round Fitness Programme

## Chan Ling Yap

Foreword by Stephanie Cook

A&C Black • London

First published 2002 by
A&C Black Publishers Ltd
37 Soho Square, London W1D 3QZ
www.acblack.com

ISBN  07136 6350 2

A CIP catalogue record for this book is available from the British Library.

Typeset in Goudy 10.5/14pt

Photographs by Grant Pritchard
Medical illustrations by Peter Gardiner
Exercise drawings by Jean Ashley
Page design by James Watson
Cover design by Jocelyn Lucas
Photo of Stephanie Cook © with thanks to Matchtight Ltd and the University of Bath
Photo of T'ai Chi session by Jimmy C.K. Lee
Photo of Fusion Fitness class by Tony Loftas
Models: Chan Ling Yap, Charlotte Steptoe, Christine Oliver and Lee Webb.

**Note**: Whilst every effort has been made to ensure that the content of this book is as technically accurate and as sound as possible, neither the author nor the publishers can accept responsibility for any injury or loss sustained as a result of the use of this material.

A&C Black uses paper produced with elemental chlorine-free pulp, harvested from managed sustainable forests.

Printed and bound in Great Britain by
Biddles Ltd, Guildford and Kings Lynn

# Contents

# Illustrations

## Tables and boxes

## Figures

**Chapter**

# Foreword

**Stephanie Cook**
MBE, BM, BCh (Oxon), MA (Cantab), Modern Pentathlon Olympic Gold Medallist, Sydney 2000, Modern Pentathlon European and World Champion 2001.

Sport and exercise are an integral part of many people's lives. In winning an Olympic gold medal I reached a pinnacle that few people ever achieve, but you do not have to compete at an Olympic Games to appreciate many of the benefits that exercise can bring to your life. More women than ever before are benefiting from exercise, not just in fitness regimes but in competitive sport as well. The Sydney Olympics in 2000 marked the first time that women had the chance to compete in modern pentathlon, even though it was introduced into the Olympic Games in 1912 by the founder of the modern Olympic movement, Baron Pierre de Coubertin. *Fusion Fitness* is geared particularly towards women, encouraging them to take a more active role in improving their health and lifestyle, and increasing their understanding of important issues.

The very nature of modern pentathlon, with its five diverse disciplines of shooting, fencing, swimming, show jumping and running, embodies the idea of the fusion of different sports and the necessity of a balanced approach. Through training for all these events I have come to learn the benefits of cross training. In a similar way this book integrates the best from a wide range of exercise and fitness techniques with input from different cultures around the world.

I have always led a very active life and am thankful for the good health and fitness that I enjoy. I have been very fortunate in having the opportunity to participate in a range of different sports from a young age and I have competed internationally at both cross-country running and modern pentathlon. At school I was no remarkable athlete, but I enjoyed a variety of sports from hockey and tennis to netball and athletics. It was not until I was studying medicine at university that I took sport in any way seriously when I was selected to row for the Cambridge University Women's Lightweight crew.

Through my medical studies I became particularly interested in the way in which the human body adapts with exercise, and the importance of having a sound scientific basis to any training regime along with a careful nutritional plan. The explanations of exercise and fitness in this book are based firmly in modern medical and scientific knowledge. The reader is able to understand the derivation of certain exercises, thereby encouraging the accurate accomplishment of them and helping to prevent injury.

My life has been enriched in many different ways by sport and exercise and the consequences of being fit and healthy. From a very early age exercise provides a fun way for children to develop social skills and learn the importance of teamwork. This social element continues into adulthood with many a lifelong friendship being built up through shared experiences, whether through competitive sport, attending exercise classes, or recreational jogging. Exercise is a vital means of improving your health and well being and also serves to improve confidence levels through looking good and feeling good about yourself. It also provides a great way of reducing stress levels, and the fitter you are the more energy you have for other activities too. By integrating some form of exercise into your daily routine the positive effects will extend into all areas of your life.

*Fusion Fitness* goes a step beyond many other books in the field and will meet the needs of both fitness instructors and students, as well as appealing to a wider general audience. The author is established as a specialist in the field of health and fitness, and this book reflects the wealth of experience that she has to offer. It provides a reliable source of information which is clearly presented and easy to understand, whilst retaining technical accuracy. This constitutes a major contribution towards the body of literature on health and fitness and fills a vital gap in the market.

# About the author

Chan Ling Yap, after gaining a PhD in the UK in 1973, returned to the University of Malaya to teach. In 1978 she was seconded to the Food and Agriculture Organization of the United Nations in Rome where she remained for 19 years, eventually becoming the senior commodity expert responsible for rice and Head of the Rice Commodity Group. While in Rome, she turned to exercise for relaxation. She explored a range of fitness regimes and even on missions to countries in the Far East, Latin America or Africa maintained her fitness routine. The international nature of her work enabled her to make contact with fitness disciplines from many parts of the world and appreciate their underlying philosophies and ideas. Of Chinese extraction, she also had knowledge of Eastern practices – her mother was guided for many years by a master of Chinese martial arts. Following the family's return to the UK in 1997, she combined her knowledge of the Eastern teachings and Western sports science to develop a new regime, Fusion Fitness.

# Preface

To have good health and to be fit is a blessing. A blessing, however, is not necessarily a right. Knowledge about how our body works, a balanced diet and regular exercise are vital to fitness and health.

When I first took up exercise, I went into it unquestioningly. I did what I was instructed to do because I was told that it would be good for me. There was little explanation offered as to why. I would be told: 'this is to improve the shape of your legs.' But I wanted to know why, in what way and how! Later as the number of available exercise regimes multiplied, and different methods of improving body shape and fitness grew, so did the confusion of ideas and methods, each one claiming to be better than the other, and, even worse, that the others were wrong.

My first exposure to the 'science' of exercise was when I enrolled for a fitness instructor's course on exercising to music. I learned a lot, but my need to know more and my efforts to acquire knowledge, beyond that needed to pass exams, were frequently frustrated by what information was available. I am convinced that people have a right to know more about their body, how it works and why they are being exercised in a particular way. This, I believe, places considerable responsibility on instructors who, like other health and sports professionals, should have a wider and deeper understanding of the body than many often do today. With improved technology in all aspects of our life, and with a more educated general public, surely there should also be improved knowledge of our body? We should be aware of how and why we are asked to exercise or move in a certain way, and what fitness and nutrition can do for us.

In the field of competitive sports, much headway has been made. In books on running, for example, the training regimes offered are well grounded in science and widely available. I was impressed with the book, *Keep on Running*, co-authored by Eric Newsholme, Tony Leech and Glenda Duester, on the science of training and performance.[1] It explains the whys and wherefores of training methods. Most serious runners I have met know about muscles and the rationale and science of their training regimes. That same knowledge is not so common when I speak to people attending keep-fit and exercise classes. Most attendees place great reliance on the instructor's knowledge, and there appears to be an unquestioning acceptance of what is taught. This may be because such classes are not competitive; there is no need to win which results in a relaxed attitude to what they are told to do. Nonetheless, the exercises that people perform in classes have an important impact on their health.

The implicit trust placed in fitness instructors or gym supervisors by people attending exercise classes or the gym has to be backed up by the knowledge that what is being practised is sound. I also believe that the boundaries of rigid disciplines, boundaries that are determined as much in the interests of commercialism as for the good of people, can and should be crossed. While most disciplines have something to offer, not everything offered is either safe or beneficial. Integration of the most successful elements from the various disciplines is, I believe, the best step forward.

This book is written for educators, fitness instructors, students in sports and a general audience interested in exercise and how to stay fit. It contains information about exercise and nutrition, the body and how it works. It takes the reader stage by stage through all the elements of fitness, from discussing cardio-vascular fitness, muscle strength, tone and body shape, to looking at endurance and energy levels, flexibility and acquisition of motor skills. At each stage the relevant muscles and bones are explained, as are the reasons for adopting the different body alignments – exercise is related at each stage to the relevant anatomy and the two are not regarded as separate fields of knowledge. In this way I am able to dispel many myths of the 'miracles' attached to exercise, by showing anatomically what can and cannot be achieved. I have also included a special chapter on exercising for the over-50s.

*Fusion Fitness* is based on over twenty years' experience as a participant in a wide variety of health and fitness classes and, in more recent years, as an instructor. It contains detailed illustrated exercises, many of which are original and devised especially for this volume. I have brought together my knowledge of a wide range of disciplines, choosing only the best and the safest elements from them to produce a 'fusion exercise regime' for health and fitness. There is still further to go and more improvements to be made, but the future of fusion fitness looks promising. I hope that this book will be a positive step towards encouraging the practice of informed and holistic exercise programmes.

## Acknowledgements

I would like to thank my husband, Tony Loftas, for the encouragement, support and help he has given me in writing the book. His background as a science writer and editor made his comments invaluable. Thanks go also to my children, Hsu Min and Lee for their understanding and support. Lee deserves a special mention for his patience in teaching me the software that I used for the initial drawing of the diagrams and figures. I would also like to thank my students for their interest and encouragement. My thanks also go to Charlotte Steptoe, Christine Oliver and Lee Webb for helping in the demonstration of the exercises. I would also like to thank Stephanie Cook for taking the word of my daughter, a fellow runner, that this was a serious book and agreeing to read the manuscript and write the foreword. Finally, I would like to thank Sonia Wilson, Charlotte Jenkins and the staff of A&C Black for their help and understanding in the production of this book.

# Introduction: exercise, past and present

Individuals have long used exercise to improve health and maintain physical fitness. The practice of yoga, which combines physical and mental disciplines to still the mind and body, dates back to pre-historic India. Records of ancient Chinese civilisations abound with examples of martial art forms for improving mental discipline and physical prowess. As in yoga, physical discipline is enmeshed with meditation and breath control. In Greek and Roman civilisations, pride of place was given to excellence in a wide range of sports. In ancient Greece, home of the Olympic Games, fitness and beauty of the human form were revered, and a regime of strict physical discipline was entrenched in the social structure of free born Greeks, particularly the ruling class.

In the past, athletic activities fell almost entirely within the domain of men. It was generally men who hunted or fought on behalf of the family or state. Consequently, they were the ones most concerned with honing the necessary skills. Even in the case of disciplines that involved meditation and prayer, men were the main participants. The original sites of many martial art forms in China were the monasteries. In ancient India, gurus in yoga practices were predominantly men.

Historically, women's role in the home and in the wider society did not encourage the pursuit of, or reverence for, physical activity *per se*. A few examples exist of lady ninjas in the period of the Shogun rule in Japan; in Britain, Queen Boadacea is seen as the prototype female warrior; and in ancient China there are stories of female acrobats with martial skills. Such women are exceptions to the rule. The higher up in the social structure, the greater was the propensity to regard women as adornments. Jewellery, dress and make-up played a central role in beauty rather than athletic skills; the acquisition of the genteel arts of music, painting and embroidery were seen as all important for the well-bred woman. This demarcation between men and women resulted in a concept of beauty where muscles and a toned body were admired in men but not in women. The female form was rounder and softer.

This long-held perception of beauty still lingers on today in some societies and cultures, but on the whole the twentieth century has witnessed a profound change in what represents feminine beauty.

Industrial development and the inclusion of women in the workforce, together with emancipation, have been the engines of this change. Work outside the home provided women with income. What they should and could do, how they looked and dressed, altered as they adapted to a new way of life determined increasingly by themselves. Medical advances, including control over their fertility, and improved lay knowledge of what constitutes good health have provided additional stimulus to the evolution of a new definition of beauty. Out went the idea that physical helplessness meant femininity. Leanness is preferred to rotundity as people realise the adverse impact on health of being overweight. Even in the case of make-up, which remains important, radical changes have taken place with more emphasis on effects that reflect health.

Today, beauty is increasingly equated with good health and fitness. Globalisation has blurred the definition of what constitutes beauty. Now all men and women can be beautiful: to feel beautiful is to be so. Feeling beautiful comes from within and touches upon everything that a person does. It is the ability to exert control over the body, to move well and painlessly, to perform daily tasks efficiently and effectively. In brief, it is to be fit.

Today, both men and women pursue and participate equally in athletic events. Nowhere is this seen more clearly than in the Olympics. When first celebrated in Greece in 776 BC, women were not allowed to participate, either as competitors or spectators. It was not until 1900, in Paris, that women first participated at the Olympics and then only in golf and lawn tennis. In 1908 in London, just 36 women took part out of a total of over 2000 athletes. The first post-war Olympics, held in London in 1948, had 385 women competitors out of a total of 4000 athletes. Twenty years later the number had risen to 800, just 12 per cent of the competitors. By the 2000 Olympic Games, in Sydney, Australia, the number of women had risen to 3906, 38 per cent of the total number of competitors (see below). Equally significant

## Women take to the Olympic Games

|  |  | Male competitors | Female competitors | Total |
|---|---|---|---|---|
| Atlanta 1996 |  | 7061 | 3683 | 10744 |
| Sydney 2000 |  | 6416 | 3906 | 10321 |
| Change per cent |  | –9 | +6 | –4 |
| Individuals' medal tally: |  |  |  |  |
| 2000 | GOLD | 103 | 56 | 159 |
| Olympics | SILVER | 38 | 42 | 80 |
|  | BRONZE | 21 | 21 | 42 |

The progress of women in the Olympic Games reflects a changing emphasis among women in favour of fitness and competitive sports.

are the events now open to women, which include the modern pentathlon, weight lifting, hammer, pole vault and water polo.

The advances in sports science and training regimes do not appear to have influenced the general public to any great extent. While virtually everyone appears to agree on the importance of being fit, relatively few people exercise regularly or pursue physical activity of any sort. We have a strange paradox where parallel to ever greater athletic achievement, the population at large has probably never been so lacking in fitness.

The Allied Dunbar National Fitness Survey, published in the UK in 1992, indicated that one in six people led a sedentary life.[2] They had not undertaken a physical activity continuously for more than 20 minutes in the previous four weeks. Slightly over 30 per cent of men and two-thirds of women had difficulties in walking up a gentle slope at a moderate pace of three miles per hour. This finding, in smaller proportions, extended even to individuals between 16 and 24 years of age. Perhaps even more alarming were the numbers, even among the relatively young, who had difficulties in performing ordinary activities such as getting up from a couch and walking up the stairs.

More recent findings of the increasing number of people who are obese and the number of young people abusing alcohol add little optimism for an improvement in the malaise that seems to have gripped the population at large. The British Heart Foundation reported in 2002 that some 37 per cent of all coronary heart disease in the UK is caused by inactivity.[3] About a third of the adult population in the UK do not undertake even 30 minutes of physical activity a week. For many, pursuit of the lean look means special diets and even starvation rather than sensible exercise. The results can be anorexia, bulimia and vacillating weight losses and gains.

The contrast between the progress made in competitive sports and that of the general public results from a number of causes. Probably chief among them is a misconception of what exercise entails. Many think that exercise is a vigorous physical activity that has to be pursued separately and is therefore ruled out by work commitments, children and economic as well as time constraints. This is certainly inaccurate. Exercise is just activities that involve the use of muscles and increases the metabolism of the body. It can be easily incorporated into daily life. Moreover, if exercise is pursued for health, moderation rather then vigour is often the answer: brisk walks may well be a better option than running or even jogging.

Exercise includes a wide range of activities and is not synonymous with sports. Understanding the different forms of exercise and the different components of fitness is important in designing and selecting the exercise programme suited to the individual. Knowing what your aims are in exercise and what the different exercises can do are also important. Education is vital, both for instructors to give their best and for the student to get the best.

You need to know how your body works, what it needs, what fitness means and how to achieve it. What are the benefits of the different fitness components and exercise regimes?

What can be achieved and what cannot be changed? How do you systematically exercise your muscles? How can you tackle common 'problem areas' such as a flabby stomach? In the search for solutions I have taken a 'fusion approach', selecting and combining the best from East and West, to provide a balanced exercise regime that meets the present day needs for fitness and a release from the stress of modern life. Last, but not least, I have restored the place of eating and enjoying a varied diet back where it belongs in the spectrum of fitness and health!

# In search of fitness and its benefits for you

At its simplest, fitness means having the capacity to perform activities without exhaustion. This capacity, often taken for granted when young, is not easy to maintain throughout life. Fitness requires:

- strength to provide the force needed for pushing, lifting, pulling, walking, running and similar activities

- endurance to maintain effort long enough to finish a task and even go on to others

- flexibility to attain or maintain the full range of movements that the body should be able to do such as twisting, bending and reaching

- motor skills to enable the body to respond efficiently and effectively to external stimulus

- circulatory (cardio-vascular) and respiratory efficiency to sustain these activities and for recovery after such efforts

## A balanced fitness programme

A well-balanced programme should include training components for the achievement of these five goals. If a particular fitness programme does not cover all of them, it should be complemented with activities necessary to provide the balance.

To increase strength requires working with resistance which can be provided using your own body or weights. In floor press-ups, for example, the resistance or weight is provided by your body. The level of resistance can be adjusted to meet personal needs and capacity. Press-ups from a kneeling position involve less resistance than if they are carried out with straight legs pivoting on your toes.

Strength development with body resistance: box press-ups (A) provide less body resistance than full press-ups (B) where the arm and chest muscles take on the full weight of the body (see overleaf). Strength development with weights (C): the heavier the weights, the greater the resistance (see overleaf).

A  Box press-ups

**B  Full floor press-ups**

**C  Training with weights**

Endurance is built-up by increasing the number of repetitions and hence the duration of an activity.

Improving flexibility involves both stretching muscles and mobilising the joints. When stretching the hamstring, the knee joint is mobilised; stretching out the inner thigh muscles moves the hip joint.

Improvement in motor skills comes from practice. Generally, exercises performed in a class, such as aerobics, step and line dancing, provide a good forum for their development because participants have to follow the instructor. Initially, responses may be slow but these should improve with experience because the body can be trained to move in a coordinated manner in response to signals received from the brain's motor nervous system. Exercise trains the eye and the nervous network to be alert. The development of motor skills is often neglected, which is unfortunate since with age they decline. Motor skills can only be maintained if nerve cells receive repeated stimulation. Sports that encourage motor skill and reflex development include boxing, fencing, tennis, badminton and taekwan do.

A structured cardio-vascular work-out is essential. Effected primarily through aerobic activities, it should aim to raise the heart rate gradually from its resting rate to one above normal. The heart is a muscular organ. Like any muscle it can be strengthened by being exercised and put to work. But herein lies the tricky part. How hard should it be put to work?

At rest, the pulse or heart rate of an average person measures around 60 to 70 beats per minute. Theoretically, the maximum heart rate that a normal healthy person could work toward is 220 minus his/her age. This is known as the personal maximum heart rate. In other words, if you are 40 years old, then *the personal maximum heart rate* would be 180 beats per minute. If you have not done any sports before or have not exercised for some time, even if you have taken a holiday where you have done little, this must be substantially moderated. It would be advisable, for example, to work towards 60 per cent of the personal maximum heart rate or, in the case of the above example of a 40 year old, start with a target heart rate of about 110 beats per minute. Over a period of weeks of regular training of 3–4 times a week, this could be gradually raised to no more than 80 per cent of the personal maximum heart rate, in this case, around 145 beats per minute (see Chapter 3, section on energy systems).

A different method, called the Karvonen formula, is used in the US to determine the target heart rate. In this formula, the resting heart rate is deducted from the personal maximum heart rate. This gives the reserve heart rate. Multiply this by the intensity at which you wish to work and add it to the resting heart rate. Thus, for a 40 year old man, the personal maximum heart rate is 180 (220 minus 40). If his resting heart rate is 70, then his reserve heart rate is 110 (180 minus 70). Training at 60 per cent intensity, the target heart rate would be 136 ([0.60 x 110] + 70). Training at 70 and 80 per cent intensity using this formula the heart rate would be 147 and 158 respectively.

The recommended effective aerobic training zone is normally 60 to 80 per cent of the personal maximum allowing for age. Working below 60 per cent is of little use while at above 80 per cent, fatigue sets in rapidly.

Very rarely, unless training for specific competitive sports, would anyone be encouraged to work towards their full personal maximum heart rate. It is preferable, with increased fitness, to increase the duration of the work-out within the same training zone. It is important to note that with increased fitness, the heart beat is not raised as much by a given intensity of work. Thus, for the individual to reach the same training heart rate, he/she will have to intensify the work-out. As a result, maintaining training within 60 and 80 per cent of the personal maximum heart rate automatically involves an increase in effort.

**A note of caution: these levels of exercise are only guidelines. It is much more important that you should feel comfortable, without any sense of giddiness, pain or forced exertion. A great deal of sensible judgement is required. No one but the individual involved can fine tune his/her own fitness programme.**

A good work-out is always based on the principle of overload, that is, giving the body more work and exertion than it is accustomed to, in order to improve fitness. Thus, the greater the fitness the greater the load. Inevitably, there should be some feeling of increased exertion. How much, as illustrated above, can be indicated by taking one's pulse rate. This is easy enough when working on the treadmill or the bicycle, but can be difficult in a class situation. A general guide in this instance is to work toward a comfortable level, where you are breathing hard without being breathless or giddy, and are able to continue the same level of effort. This is referred to as the *perceived exertion rate*, a scale developed by Gunner Borg.

According to this scale, the scale 6–7 or 'somewhat hard' is the minimum in order to work aerobically. If perceived exertion is at 10–11, or 'very hard', you should slow down. If at any point you feel that you have reached this stage, moderate your work-out. Walk briskly instead of jogging, leave out any bouncy or high-impact moves, reduce the vigour of arm movements, but do not stop. An abrupt halt at the peak of the work-

| Perceived rates of exertion | |
|---|---|
| Categories of exertion | Perceived exertion by rank |
| None | 0 |
| Extremely light | 1 |
| Quite light | 2–3 |
| Moderate | 4–5 |
| Somewhat hard | 6–7 |
| Hard | 8–9 |
| Very hard | 10–11 |
| Extremely hard | 12 |
| Maximum exertion | 13 |

out would lead to a 'pooling' of blood as the work-out on the calf muscles stops. This reduces the return of blood to your heart, which in turn reduces the amount of blood that can be pumped to the rest of the body, and results in giddiness or even fainting. The perceived rate of exertion is a convenient measure for those on medication or with unusually high or low resting heart rates, where the pulse rate is a less reliable indicator of effort.

In all work-outs, whether in a class or on your own, even when jogging in the countryside, always start with a warm-up. This should consist of movements to mobilise the joints, ensuring that the synovial fluid that cushions them is warm and giving the lubrication necessary to ease their movements. Muscles, ligaments and tendons are also gradually prepared for the increased exertion that is to follow. Then do a preparatory stretch. As the word suggests, this stretch prepares the body for bigger and possibly more vigorous movements in the main work-out. These preparatory stretches help reduce the incidence of sports injury that can occur if the body is launched into vigorous activity without sufficient preparation.

On completion of the work-out, again stretch all the muscles that have been involved, paying special attention to the hamstrings and the inner thigh muscles, holding them longer than in a preparatory stretch.

Muscles shorten with age, especially with sustained muscle contractions, as is inevitable in any work-out, and even in daily activities. Unattended, shortened muscles, especially the hamstring and the back muscles, can give rise to poor posture and the bent frame, commonly associated with ageing. Stretching at the end of a work-out also helps reduce muscle aches; it maintains the flexibility needed for ordinary day-to-day activities such as bending to tie shoe laces, soaping the back, reaching up and twisting. The reduction in muscle tightness and the greater mobility of joints that accompany stretches contribute significantly to reducing accidents that cause injury and breakage of bones.

Finally, before embarking on any programme of fitness, it is advisable to have a medical check-up and a fitness test. The major questions that you should clarify are listed in the questionnaire that I use for my Fusion Fitness classes. This kind of questionnaire is usually completed when joining a fitness club or centre. The objective is to establish if there are any problems that might require referral to a medical service for clearance before starting an exercise programme. If you have an instructor, keep him/her informed of any medical problems and injury, even after you have filled in a questionnaire. It is important to discuss your needs and objectives with your instructor.

## Fitness assessment and testing

Fitness testing is carried out in most fitness centres. It is simply a means to establish a baseline from which a person embarking on an exercise regime can work and progress. It also gauges health, already covered to some extent by the screening questionnaire, and fitness. In addition to establishing height, weight, blood pressure, resting pulse rate and body fat, tests for strength, stamina/endurance and flexibility will also be conducted. The tests conducted vary in

**Sample screening questionnaire**

# Screening Questionnaire

Name. . . . . . . . . . . . . . . . . . . . . . . . . . . . . . . . . . . . . . . . . Age . . . . . . . .
Address . . . . . . . . . . . . . . . . . . . . . . . . . . . . . . . . . . . . . . Female ☐   Male ☐
. . . . . . . . . . . . . . . . . . . . . . . . . . . . . . . . . . . . . . . . . . . . Phone:
. . . . . . . . . . . . . . . . . . . . . . . . . . . . . . . . . . . . . . . . . . . . Home: . . . . . . . . . . . . . . . . . . . . . . . .
. . . . . . . . . . . . . . . . . . . . Postcode . . . . . . . . . . . . . Office: . . . . . . . . . . . . . . . . . . . . . . .

Person to be contacted in case of accident:           Home: . . . . . . . . . . . . . . . . . . . . . . .
. . . . . . . . . . . . . . . . . . . . . . . . . . . . . . . . . . . . . . . . . . . . Office: . . . . . . . . . . . . . . . . . . . . . . .

**Please answer the following questions** (Please tick appropriate box or boxes)

1. If you already exercise regularly, please state type and frequency of exercise . . . . . . . . . . . . . . .
. . . . . . . . . . . . . . . . . . . . . . . . . . . . . . . . . . . . . . . . . . . . . . . . . . . . . . . . . . . . . . . . . . . .

|  | NO | *YES/UNSURE |
|---|---|---|
| 2. Have you ever had any injury, illness, back or joint condition that may be aggravated by vigorous exercise? | ☐ | ☐ |
| 3. Have you ever had: arthritis, asthma, diabetes, epilepsy, hernia, dizziness, gout, circulation problems or an ulcer? | ☐ | ☐ |
| 4. Have your mother, father, brother or sister had any heart problem prior to age 60? | ☐ | ☐ |
| 5. Have you ever had a heart condition, high blood pressure, rheumatic fever, stroke, high cholesterol, palpitations, murmers or chest pains? | ☐ | ☐ |
| 6. Are you now or have you recently been pregnant? If yes, please state number of months into or since pregnancy: _____ months. | ☐ | ☐ |
| 7. Are you taking any medicine prescribed by a medical practitioner? | ☐ | ☐ |

*If you have ticked any yes/unsure box you should check with your doctor before starting any exercise programme.

**Please note**: You are responsible for your own health and safety. Should your health status change, please seek medical advice and inform me.

**What benefits do you want from exercise?** (Please tick appropriate box or boxes.)

☐ WEIGHT MANAGEMENT       ☐ IMPROVED CARDIO-VASCULAR SYSTEM       ☐ SOCIAL ENJOYMENT
☐ IMPROVED MUSCLE TONE    ☐ IMPROVE OR MAINTAIN OVERALL FITNESS   ☐ GOOD HEALTH
☐ OTHERS (PLEASE SPECIFY) . . . . . . . . . . . . . . . . . . . . . . . . . . . . . . . . . . . .
. . . . . . . . . . . . . . . . . . . . . . . . . . . . . . . . . . . . . . . . . . . . . . . . . . . . . . . . . . . . . . . . . . . .

**General advice on exercise**

1. Do not eat for at least two hours before exercise.
2. Drink moderate quantities of water throughout the work-out.
3. Wear appropriate footwear and clothes.
4. Work out at a sensible pace: to improve fitness, exercise at least three times per week.

I have completed the **fusion fitness** Screening Questionnaire and I understand the advice and accept the conditions detailed above.

Signed . . . . . . . . . . . . . . . . . . . . . . . . . . . . . . . . . . .        Date. . . . . . . . . . . . . . . . . . . . .

complexity depending on the activity to be pursued. The following are some of the measures most commonly used to assess fitness.

# Weight, height and body mass index

The measurement of weight and height is normally used to gauge whether a person deviates from the 'ideal body weight', and whether weight loss or gain should be pursued. Someone can be said to be obese when their weight exceeds by 20 per cent or more the standard 'weight for height' table (see below). However, this method is only broadly indicative of whether a person has excess weight or not. This is because the weight for height measures do not reveal the amount of body fat or the body composition. Since muscles weigh more than fat, being heavy does not necessarily indicate excess weight. Furthermore, the tables are usually computed for insurance purposes, and like most actuarial data are 'population averages' based on data drawn from a large sample of people. Therefore, height and weight measures are usually supplemented by measurements of Body Mass Index (BMI) and assessments of body fat.

The BMI is calculated by dividing the body weight in kilograms by the square of the height in metres. The table opposite provides readings of BMI for different height and weights. To read

## Weight and height index[4]

| | Men | | | | Women | | |
|---|---|---|---|---|---|---|---|
| Height (cm) | Small | Medium (Kgs) | Large | Height (cm) | Small | Medium (Kgs) | Large |
| 157.5 | 60 | 62 | 65 | 147.5 | 48 | 52 | 57 |
| 160 | 60 | 63 | 67 | 150 | 49 | 53 | 58 |
| 162.5 | 61 | 64 | 68 | 152.5 | 50 | 54 | 59 |
| 165 | 62 | 65 | 69 | 155 | 51 | 55 | 60 |
| 167.5 | 63 | 66 | 70 | 157.5 | 52 | 57 | 62 |
| 170 | 64 | 67 | 72 | 160 | 53 | 58 | 63 |
| 172.5 | 65 | 69 | 74 | 162.5 | 54 | 60 | 65 |
| 175.5 | 67 | 70 | 75 | 165 | 56 | 61 | 66 |
| 178 | 68 | 71 | 77 | 167.5 | 58 | 62 | 68 |
| 180.5 | 69 | 73 | 78 | 170 | 59 | 64 | 70 |
| 183 | 70 | 74 | 80 | 172.5 | 60 | 65 | 71 |
| 185.5 | 72 | 76 | 82 | 175 | 62 | 66 | 73 |
| 188 | 73 | 78 | 84 | 178 | 63 | 68 | 74 |
| 190.5 | 75 | 79 | 86 | 180.5 | 64 | 69 | 75 |
| 193 | 77 | 81 | 88 | 183 | 66 | 70 | 77 |

the table, find the appropriate height in the left column and move across the row to the weight that most represents you. The number at the top is the BMI for that height and weight. For middle-aged adults, BMIs ranging from 20 to 27 fall within the desirable range. BMIs over 27 indicate overweight and those above 29 indicate obesity. For the BMI of body weight and height in imperial measurements see Appendix 1. The BMI is an improvement over weight for height indicators because it is based on an individual's body mass rather than on a sample of people, but it still does not provide a measure of the fatness or leanness of the body.

# Body fat

A more accurate guide to ideal weight and 'fatness' is to take a direct measurement of body fat. The average fat content of a young, healthy adult male is 10–15 per cent and for a young healthy woman, 18–25 per cent. The higher the age, the greater the fat content. Therefore an

## Determining your body mass index (BMI)

| BMI (kg/m²) | 19 | 20 | 21 | 22 | 23 | 24 | 25 | 26 | 27 | 28 | 29 | 30 | 35 | 40 |
|---|---|---|---|---|---|---|---|---|---|---|---|---|---|---|
| Height (cm) | | | | | | Body Weight (kg) | | | | | | | | |
| 147 | 41 | 44 | 45 | 48 | 50 | 52 | 54 | 56 | 59 | 61 | 63 | 65 | 76 | 87 |
| 150 | 43 | 45 | 47 | 49 | 52 | 54 | 56 | 58 | 60 | 63 | 65 | 67 | 78 | 90 |
| 152 | 44 | 46 | 49 | 51 | 54 | 56 | 58 | 60 | 63 | 65 | 67 | 69 | 81 | 93 |
| 155 | 45 | 48 | 50 | 53 | 55 | 58 | 60 | 62 | 65 | 67 | 69 | 72 | 84 | 96 |
| 157 | 47 | 49 | 52 | 54 | 57 | 59 | 62 | 64 | 67 | 69 | 72 | 74 | 87 | 99 |
| 160 | 49 | 51 | 54 | 56 | 59 | 61 | 64 | 66 | 69 | 72 | 74 | 77 | 89 | 102 |
| 163 | 50 | 53 | 55 | 58 | 61 | 64 | 66 | 68 | 71 | 74 | 77 | 79 | 93 | 105 |
| 165 | 52 | 54 | 57 | 60 | 63 | 65 | 68 | 71 | 73 | 76 | 79 | 82 | 95 | 109 |
| 168 | 54 | 56 | 59 | 62 | 64 | 67 | 70 | 73 | 76 | 78 | 81 | 84 | 98 | 112 |
| 170 | 55 | 58 | 61 | 64 | 66 | 69 | 72 | 75 | 78 | 81 | 84 | 87 | 101 | 116 |
| 173 | 57 | 59 | 63 | 65 | 68 | 72 | 74 | 78 | 80 | 83 | 86 | 89 | 104 | 119 |
| 175 | 58 | 61 | 64 | 68 | 70 | 73 | 77 | 80 | 83 | 86 | 89 | 92 | 107 | 122 |
| 178 | 60 | 63 | 66 | 69 | 73 | 76 | 79 | 82 | 85 | 88 | 92 | 94 | 110 | 126 |
| 180 | 62 | 65 | 68 | 71 | 75 | 78 | 81 | 84 | 88 | 91 | 94 | 98 | 113 | 130 |
| 183 | 64 | 67 | 70 | 73 | 77 | 80 | 83 | 87 | 90 | 93 | 97 | 100 | 117 | 133 |
| 185 | 65 | 68 | 72 | 75 | 79 | 83 | 86 | 89 | 93 | 96 | 99 | 103 | 120 | 137 |
| 188 | 67 | 70 | 74 | 78 | 81 | 84 | 88 | 92 | 95 | 99 | 102 | 106 | 123 | 141 |
| 191 | 69 | 73 | 76 | 80 | 83 | 87 | 91 | 94 | 98 | 102 | 105 | 109 | 127 | 145 |
| 193 | 71 | 74 | 78 | 82 | 86 | 89 | 93 | 97 | 100 | 104 | 108 | 112 | 130 | 149 |

upward adjustment of some 10 per cent might be made to older individuals to reflect this, although, from a health perspective, such an adjustment may not necessarily be desirable.

While direct measurement has the potential to provide the most accurate assessment of body fat, the technologies available for taking such measurements have limitations. The most common technique is to measure skinfold thickness using callipers in the area of the biceps, triceps, back – just below the scapula (subscapular), top of the hip (suprailiac) and the thighs. This measure, however, can be inaccurate because skin fold callipers cannot open wide enough to measure total fat thickness in the case of the very obese. Moreover, the measure assumes that 50 per cent of body fat is located in subcutaneal tissues. This, however, is not necessarily so, because body form, nutrition and physical activity can influence how fat is distributed around the body.

## Pulse rate

The resting pulse rate is a good indicator of cardio-vascular fitness, because it shows the character and rate at which the heart contracts to pump blood to the lungs and the rest of the body. Pulse rates should be measured under calm conditions, using the pulse that can be felt on the radial artery of the wrist. Alternatively, the pulse which can be felt on the carotid artery in the neck just below the angle of the jaw can be used. The pulse is taken for either 6, 10 or 15 seconds and then multiplied by 10, 6 or 4 respectively to derive the beats per minute. The normal resting pulse rate is between 60 and 70 beats per minute.

## Blood pressure

The resting blood pressure of a person provides the pressure when the heart contracts (systolic phase) and relaxes (diastolic phase). Blood pressure outside the normal range indicates poor health and the possibility of cardio-vascular illness. A typical blood pressure for a young adult is 120 (systolic) over 70 (diastolic). The risk factor rises with blood pressure measuring 140/90 and more. Blood pressures measuring higher systolic and diastolic rates than 140/90 require medical clearance prior to exercise (see also Chapter 3, section on cardiac muscles). Medical clearance before exercise is also needed in cases of low blood pressure. The World Health Organization's classification of blood pressure is provided below.

| WHO classification of blood pressure | | |
|---|---|---|
| Classification | Systolic mm/Hg | Diastolic mm/Hg |
| Low | less than 90 | less than 60 |
| Normal | 90–139 | 60–89 |
| High normal/borderline hypertension | 140–160 | 90–95 |
| Above average | above 160 | above 95 |
| Note: mm/Hg refers to millimetres (mm) of mercury (Hg) | | |

## Muscular strength

Strength is measured by the force that can be exerted to undertake a physical task. Two measures are commonly used: handgrip and sit-ups (abdominal crunches). A handgrip dynamometer is used to measure handgrip strength.

## Stamina and endurance

Stamina is tested using several different measures. The number of abdominal crunches that can be executed is sometimes used. A 'step' test might be applied. The type of step test may vary from place to place but basically it requires the individual under test to step up and down on a step-box with alternate feet at a steady pace for a period of 3 minutes, after which the heart rate is measured and compared against a chart. The lower the heart beat after executing the steps, the greater the stamina. For a man, heart beats lower than 112 is generally rated excellent. For women, the figure is lower than 109. For both men and women, heart beats exceeding 136 are rated poor. The step test is a convenient and simple measure but its reliance on the maintenance of regular stepping frequency and variations in leg length and weight of people can all reduce the consistency of the results.

Step test

In determining cardio-respiratory endurance or stamina, the most common approach is to measure the oxygen uptake (the volume of oxygen inhaled) during exercise on a treadmill, rowing machine, bicycle or similar appliances used for aerobic activities.

## Flexibility

Flexibility tests can measure either static or dynamic flexibility. Static flexibility is determined by the extent muscles and joints can facilitate a movement, while dynamic flexibility refers to the ease of movement. Dynamic flexibility is important for exercises such as gymnastics and dance; static flexibility is important for yoga. Generally, only static flexibility is measured. A sit and reach technique is normally used to measure the flexibility of the back and hamstrings (A). These two muscles are generally a source of tightness. The further the reach, the greater the flexibility. B provides an

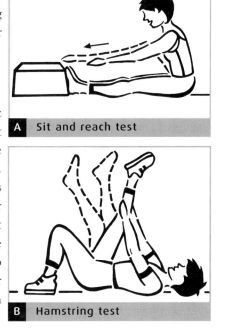
A Sit and reach test

B Hamstring test

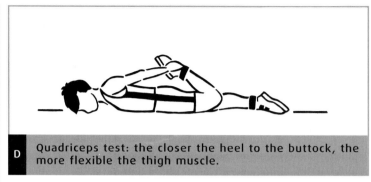

**D** Quadriceps test: the closer the heel to the buttock, the more flexible the thigh muscle.

**C** Shoulder test

alternative method for measuring the flexibility of hamstrings. Tests for shoulders and quadriceps are shown separately in C and D.

In C extending the arms behind the ears indicates greater flexibility, but arms held to the front show stiffness in the shoulders.

# Ready, steady, go!

Medical check-ups and fitness testing can seem daunting, but they are usually the prelude to years of safe and enjoyable activity that brings enormous benefits, keeping you mobile, active and young. Gaining strength, flexibility, endurance and coordination empowers you to do the things you wish to do, giving confidence and independence. It means moving better. Your posture improves so that you stand taller and reach out further. The body becomes toned and tauter. Your fatigue is reduced and your energy levels increase.

These benefits by themselves are sufficient to promote the feel-good factor. There is, however, much, much more to be gained as your muscles, bones, heart, lungs, circulatory system and body cells change in response to exercise. The efficiency and strength of muscles improve as the number of component muscle fibres rises; weight-bearing activities increase the density of bones, making them stronger and less prone to breakage; joints are more mobile; the heart and lungs become larger and stronger and better equipped to deal with the stress of modern living; and the skin improves with better circulation and respiration. Even the hormonal balance of the body is improved, bringing a tremendous sense of wellbeing.

# Understanding your body and its response to exercise

To understand and maximise the benefits of exercise, it is vital to understand how the body works. This helps to set realistic targets and objectives when setting out to improve performance, body shape and health.

## The skeleton

The human adult has a total of 213 bones (counting the fused bones in the sacrum [5] and coccyx [4] as individual bones). The bones are joined with ligaments and tendons to form a framework which supports the attached muscles and protects the soft tissues and internal organs. The cranium, for example, protects the brain; the ribs provide similar protection for the heart and lungs, as well as maintaining the chest cavity; the pelvis protects the reproductive organs; and the backbone encloses the spinal cord. This framework determines a person's basic shape.

The bony framework of the body consists of two major parts: the *axial skeleton* (87 bones) consisting of the skull, spine, ribs and sternum; and the *appendicular skeleton* (126 bones) consisting of two limb girdles – the shoulder and the pelvis, and the attached limb bones.

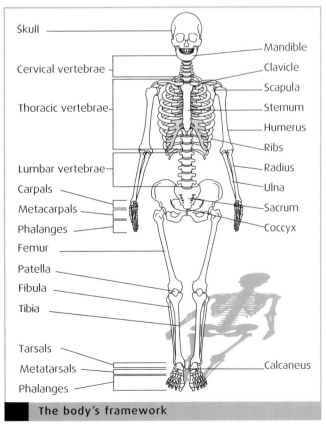

The body's framework

15

The shape and function of bones differ. Long bones, such as the humerus, ulna and radius in the arm and the femur, fibula and tibia in the leg, act as levers and are principal movers. Short bones, such as the patella (knee cap), tarsals (located in the foot) and carpals (located in the hands) have only restricted movement. Flat bones, which include the cranium, scapula, sternum and pelvis, have protective functions. Irregular bones such as the vertebrae provide support to the body. The vertebrae also have the vital job of protecting the spinal cord: each vertebra has a central passage through which the spinal cord runs. The spinal cord is a cylinder of nerve tissues and can be represented as a downward extension of the brain. Together, the brain and the spinal cord form the central nervous system which is responsible for, among other vital functions, the control of body movements.

## The spinal column

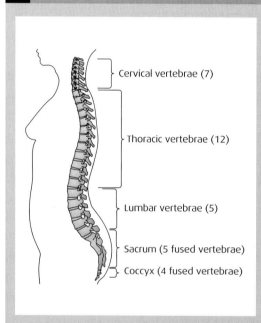

Cervical vertebrae (7)

Thoracic vertebrae (12)

Lumbar vertebrae (5)

Sacrum (5 fused vertebrae)

Coccyx (4 fused vertebrae)

The spine consists of 33 vertebrae grouped in three sections: the cervical vertebrae which support the head and neck; the thoracic vertebrae to which the ribs are attached; and the lower back consisting of the lumbar, the sacrum and the coccyx. Together, the lumbar, sacrum and coccyx form a stable centre for the body during movement.

The vertebrae are connected by facet joints which provide stability to the spine yet allow movement. Between the vertebrae are the intervertebral discs, tough fibrous cartilage discs that help cushion the force of the body's movements. Injury to these discs results in pressure on the spinal nerves which, in turn, causes pain. The vertebrae are held together by ligaments. Bony protrusions from the vertebrae provide sites for the attachment of muscles. The spinal cord, a network of nerve tissues, runs within the spinal column. Spinal nerves pass from the spinal cord to the body through gaps between the vertebrae.

Normally, the spine curves gently forward in the cervical region, slightly backward in the thoracic region and slightly forward in the lumbar region. The spinal structure limits the ability of the body to bend backwards, but allows it to bend forward easily. When this natural curvature is unbalanced, as a result of poor posture, weak abdominal muscles or because of congenital defects or bone diseases, back disorders result and these are often extremely painful. Lordosis, excessive inward curvature of the lower back, and kyphosis, the excessive rearward curvature of the upper spine, are both associated with poor posture, excess weight and weak abdominal muscles.

Correct body alignment is essential in our daily activities and in exercise if spinal disorders are to be avoided. Back pain is one of the most common afflictions of modern society and affects almost everyone sometime during the course of their lives. You will find in the chapters on exercises that special emphasis is placed on maintaining correct alignment of the spine, particularly the lower back.

# Bones and their development

Bones are not inert: they provide a mobile framework on which muscles act to produce movements. The inner core of bones, the bone marrow, is the site of red and white blood cell production. Bones also store minerals, particularly calcium and phosphorus, that other parts of the body can draw upon when needed. The stronger the bones, the greater the strength and structure of the skeleton and its mobility. Exercise can contribute significantly to this.

Development of the skeleton is a lengthy process which starts in the womb and is only completed in early adulthood. Most bones begin to develop in the human embryo in the fifth or sixth week of pregnancy. By about seven weeks, the embryo will have the rudiments of most of the bones of the body, but at this early stage they are soft and flexible. Most of these structures are made of cartilage, but a few are only membranes. For example, some of the facial bones, most of the brain case and the collar bones start as membranes in the embryo. Around the eighth week, bone begins to form in the cartilage and membranes through the process of ossification. Special cells, osteoblasts, move out from centres in the cartilages and membranes depositing calcium carbonate and calcium phosphate, the main ingredients of bone.

By the time a baby is born much of the ossification is complete, but the bones are by no means completely formed. For example, there is a conspicuous soft spot, the fontanel, at the top of a new-born baby's head that persists for several months. If the skull bone were not flexible, babies would not be able to pass through the opening in their mother's pelvic girdle.

The formation of bone can be likened to a battle between the osteoblasts, which encourage the deposition of the bone minerals, and the osteoclasts which remove mineral from the bone. Bone is continuously being made and resorbed in response to hormonal secretions, including growth hormones, the sex hormones (oestrogen and testosterone), adrenal hormones and parathyroid and thyroid hormones. These hormones control the amount of calcium in the blood.

During the growth period, bone density increases, making the bone hard and resilient as a result of the hormonal stimulation of the osteoblast. Because the bones are rigid, they grow in specific areas that remain active after the rest of the bone has become completely ossified. The long limb bones, for example, have a growth disk near each end (the epiphyses) that enables the bone to lengthen during childhood growth. After adolescence, the disks also become ossified and bone growth ceases. Some parts of the skeleton, such as the external ears, the tip of the nose and the ends of bones where they meet to form a joint, remain as cartilage.

In their mid-thirties, people start to lose bone density. This loss of bone, known as osteoporosis, is a natural part of ageing. In contrast to the growth period, the osteoclasts appear to have the upper hand. By the age of 70 the male skeleton will have lost, on average, about 10 per cent of its bone, while the bone in the female skeleton will have been reduced by about 25 per cent. The process is particularly fast in women after the menopause because of the loss of oestrogen. The reduction in bone density increases the brittleness of bones and their vulnerability to fracture. By the age of 75 about half of all women will have suffered a fracture as a result of osteoporosis.

The decrease in bone density can be slowed down by regular weight-bearing exercises such as walking, jogging, aerobics and dancing. These activities involve the skeletal framework bearing the body weight, in contrast to activities such as swimming and aqua-aerobics where the body's weight is offset by its buoyancy in water. The earlier in life that weight-bearing activities commence, the stronger the bones are likely to be because of the encouragement to bone formation. In addition, the thin membrane, the periosteum, that covers the bone and contains a network of blood and nerve vessels also benefits from the increased blood supply that results from regular physical activity.

# Joints

A joint is the junction between two or more bones. Joints feature very importantly, together with bones and muscles, in determining the type of movements that can be produced. Bones are joined together by ligaments, which are tough fibrous tissues that give joints stability. Ligaments are relatively inelastic and have a limited response to sudden movements at the joint. Sudden excessive movements can result in damage and a torn ligament can take at least 6 months and sometimes even years to repair. In some instances the damage may be permanent because ligaments have a poor blood supply, and as a result do not repair easily. Another fibrous cord, the tendon, is also involved in movement. Tendons consist of bundles of collagen

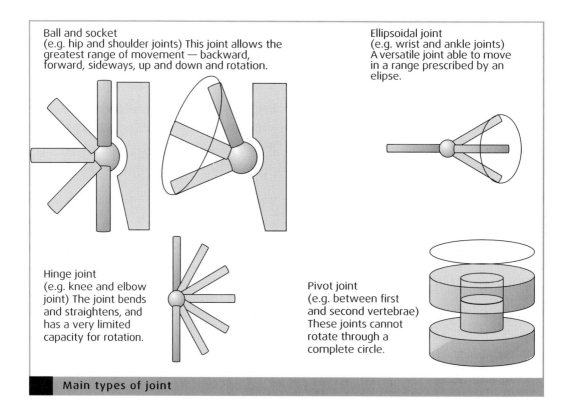

Ball and socket
(e.g. hip and shoulder joints) This joint allows the greatest range of movement — backward, forward, sideways, up and down and rotation.

Ellipsoidal joint
(e.g. wrist and ankle joints)
A versatile joint able to move in a range prescribed by an elipse.

Hinge joint
(e.g. knee and elbow joint) The joint bends and straightens, and has a very limited capacity for rotation.

Pivot joint
(e.g. between first and second vertebrae) These joints cannot rotate through a complete circle.

**Main types of joint**

(white fibrous protein) and join bone to muscle or muscle to muscle. They are strong and flexible, but inelastic. They can also be damaged by excessive sudden movements, but, because they have a blood supply, heal faster than ligaments.

Some joints such as the skull are fixed because the bones are fused or held together by collagen. Some joints, i.e. partially movable joints, allow only restricted movement. Included in this category are the ellipsoidal joints such as the wrist and ankle. They allow movement from side to side and up and down. Pivot joints allow only rotational movements. An example is the joint between the first cervical vertebra at the base of the skull which rotates around the second cervical vertebra. Mobile or movable joints include hinge joints, and ball and socket joints. Hinge joints, such as the elbows, knees, fingers and toes, allow bending and straightening. The elbow and knee also provide for limited rotation. Ball and socket joints allow the widest range of movements in all directions, including backwards and forwards, sideways and rotation (see opposite). Examples are the shoulder and the hip.

To facilitate movements, partially movable and movable joints are specially structured. The bone surface is coated with smooth cartilage to reduce friction and act as a shock absorber. The joint is enclosed by the joint capsule. This tough fibrous capsule is lined by the synovial membrane which produces a sticky fluid that acts as a lubricant where the bones meet. Each joint is surrounded by strong ligaments that support the joint, provide stability and prevent excessive movement. Movements are produced and controlled by muscles attached to the bone, usually via a tendon.

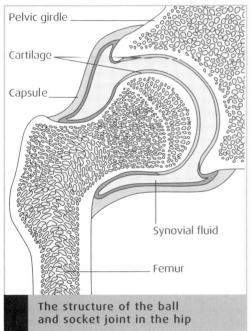

Pelvic girdle

Cartilage

Capsule

Synovial fluid

Femur

**The structure of the ball and socket joint in the hip**

It is important in any exercise regime to warm-up with mobilising movements that concentrate on the joints. The warming up process brings heat to the thick synovial fluid. Thinning of the synovial fluid helps to cushion impact and friction; the 'oiling effect' also helps increase the range of movements, preparing the ligaments and tendons for more strenuous activity.

# Muscles

Muscles consist of bundles of specialised cells that are capable of contracting and relaxing to create movement of the body or of organs within it. Three types of muscles exist in the body: *skeletal* or *striated muscle*, *smooth muscle* and *cardiac muscle*. Skeletal muscle is sometimes called voluntary muscle because, apart from reflex actions, it is subject to conscious control by the brain. Smooth muscle is often called involuntary muscle because it is not controlled consciously but responds to hormonal and involuntary nervous stimuli.

# Skeletal muscle

## How the skeletal muscle works

Skeletal muscles, as the name suggests, are linked to the skeleton of the body. There are some 600 of them and they are classified by the movements that they produce. The point where a muscle is attached to the more stable bone is generally referred to as the point of origin or attachment, while the point where the muscle connects with the movable bone is referred to as the point of insertion.

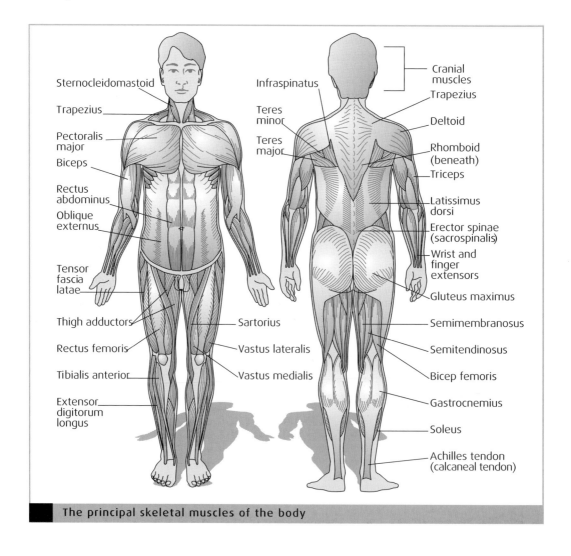

The principal skeletal muscles of the body

An *extensor muscle* extends or opens a joint. A good example is the *triceps*, a muscle situated at the back of the arm. It has three heads (hence its name) attached to corresponding points of origin, one in the *scapula* and two in the upper part of the *humerus*. The lower end of the triceps is attached to a large tendon which inserts into the *ulna* bone below the elbow joint. When the triceps contracts, the forearm straightens or extends.

A *flexor muscle* closes the joint. Keeping to the example of the arm, the *biceps* is a flexor muscle. This muscle has two points of origin, at the tip of the *coracoid process* in the scapula and the top of the scapula, respectively, and inserts into the *radius*. When the biceps contracts, the elbow bends bringing the forearm inward. Its contraction can also rotate the forearm.

Muscles responsible for moving a bone outward are classified as *abductors* and those that bring them inward are called *adductors*. The *deltoid*, the triangular muscle in the outer upper arm, and the muscles in the upper outer part of the thigh, the *tensor fascia latae*, are abductors. When they contract, they move the arm and leg respectively outward. The muscles in the upper inner thigh, the *adductor brevis, adductor longus* and *adductor magnus*, move the leg inward. Other adductor muscles include the *pectorals*, the chest muscles originating from the *sternum* and *clavicle* and inserting into the humerus, and the *teres major* and *teres minor*, originating from the edge of the scapula and inserting into the back of the humerus just below the shoulder. These work in conjunction with the *lattisimus dorsi* running from the spine to the humerus to move the arm inward.

Other categories of muscles include *levators* and *depressors* responsible, respectively, for raising and lowering, and *sphincter muscles* for constriction. The box overleaf gives basic information on the major muscle groups.

From the descriptions given it can be seen that individual muscles do not work alone. When the biceps contracts to move the forearm inward, it cannot then straighten on its own but will do so when the triceps, the opposing or antagonist muscle, contracts to extend the forearm. Thus, muscles lengthen via the action of the opposing muscle group. Movement is produced only when a muscle crosses a joint, in this case the elbow. A muscle may cross a number of joints before it reaches the site of its principal action. In order to prevent unwanted movements in the other joints, groups of muscles known as *synergist muscles* contract to stabilise them.

Muscles rely on contraction to produce movements. In other words, they pull, but they cannot push. In any single action there will be a muscle that is the prime mover (agonist), an opposing (antagonist) muscle that relaxes to support this move and synergist muscles (in the intermediate joints) that stabilise the action around the joints. Thus, in bending the forearm inward, the biceps is the prime mover or agonist and the triceps is the antagonist (see figure on p. 24), while in straightening the arm, the triceps is the prime mover and the biceps the antagonist.

## The skeletal muscles of the body

| Muscle | Origin | Insertion | Joints crossed | Movement |
|---|---|---|---|---|
| UPPER BODY Sternocleido-mastoid | Top of sternum and inner end of clavicle | Skull, mastoid process at back of head and behind ears | Neck | Flexes head drawing it towards shoulder; rotation of head |
| Biceps | Scapula | Radius | Shoulder/elbow | Flexion of forearm; supination of forearm, i.e. turn palm upwards |
| Triceps | Top and rear of humerus and edge of scapula | Ulna | Shoulder/elbow | Straightens forearm; extension of shoulder |
| Deltoids | Clavicle and the scapula | Humerus | Shoulder | Abducts or lifts shoulder away from the body, extends and flexes upper arm |
| Pectoralis major | Clavicle and sternum | Humerus | Shoulder | Adduction of humerus, moves upper arm inward across the body |
| Rectus abdominus | Pubis | Middle ribs, 5th, 6th and 7th | Pelvis and trunk | Pelvic tilt, trunk flexion |
| Transverse abdominus | Thoracic lumbar region of the spine (between iliac crest and 12th rib) | Pubis via internal obliques and rectus abdominus | Pelvis and trunk | Constricts and supports the abdomen and helps force air out of the lungs |
| External obliques | Eight lower ribs | Iliac crest | Pelvis and trunk | Flexes, rotates and bends trunk |
| Internal obliques | Iliac crest | 7th to 9th costal cartilages; lower fibres join the aponeurosis of the transverse abdominus and insert in the pubic crest | Pelvis and trunk | Flexes, rotates and side bends trunk |
| Erector spinae | Sacrum, ilium, lower spinous processes of the lumbar, lower ribs | Spinous processes stretching from 1st cervical to 5th lumbar | Trunk | Extension of back, lateral flexion, rotation of the vertebral column; lateral movement of the pelvis |
| Transverso-spinalis – multifidus | Laminae of vertebrae | Spinous process 2 or 3 vertebrae above | Trunk | Lateral flexion, rotation, extension/hyper-extension of spine |

## The skeletal muscles of the body – continued

| Muscle | Origin | Insertion | Joints crossed | Movement |
|---|---|---|---|---|
| UPPER BODY Rhomboids | Spinous processes, from 7th cervical and upper five thoracic vertebrae | Inner part of the scapula | Juncture of scapula, spine and upper ribs | Adduction of scapula towards the spine |
| Trapezius | Spinous processes from the base of skull (7th cervical vertebra) along the first to fifth thoracic spine down to the 6th to 12th thoracic vertebrae | Clavicle and upper and middle scapula | Juncture of scapula, spine, upper ribs and shoulder | Adducts, rotates and elevates scapula, laterally flexes neck |
| Latissimus dorsi | Spinous processes stretching from the six lower thoracic to the five lumbar vertebrae and the posterior crest of the ilium (pelvis) | Humerus | Shoulder | Pulls arm downward and backwards and rotates the humerus medially, i.e. draws the arm back and inward towards the body |
| LOWER BODY Iliopsoas/hip flexor | Stretching from front of 12th thoracic to 5th lumbar vertebra and front of ilium | Top inside of femur | Hip/pelvic joint | Flexes hip, lateral rotation of femur |
| Quadriceps: rectus femoris | Front of the ilium | Patella and tibia | Hip/pelvic joint and knee | Extension of knee, leg, flexion of thigh at the hip |
| Abductors: tensor fascia lata | Outer edge and front of ilium | Top, outer part of tibia | Hip/knee | Flexion, abduction and medial rotation of thigh |
| Tibialis anterior | Front, outer side of tibia, just below knee | Inner edge of foot, before big toe | Ankle | Dorsiflexion or flexing foot upwards |
| Gluteals: gluteus maximus | Back of the ilium and along sacroiliac joint | Top of femur | Hip/pelvic joint | Extension of thigh (lift leg to back), lateral rotation of leg |
| Hamstring | Ischium | Tibia | Knee | Flexes knee, extension of thigh |

## The skeletal muscles of the body – continued

| Muscle | Origin | Insertion | Joints crossed | Movement |
|---|---|---|---|---|
| LOWER BODY Adductors: adductus brevis, longus, magnus | Front part of pubic bone and lower hip bone | Femur stretching from hip to knee | Hip joint | Adduction of leg, hip flexion and lateral rotation of thigh |
| Gastrocnemius | Back of femur, just above knee | Achilles calcaneous/ heel bone | Knee/ankle | Knee flexion, plantar flexion (pointing of toes) |
| Soleus | Outside and back of tibia, just below knee | Achilles calcaneous/ heel bone | Ankle | Plantar flexion (pointing of toes) |

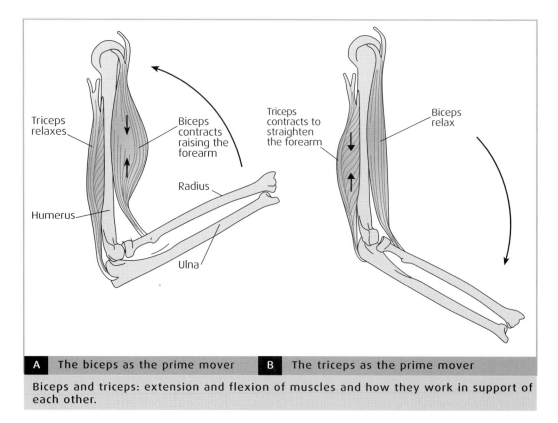

**A**   The biceps as the prime mover   **B**   The triceps as the prime mover

Biceps and triceps: extension and flexion of muscles and how they work in support of each other.

Understanding the points of origin, points of insertion and the joints/bones involved when contracting a muscle is essential for an instructor tailoring specific exercises on specific muscle groups. Not only does it help to target the muscles to be worked, it helps to reduce the strain that can occur from improper positioning of the body. The latter is often a result of inadequate understanding of the principles of muscle contraction, insertion and origin.

For example, full sit ups and 'stomach crunches' (raising the trunk by about 30 degrees), are performed to strengthen the stomach muscles, the *rectus abdominus*. If these movements are made with the legs extended straight out on the floor, there will be stress and strain on the lower back, because the *hip flexor/iliopsoas muscle* acts synergistically, contracting to stabilise the hip and allowing the trunk to come up. In doing so, it pulls the lower back and causes stress in the lumbar region. This stress can be avoided, however, if the exercise is performed with the legs bent. Bending the legs involves the iliopsoas and will stabilise the hip area *before* starting the trunk movement, thereby avoiding stress in the back that occurs when the muscles act simultaneously in an opposite direction. Even better would be to contract the *transverse abdominal muscles* as well, which would provide greater stability in the lower trunk and focus the exercise on the rectus abdominus. (A detailed, step by step, description of this exercise is given on p. 78–80 and p. 89.)

The principles governing the actions of muscles and the resulting body movements form the cornerstone of aerobic routines and fitness training. In brief, these movements are:

- *flexion* (e.g. bending the arm or leg)
- *extension* (e.g. straightening the arm or leg)
- *abduction* (e.g. lifting the arm or leg sideways away from the body)
- *adduction* (e.g. crossing the leg)
- *circumduction* (e.g. circling the arm)
- *pronation* (e.g. turning the foot or hand inward)
- *supination* (e.g. turning the foot or hand outward)
- *plantar flexion* (e.g. pointing the toes downward)
- *dorsi flexion* (e.g. flexing the foot to point the toes upwards)

These terms may seem rather technical but any one who has been to an aerobic class would easily recognise them in typical movements such as 'bicep curls' and 'hamstring curls' (flexion) or 'windmill arms' (circumduction). The 'grapevine' involves abduction, taking one leg to the side, and adduction, bringing the other leg inward. 'Squats' involve flexion of the thigh. 'Heel digs' are dorsi flexion, etc.

## How the fibres in muscles work

Skeletal muscles consist of bundles of muscle fibres composed of elongated cells enclosed in a tough sheath of tissue. Each end of a muscle is drawn out to form tendons which are attached to the tough membrane, the *periosteum*, that surrounds the bones of the skeleton. Muscles vary in size according to the number of bundles that they contain. A large muscle such as the *gluteus maximus* (the large powerful muscle in the buttocks) or the *rectus femoris* (the largest muscle in the *quadriceps*) will contain thousands of bundles of muscle fibres. A small muscle such as the triceps would contain far fewer bundles.

Each muscle fibre consists of smaller fibres or *myofibrils*, which contain alternating thick and thin microscopic filaments. The thick filament contains mainly the protein *myosin*, while the thin filament consists mainly of the protein *actin*. The alignment of the thick and thin filaments in bands accounts for the typical striated or striped appearance of these muscle fibres when viewed with a microscope. As a result, skeletal muscle is often referred to as striated muscle. The functional unit of these protein filaments which is responsible for muscular contraction is called a *sarcomere*.

Muscle contraction is produced when the brain sends out a signal that is relayed to the muscle fibre via nerve endings. The nerve impulse stimulates the muscle by releasing chemicals from the nerve endings. This starts a chain of reactions that results in the myosin and actin filaments sliding over each other in an action akin to the closing of an extendable ladder, with the filaments hooking on to each other. This shortens the sarcomere and so the muscle fibres contract.

The bigger the muscle the greater its strength, because of the larger number of fibres that can be brought into use. Lifting a small object requires the use of far fewer muscle fibres than when lifting large objects. Hence, if you were to lift a small plant pot, the number of muscle fibres you recruit would be much smaller than if you were to lift a big plant pot. This *recruitment* of muscle fibres can be learned and modified through experience.

Most of us are totally unaware of the process of brain, eye and muscle coordination that is involved routinely in controlling our movements and posture. It can

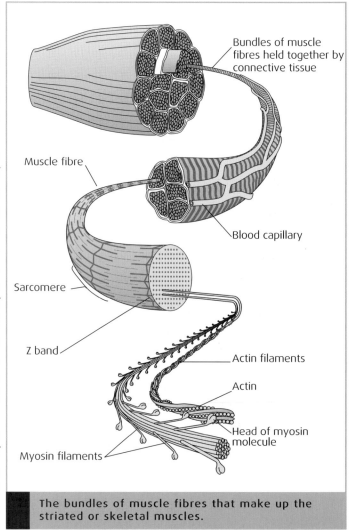

Bundles of muscle fibres held together by connective tissue

Muscle fibre

Blood capillary

Sarcomere

Z band

Actin filaments

Actin

Head of myosin molecule

Myosin filaments

The bundles of muscle fibres that make up the striated or skeletal muscles.

### Actin and myosin: how muscles work

Muscle fibres consist of myofibrils, which in turn are made up of two myofilaments, a thin one consisting mainly of the protein actin, and a thicker one made up mainly of the protein myosin. During muscle contraction, hook-like attachments between the filaments change, powered by chemical energy, sliding them together. The boundary between each contractile unit, known as a sarcomere, is called the Z-band which provides an anchorage for the myofilaments.

be very startling, therefore, if for some reason the strength required to move an object is wrongly judged. This can be demonstrated by a very simple experiment. Take two identical cans with lids, leave one empty and fill the other with sand. Put them on a table and ask an unsuspecting friend to pass you the filled can and then ask immediately afterward for the empty one. The recruitment of muscle fibres necessary to lift the first heavy can will have been registered in the brain. Invariably, with no contradictory visual or other clues the same force will be applied to the empty light can. As a result the hand and can will move quickly and involuntarily upward before the brain can correct its error.

It is difficult to repeat the experiment with the same individual or someone who has seen it done, even if the identical cans are rearranged while their backs are turned, such is the 'shock' of this failure in coordination. The next time you ask them to pass the cans, they will assess the weight of each one before lifting them. Of course, some experiences are deep-seated and require an effort to readjust as anyone who has walked down a stationary escalator or come ashore after a long sailing trip will know.

We are able to control and modify the actions of skeletal muscles because structures called *proprioceptors* provide feedback on the physical movement and changes in tension or force to the brain which can then send the appropriate stimuli to the muscles.

Essentially, there are three kinds of proprioceptors, although they can be sub-divided according to form and specific function:

- *neuromuscular* or *muscle spindles* which are embedded in the muscles
- *Golgi tendon organs* which lie close to where the muscle sheath attaches to the tendon

- *joint receptors* situated mainly in and near the articular capsules of joints, close to the Golgi tendon organs.

The muscle spindles, which lie parallel to the muscle fibres, provide feedback on the length of the muscle, and during movement they monitor the degree and speed with which it is being stretched. If the muscle is being overstretched the spindles signal the need to contract the muscle. The Golgi tendon organs monitor the force exerted on the tendons by the muscle at rest, but they become particularly active when it contracts. In contrast to the muscle spindles they signal the need for the muscle to relax in order to reduce the force being exerted. Both proprioceptors work together, the spindles regulating muscular tension to produce a smooth movement and the tendon organs regulating the force applied by the muscles to prevent injury and damage to the muscles, tendons and bones. The picture is completed by the joint receptors, which provide information

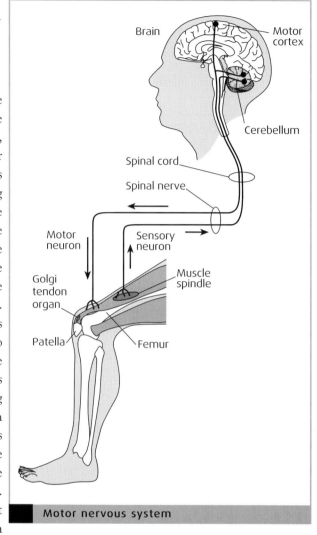

Motor nervous system

on the angle of joints, the pressure exerted on them and, when moving, acceleration.

It is easy to imagine how all these elements combine with other sensory information in the case of the can experiment to supply the brain with the information necessary to coordinate the movement and to correct its mistake. Being aware of the proprioceptors is important when exercising. Most importantly you should be guided by messages delivered by the tendon organs and avoid overriding their messages, for example by trying to lift excessively heavy weights or attempting to exert excessive force when using equipment. On the other hand, if you are to stretch adequately at the end of a work-out, you must hold the stretch for at least 25 to 30 seconds beyond the point when the muscle first tightens as a result of the response of the muscle spindles.

# Fast and slow twitch muscle fibres

Skeletal muscles consist of two different kinds of muscle fibre, *fast twitch* and *slow twitch* fibres, the preponderance of which determines both the appearance and capacities of muscles. Fast twitch muscles are white and respond very quickly to stimulation. They have a better capacity for anaerobic metabolism which means that they do not need oxygen to power them (see 'Energy and energy systems' p. 34). In contrast, slow twitch muscle fibres are red in colour and have a slower contraction rate. They depend entirely on energy generated by aerobic activities (oxygen) and are red because of the reliance on oxygenated blood supply for energy.

Sports such as sprinting make use of fast twitch muscles, as do those requiring quick changes of pace, including football, rugby and basketball. Strength training activities, which tend to employ anaerobic energy, also use predominantly fast twitch muscles. In contrast, endurance sports such as marathon and long distance running, use predominantly slow twitch muscles.

All muscles contain red and white muscle fibres. A cross section of a muscle would illustrate this. But the preponderance of red versus white muscles differs from one part of the body to another and from person to person. A sprinter, for example, would have a very small proportion of slow twitch muscles compared to middle or long distance runners. A sprinter might have as much as 70 per cent of muscle fibres in the fast twitch form whereas a long distance runner might have only 20 per cent in this form. An analogy can be made with respect to the colour of the breast meat of a domestic chicken and a wild pigeon. A chicken uses its wings to take off suddenly in order to avoid being caught, not for flying as such. Hence the breast muscle which powers the wings is predominantly white with fast twitch fibres for a quick response. A pigeon, however, uses its wings to fly long distances so the breast muscle is red with predominantly slow twitch muscle fibres for endurance. Muscles within the chicken itself vary. In contrast to the white muscle fibres of the breast, the leg muscles are much darker because the bird spends most of its time running around on the ground.

This division of the muscle fibres has become blurred, however, in light of recent research showing that training can change the characteristics of muscles. Fast twitch muscle which relies primarily on anaerobic energy conversion can be trained to acquire the slow twitch characteristic of aerobic respiration. There is some evidence also that slow twitch muscles can be converted to fast twitch if, for example, a marathon runner is trained to sprint. This discovery is important because it shows that training can help to improve strength and endurance.

The basic structure of the muscle, however, remains all important in shaping athletic and related capacities, and largely determines how individuals respond to training regimes. Fast twitch muscles bulk more in response to resistance training, for example, although the situation for women in this respect is a little different because they lack the male hormone testosterone. Even so, the predominance of one or other muscle fibre does influence the results of resistance training. Increased strength in women does not necessarily mean muscle bulk, but increasing the intensity and duration of training can also lead to greater muscle definition than usual.

## Smooth muscles

This muscle is responsible for movements in internal organs, such as the uterus, intestines, lungs, bladder and blood vessels. Smooth muscle does not contain myofibrils. It has thick myosin filaments and thin actin filaments but these are distributed throughout the muscle cell. Also, smooth muscle has only half the myosin found in skeletal muscle and does not have the sarcomere structure of skeletal muscle. As a result, smooth muscle does not have a striated appearance. Its contraction speed is very slow. Because smooth muscles are not under conscious control, they cannot be trained, but their efficiency and function can be improved indirectly through exercise, especially those geared toward improving the function of the cardio-vascular respiratory system.

## Cardiac muscles

The cardiac muscle or *myocardium* makes up much of the heart. It contracts rhythmically to propel blood through the circulatory system. It does not need nervous stimulation to contract: isolated cardiac muscle cells, for example, will continue to contract for many hours providing they are bathed in oxygen-rich, nutritious saline. Contraction of the heart is influenced, however, by the involuntary nervous system, hormones and the stretching of the muscles. Contractions start in the right atrium of the heart, spreading through both atria and then both ventricles alternately.

The pumping action of the heart varies considerably in response to the demands of the body muscles for oxygen. At rest, the heart contracts at around 60 to 70 beats per minute and pushes out some 80 mls of blood at each stroke. During exercise, when more oxygen is needed, the heart can contract at a maximum of 200 to 220 beats per minute to pump over three times the amount of blood. The maximum number of contractions generally reduces with age.

Increases in the heart beat or myocardial contractions occur during exercise because the active muscles not only require more blood/oxygen but are also returning more blood. The more blood returning to the heart, the more forcibly the heart can contract to push the blood to the lungs and back around the body. An increase in the contractions of the myocardium contributes to an increase in the strength and size of the heart, just as exercise helps to strengthen skeletal muscles.

Over time exercise causes advantageous changes to the cardio-vascular system. The demands for more blood during exercise lead to an increase in blood capillaries which helps lower blood pressure. The importance of this is self-evident at a time when the incidence of hypertension (abnormally high blood pressure when at rest) is rising dramatically in the industrialised countries (see 'Cardiac cycle and hypertension', p. 32). As the heart becomes stronger, the volume of blood it pushes out at each contraction (*stroke volume*) increases while the resting pulse rate falls. Both changes lower the workload of the heart, reducing the stress and strain.

## The heart and circulatory system

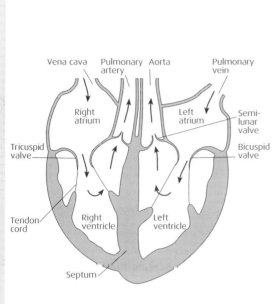
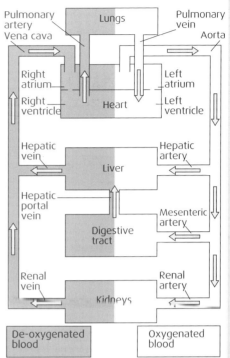

The heart is divided into four chambers: the upper two are called atria and the lower two, ventricles. The septum, which is a thick muscular wall, runs in the centre to separate the left atrium and ventricle from the right atrium and ventricle.

The right half of the heart receives deoxygenated blood from the body via the *vena cava* vein. The build up of pressure in the right atrium as a result of the inflow pushes the *tricuspid valve* open and deoxygenated blood is pumped into the right ventricle. The right ventricle contracts to push the blood into the *pulmonary artery* which leads to the lungs. In the lungs the carbon dioxide carried in the blood diffuses into the air sacs (*alveoli*) and is subsequently exhaled while the oxygen in the alveoli diffuses into the blood. The oxygenated blood is then carried by the *pulmonary vein* to the left atrium of the heart. The *bicuspid valve*, separating the left atrium from the left ventricle, opens allowing the oxygenated blood to pass into the left ventricle which then contracts, sending it into the *aorta*. The arterial system distributes the blood throughout the body. The oxygen from the blood is diffused through the capillary walls into the spaces between the body cells. Carbon dioxide passes from body cells via tissue fluids to the capillaries of the venous system returning eventually to the vena cava.

## The cardiac cycle and hypertension

The cardiac cycle has three phases: the diastolic, atrial systolic and ventricle systolic. Together, they make up one heart beat.

The *diastolic phase* is the resting phase, during which deoxygenated blood flows into the right atrium and oxygenated blood flows into the left atrium. As the blood flows into the atria, the build up of pressure causes the valves that separate the atria from the ventricles to open so that blood goes simultaneously into the ventricles. About 80 per cent of the ventricle is filled with blood at the diastolic phase.

In the *atrial systolic phase*, the atria (both left and right) contract to push more blood into the ventricles to fill them completely. The ventricles then contract, referred to as the the *ventricle systolic phase*, and the valves that separate the atria from the ventricles close to prevent any flow back. The contraction of the ventricles sends blood out into the arteries: from the right ventricle to the pulmonary artery and from the left ventricle to the aorta.

The amount of blood ejected into the arteries by this contraction is called the stroke volume. The amount of blood pushed out per minute is referred to as the cardiac output, which is simply stroke volume multiplied by the number of heart beats that occur during the minute.

Blood pressure generally refers to the pressure exerted on the arteries in the different phases of the cardiac cycle. Blood pressure increases with activity. This is normal. *Hypertension* is when the pressure remains high even at rest.

Blood pressure is measured in two values: the systolic rate over the diastolic rate, or the pressure exerted on the arteries when the ventricles contract over the pressure exerted in the diastolic phase. Normal blood pressure is not strictly defined and varies with age. As people grow older, the resistance to blood flow rises because the blood vessels become more rigid and so blood pressure increases. Generally, blood pressure is normal if it is below 140/90. Those with a systolic value between 140 and 160 and diastolic rate between 90 and 95 have moderate hypertension. Those exceeding these values are classified as having severe hypertension.

Between 10 and 20 per cent of the adult population in many countries, including the UK and the USA, are estimated to have hypertension. Men are more prone to it than women, but after the menopause, women become equally susceptible.

Hypertension exists in two forms:

- primary or essential hypertension, which is without obvious cause, but is linked to gender, lifestyle (smoking, obesity, alcohol) and hereditary factors
- secondary, which is linked to specific causes including kidney disorders, congenital heart defects and taking certain drugs

Hypertension often passes undetected because there are few obvious symptoms. This is why it is sometimes called the silent killer. Despite the lack of symptoms, hypertension increases the stress and strain on the heart severely, making it susceptible to myocardial infarction (heart attack), stroke and other coronary heart diseases.

Research studies have proven that regular exercises will help lower blood pressure in all persons suffering from hypertension and protect against heart diseases.

# The respiratory system

The efficient delivery of oxygen is of paramount importance to the body and brain. This is the job of the pulmonary or respiratory system. Air enters through the nose and mouth and passes down the windpipe or *trachea*. This divides into two *bronchi* which lead to the left and right lungs set on either side of the heart. Inside the spongy lung the bronchi sub-divide into smaller airways, the *bronchioles*. There are some 30,000 of these tiny bronchioles in each lung. Each bronchiole divides into two or more respiratory bronchioles which lead into numerous tiny air sacs, the *alveoli*. Oxygen passes through the thin walls of the alveoli into the blood stream, and carbon dioxide (the waste product of respiration) passes from the blood into the alveoli to be exhaled.

Each lung is cone-shaped with the base resting on the *diaphragm*, a sheet of muscle that separates the airtight chest cavity from the abdominal cavity. The right lung is divided into

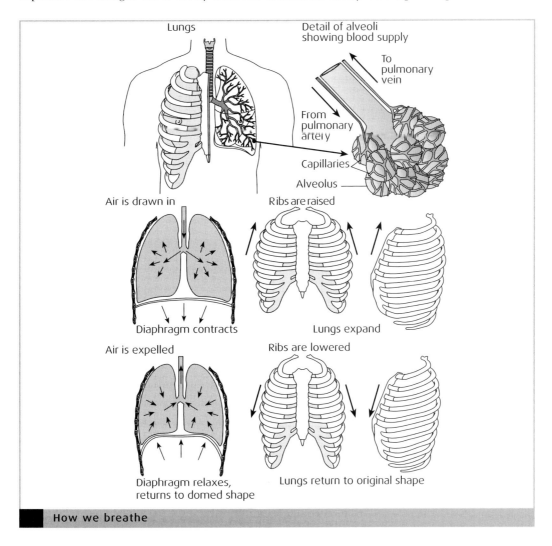

Lungs

Detail of alveoli showing blood supply

To pulmonary vein

From pulmonary artery

Capillaries

Alveolus

Air is drawn in

Diaphragm contracts

Ribs are raised

Lungs expand

Air is expelled

Diaphragm relaxes, returns to domed shape

Ribs are lowered

Lungs return to original shape

**How we breathe**

three lobes while the smaller left lung is divided into two lobes. Together the lungs form one of the body's largest organs. They provide an internal surface area for the exchange of respiratory gases that is some 40 times greater than the body's outer surface. A *pleural membrane* covers the lungs and lines the thoracic cavity. The membrane produces *pleural fluid* which lubricates the surfaces of the lungs and thoracic cavity so that they move easily against one another during breathing.

Air is inhaled and exhaled by the action of the chest muscles (intercostal muscles between the ribs) and the *diaphragm*. When we inhale, the external intercostal muscles contract causing the ribs to move upwards and outward and the diaphragm contracts and flattens, pushing down on the viscera (guts) which are allowed to descend by relaxation of the abdominal wall. This increases the volume of the thorax and of the lungs. The increase in volume raises the capacity of the lungs so that atmospheric pressure forces air into them. When we exhale, the external intercostal muscles relax and the internal intercostal muscles contract, pushing the ribs downward and inward, while the viscera, under pressure from the muscular walls of the abdomen, push the relaxed diaphragm back up into position. This reduces the thoracic and lung volume and increases the internal pressure, expelling from the lungs air which now contains less oxygen and more carbon dioxide and water vapour than when it entered them. The lungs, as a result of their elasticity, return to their original shape.

Our rhythmic breathing movements are usually made without any conscious interference at a rate of about 18 times per minute when at rest. Breathing in takes about a second and breathing out a little less than three seconds. Breathing is controlled by a region of the brain that is very sensitive to the concentration of carbon dioxide in the blood. If there is a rise in concentration, nerve impulses are sent automatically to the diaphragm and intercostal muscles to increase the rate and depth of breathing.

The *maximum* or *vital capacity* of the lungs is about 5 litres, but during quiet breathing the *tidal volume*, the volume of air moving in and out of the lungs, is between 500 and 750 mls. Furthermore, when breathing at rest often the only active muscle is the diaphragm. Exercise increases the lung capacity. The vital capacity of a trained male athlete can be 6 litres or more. The greater the capacity of the lungs to expand and take in air, the greater the supply of oxygen for the vital functions of the body cells. During heavy exercise the tidal volume can be as much as 4.5 litres. This increase in oxygen intake helps increase the release of available energy for physical activity.

# Energy and energy systems

Energy refers to the capacity to do work or carry out physical activities. Energy is needed to maintain the body temperature, to keep the heart beating and the lungs functioning, as well as all other bodily functions even when at rest. It is measured in either *calories* or *Joules* (named after the nineteenth century British physicist, J. P. Joule). Most popular books on diets and nutrition use calories, usually kilocalories (C) because a calorie is a comparatively small measure. The amount of energy required to maintain the body at rest is referred to as the *basal metabolic rate* (BMR). Any movements or physical activity (including the additional energy required for growth, pregnancy and lactation) beyond these basic body processes raises energy expenditure above the basal metabolic rate.

Energy is derived from the nutrients in our food, which are broken down and stored as chemical energy in the form of *adenosine triphosphate* (ATP) in body cells. When a muscle contracts the ATP is broken down into *adenosine diphosphate* (ADP) and *phosphate* with the release of energy. The amount of ATP stored in muscles however is limited, so that if energy is to continue to be released ATP synthesis must keep pace with its consumption. The ADP and its split phosphate must therefore be restored to ATP. This resynthesis requires energy which is supplied through one of two energy systems: the *aerobic system* or the *anaerobic system*.

# The aerobic system

*Aerobics* means working with air or, to be precise, oxygen. Aerobics refers to activities or exercises that allow muscles to work at a steady rate over an extended period of time with a continuous and adequate supply of oxygenated blood. The heart rate is increased by the activity to encourage the necessary blood supply. Aerobic activities can be sustained as long as the demand for oxygen to resynthesise ATP is satisfied.

Equally important are the sources of energy for the process. Carbohydrates are the main source of energy in our food. They are stored in the cells of the body in two usable forms, *glucose* and *glycogen* (thousands of glucose molecules linked together). *Cortisol*, a hormone produced by the adrenal glands, promotes the synthesis and storage of glucose. Glucose, sometimes referred to as blood sugar, is important to the normal functioning of the body; it is the only fuel used by the brain.

Aerobic activities use glycogen and fatty acids primarily as their source of energy. Glycogen is stored in the muscle and liver. If the glycogen store is full, the excess is converted and stored as fat. Fat in the form of free fatty acids is stored in the *adipose* (fat) *tissue* and in skeletal muscle. These fatty acids can be mobilised for energy only by the aerobic energy system.

Generally, the release of energy in the body, whether aerobic or anaerobic, starts with the breakdown of glycogen into glucose and *pyruvates*. This process, called *glycolysis*, generates two molecules of ATP for each glucose molecule (see overleaf). In aerobic respiration, the pyruvates then enter a cycle of reactions, usually called the *Krebs Cycle* after its discoverer, Sir Hans Krebs. The cycle of reactions is made possible by enzymes, assisted by co-enzymes which enable them to do their work. Like all catalysts, the enzymes are not destroyed, but return to their original state after doing their specific chemical task enabling the cycle to continue. Each 'circuit' of the Krebs Cycle yields one molecule of carbon dioxide and one molecule of ATP and 'spins off' hydrogen ions that combine with oxygen to produce water and energy. It is this oxidation of the hydrogen that releases most of the energy, 12 ATP molecules.

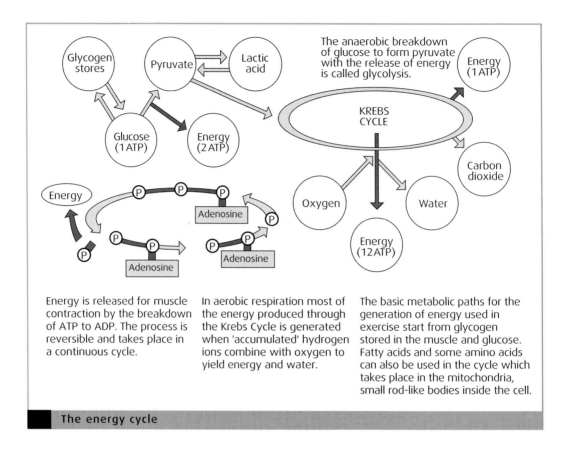

Energy is released for muscle contraction by the breakdown of ATP to ADP. The process is reversible and takes place in a continuous cycle.

In aerobic respiration most of the energy produced through the Krebs Cycle is generated when 'accumulated' hydrogen ions combine with oxygen to yield energy and water.

The basic metabolic paths for the generation of energy used in exercise start from glycogen stored in the muscle and glucose. Fatty acids and some amino acids can also be used in the cycle which takes place in the mitochondria, small rod-like bodies inside the cell.

**The energy cycle**

The process takes place within cells in rod-shaped structures called *mitochondria*, where the enzymes that drive the Krebs Cycle are found. For this reason the mitochondria are often called the cell's 'powerhouse'. Glucose is obtained from the blood and is drawn from the stores of glycogen. Fatty acids are also a source of energy, being broken down into components that join directly into the Krebs Cycle in the mitochondria. Although used continuously, fatty acids do not become a major source of energy until the body's carbohydrate resources are depleted. In extreme cases of starvation, when the body has insufficient carbohydrate or fat available, protein is also broken down to provide energy.

In practical terms, the use of glycogen and fat stores makes aerobic activities a vital tool for the control of body weight. If the objective is to reduce weight, an exercise programme should be structured in its early stage around gentle, rhythmic exercises rather than high intensity exercises that can take you outside the aerobic energy system to anaerobic energy systems (see below). The burning of fat generally takes place some 20 minutes from the start of the activity. Aerobic sessions of 20 to 30 minutes performed with moderate intensity at least three times a week can have tremendous health benefits. They improve stamina and endurance, and the cardio-vascular system. As mentioned previously, the heart rate slows down both at rest and in activity, reducing stress to the organ. The *stroke volume*, the volume of blood pushed out per heart beat, increases reducing the work that the heart has to do to circulate blood. The number of mitochondria also increases, improving the capacity of cells to use oxygen.

# Anaerobic energy systems

Anaerobic energy systems produce energy without the use of oxygen. These systems come into use when the intensity of the activity is so great that the cardiorespiratory system cannot supply sufficient oxygen to meet the demand of the body. There are two different means of producing energy without oxygen: the lactate system; and the creatine phosphate system.

## The lactate system

In physical exertion, such as sprinting, the process of energy release stops at the first stage of the energy cycle, known as glycolysis, described earlier. Glycogen in the muscles is broken down to glucose to form *pyruvic acid* and to provide the energy required for the resynthesis of ATP. Glycolysis does not break down the glycogen completely and provides only a fraction of the ATP produced under the aerobic system. What is more, the end product of the process is lactic acid rather than water and carbon dioxide, the harmless products of the aerobic process. It is the accumulation of lactic acid in the muscles that causes fatigue, 'stitch', cramps and aches. The combined effect of this is that the intensity of the activity cannot be maintained for more than a matter of minutes. Fatigue may start to set in after 35 to 40 seconds and exhaustion after 55 to 60 seconds if the intensity of activity is high. Hence, the lactate system can only provide ATP energy for relatively short bursts of activity, such as a 400 metre sprint, or sprint finishes by middle or long distance runners. (These numbers are no more than approximate because the duration varies depending on the intensity of effort. If, for example, the sprint is done at 95 per cent of the maximum intensity possible, the energy would be expended within 30 seconds.)

## The creatine phosphate system

The body draws upon this system when the energy requirement is so great that there is insufficient time to break down the glycogen to produce ATP energy. An example would be lifting very heavy weights. For this spurt of energy, the ADP stored in the muscle cells combines with creatine phosphate which is also present, to provide energy for about 5 seconds of maximum effort. The reaction is reversible at rest when the level of ATP is relatively high. The recovery time depends on the intensity of effort and can range from 30 seconds with a 50 per cent effort expenditure to 2 minutes on maximum effort. Although the energy from the creatine phosphate system is available for only a very short period, it can be drawn upon repeatedly because of the quick recovery of the supply.

# How energy systems relate to exercise

Most sports and exercises use a combination of energy systems (see below). In an exercise to music class, for example, the warm-up would use movements involving the big muscle groups in a series of low impact and travelling moves to raise the heart beat and increase the supply of blood to muscles. This would involve the aerobic energy system, but after a period of increased heart activity of 10 to 15 minutes the work-out could increase in intensity to a level where the energy requirement begins to exceed that provided by the aerobic system, for example in a series of explosive movements such as high kicks and jumping jacks. The anaerobic energy system would then come into play. Certainly the lactate system would set in, at least intermittently, if the class were to move on to training activities to strengthen muscles, and the heart rate is brought down even further.

In general, exercises that concentrate on building strength tend to rely principally on anaerobic energy while those that focus on endurance rely on aerobic energy. Hence, it is technically incorrect to refer to exercise to music classes as aerobic. Circuit classes also tend to combine aerobic with anaerobic energy use. Soccer players use both aerobic and anaerobic energy systems. Even when jogging, different energy systems can be brought into play in different terrains. However, some exercise regimes use more of one energy system than the other. This may have a crucial influence on what types of exercise are chosen to meet specific objectives. (Chapter 5 reviews in more detail the different exercise regimes available.)

**A comparison of energy systems**

|  | Aerobic | Lactate | Creatine phosphate |
|---|---|---|---|
| Energy sources | carbohydrates (glycogen), fats and proteins | carbohydrates (glycogen and blood glucose) | creatine phosphate |
| Level of activity | low intensity | high intensity | extremely high |
| Examples of sport/ activity | walking, long distance running, swimming | sustained sprint, uphill running | short sprint, weight lifting, squash |
| Duration (approx. depending on individual and effort exerted) | varies, but normally for hours if level of intensity is low | varies depending on intensity, max. duration within minutes | seconds |
| Recovery time | varies depending on glycogen availability | varies but < 2 hours | full recovery in 2 minutes |
| Waste products | carbon dioxide and water | lactic acid | none |

# Setting yourself sensible targets for exercise

People take up sports or exercise for many reasons. The most common ones are to meet other people, improve health and fitness, prepare for a particular sport or activity and for enjoyment and relaxation. The objectives for improving health and fitness vary significantly from person to person. Some hope to gain greater strength, others seek increased stamina, while yet others want to lose weight, re-shape their body or increase their flexibility. Very often, people in sedentary occupations go to the gym for a hard work-out in order to remove surplus energy and to find relief from the dullness and stress of their working day. A common goal, particularly among middle-aged men, is to increase their cardio-vascular and respiratory fitness. Increasingly, people are using exercise as a way of gaining tranquillity and calmness, and as a cure for anxiety, restlessness and sleeplessness. Most people, however, seek a combination of these objectives with greater or less emphasis on one or the other. Whatever the specific objectives, the final overall target is to feel healthier and to look better.

Understanding our body is essential if we are to set sensible objectives for ourselves. In Chapter 3, we learned that the make-up of our muscles has an important influence on what we can do. From the bone structure and information on bone formation, we learned the importance of weight-bearing activities and joint mobility. The coverage on energy systems illustrated the importance of aerobic training for cardio-vascular health as well as for weight control. However, other influences come into play, particularly what might be described as our natural endowments, in the search to understand what exercise and sports can or cannot achieve.

## Body shape or somatotype

The basic shape of a person is determined by hereditary or genetic factors, nutrition, environment and culture. Much controversy has surrounded the subject of how much of what we are is determined by the environment and how much by genetic factors: the age-old argument of nature versus nurture. Over the life time of a single generation, hereditary and genetic factors undoubtedly have an overwhelming influence on body type. Our genetic inheritance greatly determines how we look. In fact human populations can be categorised or distinguished by genetic differences, including blood type and even susceptibility to some kinds of disease.

Taken over many generations, environmental factors such as climate and food patterns have had an impact on the genetic constitution of humanity. Human evolution has demonstrated the influence of different environmental conditions. People tend to be tall and thin in very hot climates because a larger surface area relative to body mass allows for greater heat loss. Thus, African groups such as the Nilotes have probably the highest surface to body mass ratio. In cold climates the reverse is true and people tend to be short and stocky, thereby reducing the surface to mass ratio. The inuits of the Arctic region are prime examples. In climates with intense sunshine the iris is deeply pigmented to reduce the impact of injurious ultra-violet light on the eye. Studies on how humans are adapted to their environment have shown a direct link between levels of sunlight and pigmentation.

Access to different foods under different climates also influence body form. Although body measurements are linked to hereditary/genetic factors, they are also affected by nutrition. Better nourished people tend to grow larger because an improved diet allows the building of greater bone and muscle mass. A feature of emigration is that the children of people who as a rule are short may grow surprisingly tall in their new homeland.

The physical differences that emerge as a result of geography, climate and nutrition help to explain why within each of the broad racial groups, Caucasoid, Negroid and Mongoloid, such wide differences in build and facial features can develop. Africans south of the Sahara are characterised by heavy concentrations of melanin in the skin, while in Ethiopia and Somalia, towards the Gulf of Aden and in the Cape area in the far south, people have less pigmentation. In fact, such diversity has made the rigid demarcation of racial groups into Caucasoid, Negroid and Mongoloid untenable. This is reinforced by DNA analysis which reveals very little difference among the peoples of the world.

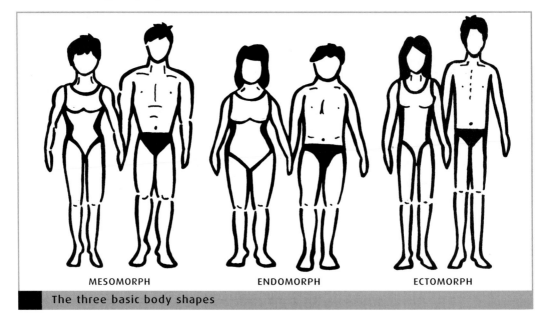

MESOMORPH     ENDOMORPH     ECTOMORPH

**The three basic body shapes**

Setting aside any consideration of human evolution or racial groups, the human body can be broadly categorised into three types: *ectomorph*, *endomorph* and *mesomorph* (see opposite). People classified as ectomorphs usually have a long lean frame, narrow shoulders and hips. Long distance runners often fall into this category. Endomorphs by contrast are short and broad with wide hips and a tendency to gain weight. Mesomorphs are athletic in build with broad shoulders, narrow waist and powerful, but not wide, hips. Gymnasts and sprinters are often this shape.

The basic shape or skeletal framework of a person, whether ectomorph, mesomorph, endomorph or a combination (few people fall neatly into one specific category), cannot be changed by exercise. Exercise and food intake, however, can influence how you look. A mesomorph who takes no exercise and over-eats can look like an endomorph. An endomorph can, through sensible exercise and eating habits, acquire a toned body that is significantly better than a mesomorph who leads a sedentary life. Even if you are born with what current fashion dictates as the 'right body type', this does not necessarily mean it will be easy to maintain. It is vital to start the pursuit of health and fitness at an early age through good food habits and regular exercise. Although everyone is born with what they have in terms of basic shape, a great deal can be done to influence how it looks and, equally important, how you feel about your physical appearance, health and fitness.

# Keeping the body ticking over

The energy needed to keep the body functioning at rest and in a fasting state is called the *basal metabolic rate* (BMR). This would include the energy required for breathing, heartbeat, maintenance of nerve functions, secretions from body glands and cells, body temperature and tension in muscles. In short, it is the minimum energy required to maintain life.

The BMR varies from person to person depending on body weight, height, body composition, age, environmental factors and sex. A muscular person will have a higher BMR than a person with the same weight but a higher fat content. Muscles are metabolically more active. Women, whose bodies naturally have a higher fat content than men, have a lower BMR. A tall thin person with a large body surface relative to her/his weight will have a higher BMR than a short thin person because of the greater loss of heat and the need to maintain body temperature. If, however, the ambient temperature is greater than the body temperature (37.5°C), the reverse is true, because the larger surface area of the tall thin person allows greater absorption of heat, reducing the need for energy to maintain body temperature. In hot climates the BMR of any individual, whether fat or thin, is generally 10 to 20 per cent lower than it would be if they were living in a temperate clime.

The BMR on a per unit weight basis generally declines with age, as the composition of the body changes. It is highest on a per unit weight basis in young children during the growth spurts associated with puberty (between 10 and 15 years of age). More energy is required for bone formation and growth. At a later stage in adulthood the BMR generally declines at about 2 per cent per annum. If a person were to maintain the same food intake and physical activity in old age as when young, there would be an inevitable gain in weight. During sleep the BMR is lowered. Interestingly, the BMR is lowered when people on a slimming 'diet' reduce their food intake, because muscle as well as fat tissue is lost. Women who are lactating or pregnant have a higher BMR.

The BMR in calories can be calculated, using a simplified formula, by multiplying the weight in kilograms by 0.9 (for women) or 1.0 (for men) and 24 (the hours in a day). Thus a woman who weighs 63 kg will have an estimated BMR of 63 x 0.9 x 24 = 1361 Calories. This is only an approximation because height, muscle tone and age also affect the BMR. Using different formulae in the calculation also produces different approximations. Appendix 2 provides examples of the different methods that can be used to estimate the BMR. See the table on p. 45 for a general guideline on BMR, taking into account sex, age and height.

While the BMR is the minimum energy needed to sustain life, energy is also required for the digestion of food, absorption of nutrients and for coping with sudden changes in temperature, emotion and stress – *facultative thermogenesis*. Additional energy is also needed for day-to-day physical activities. The sum total of all these (BMR, facultative thermogenesis and physical activities) makes up our total energy need.

*Metabolism* is the sum of all the chemical reactions within the body, whether involving the breakdown of substances such as glycogen, or the synthesis of complex substances such as proteins. The *metabolic rate* is a measure of the energy used in these processes. The metabolism includes both catabolic and the anabolic processes. A *catabolic* process is where a complex substance is broken into simpler ones for the release of energy, for example when glucose is broken down into water and carbon dioxide. An *anabolic* process is where a complex substance is built up from simpler substances, such as the synthesis of complex proteins from amino acids. This consumes energy.

The metabolic rate increases following food consumption, exertion, during fluctuations in temperature and during emotional stress or illness. Digestion alone can use as much as 5–10 per cent of the calorie intake. The metabolic rate is controlled principally by hormones (such as adrenaline, noradrenaline, insulin, thyroid hormones and corticosteroid hormones) which influence the chemical processes within the body.

During exercise, the metabolic rate is raised. Sustained exercise also increases the BMR which can stay some 10 per cent above its normal level for up to 48 hours after the exercise has ceased. This post-exercise elevation of BMR contributes to fat loss, especially when exercise is taken on a regular and sustained basis. Exercise also raises the BMR over time by increasing body muscle.

# Food and diet

The metabolic rate is only one side of the equation determining body weight. Whether the body increases in weight depends on the calorific value of food consumed relative to energy expenditure. Food intake in excess of what the body needs leads to weight gain through the deposition of fat, and eventually obesity.

Fat is stored in *adipose tissue* in a layer just beneath the skin, around internal organs, including the heart, kidneys and liver, and in the abdominal walls. Left to accumulate, this fat is not only unattractive but poses a cardio-vascular risk, increasing the risk of hypertension, heart disease, stroke, diabetes and gallstones. In men, adipose tissue tends to accumulate around the shoulders, waist and abdomen, while in women, it tends to lodge in the breasts, hips and thighs. Dr Pamela Peeke of the National Institute of Health found in a study on the link between stress and fat that both men and women when under persistent mental stress tend to accumulate fat in the abdominal walls.[5] The stress raises the levels of cortisol in the blood resulting in a surge in appetite and a search for comfort foods. (Cortisol is a hormone produced by the adrenal glands.)

Many factors influence the deposition of adipose tissues. There are people who tend to gain weight more easily than others at a given level of food intake. This might be attributed to a lower BMR. Hereditary factors can play a part. It is also possible that in some cases the weight problem is created because parents pass on bad eating habits to their children.

Persistent over-consumption of food, especially food rich in fat and sugar, can cause *hypertrophy*, where the existing fat cells increase in size or *hyperplasia*, where the number of fat cells increase. Once the number of fat cells has risen, it cannot be reduced. By contrast, the size of fat cells is reducible. The foundation for the development of fat cell numbers is believed to be laid down in three phases: before birth; between one and two years; and in adolescence. The subject is still controversial, however, because the propensity to gain weight varies so widely between people. Despite a lack of consensus, there is general agreement on the importance of balancing calorie consumption with energy expenditure, although the 'balance' seems to differ from person to person.

The table on the following page contains a list of selected foods and their calorie equivalent, set against the time that needs to be spent on activities for their consumption. The table is not a guide on how to 'spend' the energy of the foods that you consume, but demonstrates how difficult it is to achieve a balance in energy expenditure and consumption in the face of persistent over-eating. It is estimated that to lose 0.5 kg of fat, 3500 Calories would have to be expended. The first table on page 45 provides a summary of the average energy expenditure of everyday activities at home, the workplace and at leisure.

Between the ages of 25 and 50 years, an average *recommended daily allowance* (RDA) of 2200 Calories is required by women and 2900 Calories by men, to sustain life and carry out normal activity. This estimate is derived by multiplying the BMR by a factor of 1.6, assuming moderate physical activity, and then adjusted upwards for young and downwards for older people. For those engaged in high levels of physical activity, the daily calorie intake will be substantially more. If the level of physical activity is higher than 'average', then a factor of 1.8 is applicable. Athletes engaged in regular training for cross-country skiing, cycling or marathon running may need even more (see the table on p. 161). In the UK, the factor used in the calculation of the

| Calories of selected foods and duration (in mins) of activities required for their utilisation* |||||| |
|---|---|---|---|---|---|
| Food | Calories | Walking 3.2 km/h | Jogging 8.8 km/h | Aerobic dancing | Swimming (slow crawl) 3.2 km/h |
| whole medium apple (125 g) | 40 | 16 | 5 | 7 | 10 |
| Rump steak (100 g) fried | 224 | 93 | 26 | 38 | 57 |
| Roast chicken with skin (100 g) | 244 | 102 | 28 | 42 | 62 |
| Bread (one slice) (25 g) | 60 | 25 | 7 | 10 | 15 |
| Jacket potato (200 g) | 170 | 71 | 20 | 29 | 43 |

*The figures are all approximate based on a person of 50 kg weight (110 lb) working at low intensity and effort. The greater the weight, the greater the calorie consumption; the greater the effort, the more calories consumed.

average requirements for energy is 1.4 because of an underlying assumption that on average people have a comparatively sedentary lifestyle with little physical activity at work and at leisure. The UK *estimated average requirement of energy* (EAR) has also been incorporated into the table opposite to illustrate the influence on energy requirements of a sedentary lifestyle. It should be noted, however, that part of the difference between the EAR established in the UK and the RDA set in the US and elsewhere is the product of differences in weight and height in the population samples used. The RDA figures are also used by the Food and Agriculture Organization (FAO) and the World Health Organization (WHO) Consultative Group on Nutrition. It should be stressed that important differences in RDA exist depending upon climate, temperature, geography and people.

In general, restricting food intake to below what the body requires is a dubious way of losing weight. Starving sends confusing signals to the body and, as a result, body cells will respond by storing food on return to regular eating. Weight lost during this kind of extreme dieting consists of both fat and lean body mass resulting in a lowering of the BMR. As a result, less energy is spent on maintaining body functions and more is left over for storage. Reducing food intake can also cause depression and anxiety.

A combination of sensible food intake and regular exercise offers a much more viable route to weight loss. Exercise stimulates the release in the brain of *endorphins*, natural painkillers

## Average energy expenditure of everyday activities and selected sports[6]

|  | Calories/min |  | Calories/min |
|---|---|---|---|
| Everyday activities |  | (cont.) |  |
| sitting | 1.4 | bowling | 3.9 |
| standing | 1.7 | calisthenics, light | 4 |
| washing/dressing | 3.5 | cycling (6 mph) | 3.5 |
| walking slowly | 3 | cycling (10 mph) | 5.5 |
| walking moderately quickly | 5 | cycling (12 mph) | 7.5 |
| walking up and down | 9 | jogging (1mile/9 min) | 10 |
|  |  | jogging (1 mile/15 min) | 5 |
| At work |  | rowing (11 miles/hr) | 13 |
| light (most domestic work) | 2.5–4.9 | running (1 mile/5 mins) | 18 |
| moderate (gardening) | 5.0 | running (1 mile/7 mins) | 13.5 |
| strenuous (coal mining) | >7.5 | swimming, fast | 9.4 |
|  |  | swimming, slow | 7.7 |
| Sports |  | tennis, doubles | 5.0 |
| aerobics, heavy | 8 | tennis, singles | 6.5 |
| aerobics, moderate | 5 | volleyball | 5.1 |
| aerobics, light | 3 |  |  |
| badminton, doubles | 4 |  |  |
| badminton, single | 5.1 |  |  |

## Average BMR, RDA in the US and EAR of energy in the UK, by gender/age[7]

|  | Age | Weight (kg) | Height (metres) | BMR Cal/day | RDA Cal/day | EAR Cal/day |
|---|---|---|---|---|---|---|
| Male- | 11–14 | 45 | 1.57 | 1440 | 2500 | 2220 |
|  | 15–18 | 66 | 1.76 | 1760 | 3000 | 2755 |
|  | 19–24 | 72 | 1.77 | 1780 | 2900 | 2550 |
|  | 25–50 | 79 | 1.76 | 1800 | 2900 | 2550 |
|  | 51+ | 77 | 1.73 | 1530 | 2300 | 2340 |
| Female | 11–14 | 46 | 1.57 | 1310 | 2200 | 1845 |
|  | 15–18 | 55 | 1.63 | 1370 | 2200 | 2110 |
|  | 19–24 | 58 | 1.64 | 1350 | 2200 | 1940 |
|  | 25–50 | 63 | 1.63 | 1380 | 2200 | 1940 |
|  | 51+ | 65 | 1.60 | 1280 | 1900 | 1880 |

with a similar chemical structure to morphine, that give a sense of well-being. They also help to counteract the influence of the hormone cortisol in the blood, moderating the desire for food. In fact, studies have shown that a modest increase in the intensity of exercise may be mirrored by a decrease in appetite and food consumption (see Chapter 12 for more on food and nutrition).

# Spot reduction of fat

Body fat is not evenly distributed. There are particular areas where it tends to accumulate. For women, bottoms and tummies are not the only areas of concern. Flabby under arms and the build up of fat in the inner and outer thighs are just as worrying. For men, the so-called 'love handles' and 'beer bellies' very often go hand in hand with age. People can be divided into apple and pear shapes according to where the fat accumulates. Apple shapes are associated with upper body obesity and pear shapes with lower body obesity. However, this division can have implications beyond mere shape. Apple-shape people seem to be more susceptible to hypertension, coronary diseases and diabetes than pear-shaped ones. One explanation may be that the higher metabolic activity which accompanies abdominal fat results in higher levels of fat in the blood. Another is the sedentary lifestyle often associated with pot bellies.

The tendency of fat to accumulate in specific parts of the body means that, for many people, the objective of a work-out is to concentrate on reducing the fat in one part of their body. This, however, is a highly controversial topic. Many specialists are of the view that this spot reduction is not feasible because the loss of fat is not point specific.

While the general thrust of this argument is logical, it is not altogether accurate to say that exercise has no spot reduction effect. Aerobic exercises draw fat from wherever it is located. While this may mean that the fat is not drawn initially from the target areas, with time and perseverance this specific fat can eventually be used. It takes time. Moreover, the argument is, perhaps, not only how much fat is reduced from a specific spot, but whether muscles become stronger and better toned. A bottom that is toned looks different from one that is flabby even if its size remains unchanged. Here, strength building exercises play a significant part. What is important to stress is that these strength building (toning) regimes need to be complemented by aerobic activities if they are to be effective. More of these are covered in Chapters 7 and 8.

# Getting older

Ageing is inevitable. How we age is determined by hereditary factors and lifestyle. In general, a progressive physiological decline occurs. The efficiency of the body's organs such as the heart, kidneys, lungs and liver function declines. The skin loses elasticity, causing it to sag, wrinkle and bruise easily. Muscles lose bulk and strength. Reflexes slow as muscle fibres change with a reduction in fast twitch fibres. Postural muscles shorten. Bones become more porous and joints become less stable as a result of wear and tear. The pressure exerted on the intervertebral discs compresses them with a resultant loss of height. The sense of smell, touch and hearing become less sharp as nerve cells decline. The loss of brain cells reduces the ability to acquire new skills. These degenerative processes are accelerated by an excessive consumption of alcohol, drugs and food, poor diet, smoking tobacco, environmental pollution, a lack of exercise, sports injuries and so on. Resistance to disease and the capacity for body repair decline. There is also a tendency for the BMR to fall and body weight to rise.

Exercise can help slow down some of the degenerative processes. With regular exercise, an old person can retain a large proportion of his/her strength and stamina. Muscles are seldom lost unless through disease and lack of use. The ability to maintain strength and endurance helps preserve physical performance. The intensity of the exercises, however, might have to be reduced because of decreased lung capacity.

The extent and speed of decline varies from person to person and the sports arena abounds with examples of fit 60 year olds. In the book, *Survival of the Fittest*, Mike Stroud described the phenomenal prowess of Helen Klein, one of the greatest long-distance runners in the world. When they met she was 72 years old and had recently joined in the team for Eco-Challenge, a long-distance race which involved crossing more than 300 miles of the south west of the United States, using a combination of running, horse riding, mountain biking and hiking.[8] She first took up long-distance running at the age of 55 and by the time she joined the team for Eco-Challenge at 72 years old she had completed 75 marathons and 150 ultra-marathons and was still capable of running 100 miles in 20 hours. While not everyone can be a Helen Klein, and jogging might well be suitable for some and not others, regular exercise, especially begun early in life, contributes to the maintenance of cardio-respiratory fitness, muscular strength and endurance when old.

# Gender differences

People vary because of differences in their anatomy and physiology. Differences may relate to factors such as race, geographical location, climate, food, age and livelihood. But nowhere are differences more obvious and significant than those related to gender. The differences between men and women have to be understood before appropriate training or exercise regimes and targets can be set.

In terms of anatomy, taking an average man and woman, the man would have broader shoulders, longer arms and greater upper-body strength. He would also have longer legs, narrower hips, a smaller slant of the femur. He is taller. His body would contain 42 per cent muscle and between 12 and 14 per cent fat, compared with the woman's 36 per cent muscle and 20–24 per cent fat. The man's body would contain 4 per cent more water than the woman's.

Anatomical differences already make the man a more efficient runner with a longer stride and more powerful muscular output. The wider pelvis of the woman makes it difficult to bring the knees close together, making running more difficult. The achilles tendon in the woman is also shorter and tighter, impairing take-off. But the man also has other important advantages, with a larger heart, larger stroke volume and cardiac output, greater blood volume (some 5–6 litres compared to 4–4.5 litres the woman), larger volume of body fluid, larger lungs (some 10 per cent more), and higher respiratory and ventilation rate. The haemoglobin count in the woman is 10 per cent lower than in a man with the same volume of blood. Oxygen uptake is more efficient in the man and some 15–20 per cent higher than in the woman, allowing the man a greater release of energy to power the muscles. The woman, however, has greater joint mobility and greater flexibility in her muscles.

The reproductive physiology of women must also be taken into consideration. Strenuous training can disrupt the menstrual cycle in a number of ways. The onset of menstruation, which usually occurs around the age of 12, is often delayed in girls training for events such as gymnastics, dance and swimming. For those already menstruating, ovulation and menstruation can be disrupted. *Amenorrhoea* or absence of periods (sometimes with gaps of 6 months to a year) is not considered dangerous in itself, but may have an adverse effect on the bone structure. The lowering of oestrogen levels in the blood that arises as a result of amenorrhoea reduces the deposition of calcium phosphate in the bones. Osteoporosis weakens the bones and increases the risk of bone injury. In young athletes a failure to lay down sufficient calcium phosphates in the early years of development increases the problem of osteoporosis in menopause. Intense training can also contribute to increased injuries because the hormonal changes during the menstrual cycle affect bones, muscles and tendons that are already being subjected to intense stress.

The anatomical and physiological differences between men and women clearly affect athletic performance. Men, with their higher aerobic capacity, strength and endurance have a clear advantage in power sports and activities such as running. Women have an advantage in physical regimes which require mobility and flexibility, such as floor gymnastics. These are important factors determining the formulation of exercise regimes and should be applied even to body-conditioning exercises. This subject is covered in more detail in Chapter 8, which deals with training for muscular strength and endurance.

# Fusion fitness: the broad approach to exercise

Exercise regimes for improving fitness, health and beauty, like fashion, have gone through tremendous changes over the years. In the 1970s and 1980s, the hard work-out with its famous 'burn' was all the rage. It gave rise to high energy, high impact moves in aerobic training. People preferred these classes because they were associated with a certain level of fitness and, in a sense, status. Muscular and endurance training programmes similarly focused on big movements that allow people to take joints and muscles to their 'full range' of movements. Once again they were executed in an energetic way, with arms and legs swinging in great arcs. Sit-ups were done rapidly. Squats were deep, taking the buttocks well below knee level. Weights were incorporated in work-outs. Explosive movements were in vogue and stretches were often ballistic. The saying 'no pain, no gain' became the password of the cognoscenti.

Widespread incidences of injuries and improvements in sports science over the past decade or so have modified the view that pace and burn are everything. Gradually, high-impact aerobics, although still popular, is giving way to combinations of 'hi/lo' to low movements, encouraged perhaps by the growing number of people in their middle and later years now taking up exercise.

In the building of muscle strength and endurance, two contrasting 'new' trends are being superimposed on the old. The first is a modified traditional approach which continues to focus on promoting the full range of movements in joints and muscles, but is very cautious. All positions that require extreme flexion have been taken off the list of recommended exercises. For example, while touching the toes from an upright position was once an almost universal exercise in Physical Education (PE) lessons in schools, it is now considered dangerous. Fear that class participants may hurt themselves have led instructors to avoid any possibility of danger. 'Do not work through pain' has now become the motto.

The second development, running parallel to this cautious approach, incorporates little or no aerobic training. It includes exercise disciplines initiated by Lotte Berk and also what has been generally classified as *callanetics*. The exercise techniques are especially focused on getting into the right position before beginning any movement. Movements are slow and controlled.

Based, in the case of Lotte Berk's method, on her experience of dancing and later of orthopedic exercises, they promote awareness of joints and especially the spine. Her knowledge of orthopedic methods was acquired during her fight to recover from a spinal injury caused by an accident. Some of the positions did require extreme flexion of the body, but getting into them involved first getting the joints stable and controlled. The 'rolling in of the pelvis', for example, was a cornerstone of her abdominal exercises. Movements varied from full range to smaller ones, but all were difficult: just getting into the right position could take weeks of practice. The 'barre' was a prerequisite tool for supporting some of the positions.

In many ways, callanetics is similar to Lotte Berk's style of exercise. Developed and refined by Callan Pinckney, who had also trained under Lotte Berk, there appear, however, to be two main differences between the disciplines. In callanetics, almost all the movements are small and some of the movements are also very repetitive, with targets for abdominal contractions set at 100, for example. Muscle groups are isolated and their small, almost imperceptible movements are consistently applied as though against an invisible and immovable resistance.

While these two disciplines gained widespread support in some quarters, they were less accepted in others. Amongst those training for sports and athletics, there emerged a trend away from isometric training, i.e. the practice of developing muscle tension without changing muscle length, and with it, exercises involving small movements that facilitated such muscle tension became less popular because of their similarities to isometric training. Isometric training for weight lifting, which had been all the rage previously also declined. While isometric contractions are useful as a rehabilitative exercise for developing strength in specific places, they have to be used with caution because of potential adverse results, of which raised blood pressure ranks as one of the most serious (Chapter 8 discusses in greater detail the advantages and disadvantages of isometric training). In athletic training today, as opposed to the general fitness industry, isometric exercises are rarely practised except in conjunction with other training methods.

More recently, 'holistic exercise regimes' have been added to the fitness brew. These regimes have their roots, if anything, in the 'Age of Aquarius'. Stress and strife in the modern industrialised world have encouraged a search for nature and tranquillity. Just as homeopathic medicines have revived in popularity and organic foods are a must for many consumers, yoga, t'ai chi, Pilates, the Alexander Technique and a host of other similar forms of holistic exercise regimes have become either popular or revived in popularity in the West. Their practitioners consider them holistic or complete because they involve both the mind and the body, and some, such as t'ai chi and yoga, have their origins in antiquity. The latter two offer a sense of security during times of rapid change in society by returning to age-old traditions. The question remains, however, as to whether such regimes have lost some of their force in the translation from one very different culture to another.

# Holistic regimes

## Yoga

Yoga, practised for literally thousands of years in the Indus Valley in India, means 'union with God'. As in the eightfold path of Buddhism, there are eight components to the achievement of this union prescribed by Patanjali, the father of yoga. The first concerns moral disciplines, the second personal disciplines of purity, contentment, devotion to God, study and contentment, the third and fourth revolve around the practice of posture and breath control, the fifth to the eighth involve the practice of concentration – meditation to allow the mind to become quiet and in the process discover pure consciousness, a oneness with the Universe. These components form the wheel of yoga, which makes up all aspects of living – a complete way of life.

Two main schools predominate in the modern practice of yoga:

- *Hatha yoga* concentrates on the more physical aspects such as postures, based principally on the stretching movements of animals, and breath control.

- *Raja yoga* teaches concentration, meditation and discovery of oneness with the universe, a sense of withdrawal.

In the western world, Hatha yoga has the most appeal. For many, yoga is a means to relax, to overcome stress, to increase flexibility and have greater body control. In effect, it has become an exercise regime.

As an exercise regime, especially in flexibility training, yoga has much to offer. Its use of breath control to get into the various postures (*asanas*) helps to relax the body, and relaxed muscles are easier to stretch than tight ones. Greater awareness of the body is promoted through concentration. The stretches or postures are done symmetrically, which illustrates an understanding of balanced muscle development. A forward bend is complemented by a backward bend; a stretch to the left is followed by one to the right. Given that yoga originated long before sports science was born, this is remarkable. The use of 'recti breathing' techniques to isolate the abdominal muscle and retraction abdominal controls were only recently recognised in the sports world, giving rise to the so called 'abdominal revolution', the concept of *core stability* and Pilates.

Not all positions in yoga are suitable for all people and some positions, I believe, could be dangerous.[10] In many yoga postures the muscles involved (muscles work in pairs – agonist and antagonist) are both contracted and stretched, i.e. one set of muscle is contracting to 'hold' the stretch of the opposing muscle group. Yoga stretches are generally held for a significant length of time; much longer than the 25 to 30 seconds typical of developmental stretches, and certainly for much longer than the holds generally recommended for active stretches to which many of the yoga stretches belong (see Chapter 10 on active stretches). It is suggested in yoga, for example, that head and shoulder stands are held for some minutes, with the knees kept very straight and the spine and legs kept elongated upwards.[11] Holding such an unchanged posture would necessarily involve the tensing of the agonist muscle, without much change in the length of the muscle fibres. In inverted postures such as head stands (*Sirisana*), shoulder stands (*Sarvangasana*), the plough (*Halasana*) and the wheel or back arch (*Chakrasana*), blood rushes not only to the head but also to the heart, which needs to contract with much greater force to drive blood through the circulatory system, increasing both its systolic and diastolic pressure.

Many people pursue such postures in the belief that they are beneficial for health. The plough is supposed to tone the nervous system, stimulate the endocrine glands, the liver and spleen, correct menstrual disorder, prevent disorders of the stomach and 'normalise' obesity. Shoulder stands supposedly increase the sexual fitness of both men and women, reduce excess fat and soothe and tone the nervous system.[12] These claims need scientific verification and in the case of individuals with hypertension, these postures could be risky. Inverted postures carry with them yet another possible risk, namely the considerable pressure and weight exerted on the spine. This danger is magnified in the case of overweight individuals.

In the plough and shoulder stands the pressure is on the cervical spine, just at the back of the neck and base of the head. This is an important centre for the nervous network. Even when the body is supported with the hands, the cervical vertebrae are engaged in an acute angle and subjected to compression by the weight they have to bear from the body when it is centred directly above. In shoulder stands gravity would most likely off-set any stretch or 'lengthening' of the spine. To hold the position muscles would have to contract rather than relax. In the back arch it is the small of the back that is compressed, and the neck muscle is either isometrically contracted to

The plough

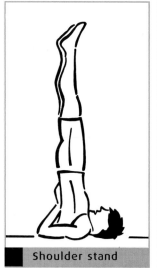

Shoulder stand

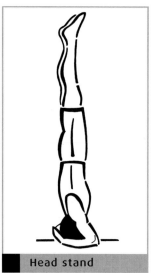

Head stand

Back arch

The dog pose

The peacock

keep the chin towards the chest (the recommended position) or hyper-extended when it hangs back; the wrists are also subject to the substantial weight of the body. In headstands the shoulders and elbows carry most of the body weight, for which they are not suited. Some non-inverted postures, such as the peacock, are similarly stressful for the wrists.

In some of the forward poses, the problem of extreme flexion is met to an extent by yoga breathing techniques and abdominal muscle control. They allow practitioners to bend without experiencing the pressure that otherwise would be exerted on the joints. A good example is the dog pose where, by holding the stomach in, much of the pressure on the back is removed. It is for this reason that some of the forward bend yoga postures have been adopted and modified to feature in the stretch positions of the sports world. With the correct techniques of breathing and abdominal muscle control, and modification of the postures to exclude movements that take joints beyond their natural range, more of these stretches could be used.

Thus, as an exercise regime, yoga has benefits including flexibility training and muscle control, but it is not a complete programme of fitness. It provides little aerobic training, which is important for cardio-vascular benefits as well as weight control, and involves virtually no or very limited motor skill development in terms of eye–limb response and coordination. Its relaxation and withdrawal techniques are useful for coping with stress, but it is not a technique that can be easily applied, for example, in the workplace where the stress occurs. Most importantly, some of the postures could be dangerous.

## T'ai Chi Chuan

T'ai Chi Chuan is an ancient Chinese martial art that dates back to the early third century. By the fifth century T'ai Chi Chuan had made further advances, becoming a key form of martial art and exercise in the Buddhist monastery of Shao Lin.

The term t'ai chi has been variously translated as 'great gargantuan fist', 'great polarity boxing' and 'shadow boxing'. There is in fact no single definition because it is an art form that has been modified and changed with time. The only central intrinsic concept is the idea of internal energy or 'chi' (sometimes spelled 'qi'). Chi is derived from three sources: there is the chi we are born with; the chi we obtain from food; and the chi derived from breathing. The last is central to the physical regime because the reservoir of chi is believed to lie in the stomach. The thrust is, therefore, to breathe using the 'stomach' or diaphragm to replenish our energy levels.

This belief cuts across practically all Chinese martial arts and methods for healing. In fact the practice of breath control in China dates further back to the period 221 BC to AD 906, when Taoism flourished. The Taoists developed breathing techniques call Qi Gong to control the flow of energy in the body. Used also to preserve and regulate the flow of semen, for healing and in martial arts, Qi Gong has revived in popularity in recent years. In Chinese acupressure, the point lying three fingers' width below the navel is referred to as the 'sea of energy'. In t'ai chi this is referred to as *tan tien*.

In t'ai chi the body is a unified entity and the tan tien is the centre of movement, with the arms and legs mere extensions of it. These vital points of energy are beliefs also shared by other Far Eastern practices such as Shiatsu in Japan and in Thai massage.

As a means of attack or defence t'ai chi is practised both with and without weapons. As an exercise discipline it seeks to promote health and relaxation through body conditioning which involves smooth, deliberate and rhythmic movements with carefully choreographed positions and stances. The stances emulate the movements of the bear, deer, monkey, tiger, snake and bird. Most of the movements are performed slowly, intercepted by occasional fast and rapid moves that might imitate, for example, an animal in flight.

Balance, coordination and breathing control are required. The entire body is involved, including movements of the eye, facial expressions (for example, raising the eyebrow), arms, legs, torso, hands, fingers, feet and toes. All movements flow one to another without any break and, depending on the school or the master, there can be 24 to over 100 prescribed exercise forms or chapters. Complete concentration and quiet is required. The ability to complete the prescribed chapters requires considerable memory power and patience. The underlying principle that binds the movements is the harmonisation of the two important forces in the universe, the *yin* (passive, female) and the *yang* (active, male). When they are in balance, equilibrium, peace and harmony are believed to have been achieved.

Many schools of T'ai Chi Chuan have existed and of these two remain today, the Wu and the Yang. In China, the discipline is handed down from master to student and no master teaches the system exactly like the other because the choreography has a story as its underlying base. There are however common moves based on the movements of creatures. Three main stances exist for the feet: weight forward, weight on the rear foot and weight to the side.

T'ai Chi Chuan is widely practised in China and by Chinese living outside China. Besides being an art form and exercise regime, it is a social activity, especially for the elderly. Early one morning, looking out from my hotel window in Beijing, I saw t'ai chi being practised in a nearby park. A sea of people in loose jackets moved in unison in a series of graceful movements in a ballet without music. When I was young my mother would go through a t'ai chi routine at the start of her day.

Open-air participation in t'ai chi is a common sight in Malaysia

In the western world, t'ai chi is generally used as an exercise. It provides moderate aerobic training, good motor skill development, memory training and concentration, moderate muscular strength and endurance, as well as flexibility training. The movements are largely low impact. The regime provides for the overall well-being of both mind and body. T'ai chi is not, however, geared to specific muscle development or body conditioning, although martial forms of t'ai chi provide for greater development of muscle strength and power.

## The Alexander technique

The Alexander technique was developed by Frederick Matthias Alexander. The first training school for teachers of the technique was set up by him in 1931, but practice of the technique dates back to the late 1890s and early 1900s. The Alexander technique does not involve an exercise programme and does not purport to be an exercise. It is basically tuned toward promoting an awareness of how we perform our daily activities, our posture, balance and coordination. By becoming aware of our body, we become conscious of the excessive muscular tension within it. This awareness is important because muscular tension is ultimately responsible for poor posture; poor posture, in turn, causes many of the ailments that people ascribe to ageing and wear and tear. From awareness, the next step is to re-educate the body to move and stand better so that equilibrium is restored.

To become free of muscular tension is an important objective of the discipline. To achieve it, people are prompted to stop and do nothing for a few minutes in order to prevent muscle tension from building up. The exercises prescribed relate mainly to matters of observation. First, comes the observation of ourselves in the mirror to see how we stand, sit and move, the angle of our head, whether one shoulder is up or down, the alignment of our spine and so on; second comes observing and executing moves without the mirror but mentally registering them, and finally, checking with the mirror to see if what is perceived as being executed has in fact been done. For example, if, with eyes closed, you attempt to stand 'correctly' with a straight back and feet aligned and pointing forward, when you open your eyes and look in a mirror you may well find that in reality your feet are not aligned and your body might be slightly to one side or the other. After the observation comes the education. To re-educate and bring about an improved way of standing or moving under the Alexander technique may require doing the very thing that feels wrong. The problem is complicated by the fact that people usually move in the way that they find most comfortable. There is also a need to re-educate response patterns by inhibiting the immediate automatic reaction in order to provide the opportunity for a different, better informed reaction.

The Alexander technique gives priority and importance to how the neck is held. When the neck muscles are overly tight, they interfere with the body's movements and throw it out of balance because the head, which leads the body, is not aligned properly with the spine. The dynamic relationship between the neck and head is referred to as primary control. When this is not in balance, then our reflexes will not be coordinated. Alexander illustrated the point with the example of a horse. When a rider pulls the horse's head back, the animal loses coordination and comes to a standstill.

The Alexander technique is not an exercise programme in the normal sense of the word. It uses body awareness, improved posture, movements and coordination to reduce muscle tension which he identified as a major cause of many stress-related illnesses such as hypertension, coronary heart disease, gastro-intestinal problems, headaches, migraine, insomnia, arthritis and backache.

## Pilates

Pilates is a body conditioning programme founded by Joseph H. Pilates in the 1920s. It focuses on three areas of the body, the abdomen, lower back and buttocks which are referred to as the core or power centre of the body. Like the Alexander technique, t'ai chi and yoga, it promotes body awareness and correct breathing to promote efficient movements, flexibility and muscle strength. The emphasis is on breathing with the diaphragm. Pilates, yoga, t'ai chi and the Alexander technique teach that if we breathe shallowly, the diaphragm does not flatten out as much. This is in part a result of not exhaling fully, hence, the emphasis in yoga on long exhalation. When the lungs are emptied they can be filled more efficiently. By being aware of a need to create space within the thorax for expansion of the lungs and going through the motion of actually creating it during the exercise (what in Pilates is call 'zipping up' and 'zipping down'), we breathe more effectively and efficiently.

Pilates takes two forms: fitness Pilates and rehabilitation Pilates. The former is for those interested in general fitness, sports training or postural improvement. The latter is used mainly by people who have been injured and need muscle rehabilitation and is mainly taught one to one and using equipment.

Fitness Pilates work-outs can be carried out either on mats using body resistance, the most widely used, or using apparatus. Apparatus sessions use a wide range of equipment – the reformer, cadillac, wall unit, chairs, pedipull, ladder barrel and barrels – to provide the resistance required for pushing and pulling activities. Irrespective of whether it is mat-based or using apparatus, the focus is on correct breathing and body alignment. Pilates has many features in common with yoga and Alexander technique. It is primarily a body conditioning and relaxation programme.

This very quick look at yoga, t'ai chi, the Alexander technique and Pilates reveals a common factor: they all emphasise body control, through improved breathing and body alignment. Through slow and controlled movement, they allow the mind to become more aware of the body. The focus on breathing and relaxing helps to de-stress muscles. They are holistic in the sense of bringing self-awareness and body movements together. They contrast with physical regimes such as aerobics and exercise to music classes where mental awareness is tuned to respond to external forces in a quick and coordinated way. They also contrast with energetic regimes because relaxation comes during the process of self-concentration (or withdrawal) whereas in energetic regimes, relaxation follows from the exercise.

As physical regimes, yoga, the Alexander technique and Pilates are incomplete. With the exception of t'ai chi there is little aerobic training in these exercises in the sense of raising the heart rate towards the personal maximum. If you breathe slowly you are bringing the heart rate down. Relaxation is good for the heart but to build greater strength in your cardiac muscle there is little to equal a good aerobic work-out. Hence, these exercises should be used to complement other more aerobic activities. Finally, as illustrated, all activities carry with them risks of injuries and the same applies to these four regimes. Much depends upon instructors and how they school and supervise their students. It is during the training to gain the muscle control needed for movements that the danger of injury is greatest.

# Finding the best combination: the art of 'fusion' exercise

Choosing what is best for you is entirely personal. For those seeking all five fitness components, one option is to have separate sessions of body conditioning, aerobics, stretching, motor-skill development to build up muscle strength and endurance, cardiac fitness, flexibility and coordination. The only problem is the time constraint: there are only seven days in a week! Taking each component in rotation would leave just two days for anything extra. Once a week for each is not enough, but fitting in more might be difficult.

Combining all the different fitness components in one work-out is, for many, the best way forward. It leaves extra time for focusing on priorities. For example, if you have three 'complete' work-outs there is still time for extra flexibility training or extra body conditioning. If you are unable to find that extra time, you are at least adequately covered.

To provide an all embracing session, teachers and instructors of fitness should seek to combine the best of all disciplines. The different disciplines do not have to be mutually exclusive and in fact, as I have shown, they are related. Rather than battle over what is 'right' and 'wrong', instructors should pause to re-examine the possibilities offered by the various disciplines.

Aerobic training is essential for the pursuit of a full fitness programme. To avoid teaching aerobics because of fears about the possibility of injury is opting out of the problem. People would still have to work-out aerobically to complement their holistic regimes. The same is true for teachers of aerobics, step and exercise to music classes. We have seen these same fears lead to a host of positions being removed from the recommended list of exercises. Perhaps more time should be spent on seeing how the dangers of getting into certain positions could be removed by incorporating breathing techniques and greater body awareness to promote correct body alignment.

Obviously there are certain fundamental principles that have to be observed for safety, but we would have at least examined all angles for the benefit of the user and increased the options available. The time has arrived to integrate all that is best into one.

To this end, I have incorporated the technique of breathing with the diaphragm and the use of pelvic and abdominal muscle control for achieving core stability in the step-by-step illustrated exercises presented in the following chapters on body conditioning and flexibility training, modifying and reinforcing them as necessary. It should be noted that 'breathing with the diaphragm' is not a human invention: it is simply a matter of human anatomy and physiology, as we have seen in Chapter 3 (pp. 33–4). By focusing on its importance, however, we will breathe more efficiently and deeply. (For more details on the concept, science and philosophy of fusion theory and exercises, see Chapters 8 and 9.)

I would also like to stress that I have not adopted available exercises piecemeal. The foundations of many holistic practices lie in antiquity. My approach has been to go back to the drawing board and revisit the musculo-skeletal structure, the movements of muscles, points of insertion and attachment, and energy systems in order to develop new or adapt existing exercises to make them more effective and safe. By placing this 'fusion' on a more scientific base and explaining the wherewithal, I hope to move beyond the myth and the 'good for you' approach. As sports science evolves and matures, more changes are likely to occur. This is just a beginning but I hope a constructive one. Now let us move first to the warm-up.

# The warm-up: getting ready to exercise

The importance of a warm-up was touched upon in the opening chapter when I introduced the need for a well-balanced work-out for fitness. This chapter considers the benefits of a warm-up in greater detail, what it should include and gives examples of how to prepare for different sports activities.

## What is a warm-up?

A warm-up is simply the performance of movements that prepare the body for more strenuous activities to follow. It includes movements that mobilise the joints, movements that raise the pulse rate to increase the blood supply to working muscles and a preparatory stretch.

The preparatory stretch is always done after the joints have been mobilised and the pulse rate raised. Whether we mobilise first before raising the pulse rate or vice versa varies with the activity and the environment. In exercise to music classes, the mobiliser comes before the pulse raiser, but if it is very cold, it may be better to boost blood circulation first by raising the heart beat. So some judgement is needed. Moreover, the distinction between the two activities is not always absolute. Activities that raise the pulse rate inevitably involve movement of joints, but they are not usually focused on the joints as such. For example, marching briskly, a typical pulse-raising activity, moves the hip joint slightly but mobilisation of this joint would involve actions focused specifically on the hip joint such as pelvic tilts and rotating the hips with the feet stationary.

## Mobilising joints

Muscles can only bring about movement when they cross a movable joint. It follows that if the joints are stiff, any strong muscle movement will cause stress on the joint it crosses and could easily result in injury. The muscles, including the tendons via which they insert into the bones, can also be damaged. Joints need to be introduced gently to the full range of their natural movements before embarking on strenuous activities. This ensures that the synovial fluid is warm and can act efficiently both as a lubricant and a buffer against impact.

The emphasis given to particular joints depends on the physical activities that follow, as well as those preceding, the exercise. Someone coming straight from the office where they have been sitting at a computer would require more shoulder and hip mobilising moves. These ball and socket joints, which are capable of the most diverse movement, are also the most susceptible to injury. The ankle and knee too are highly susceptible, largely because they carry the weight of the body and partly because the attached muscles are of unequal strength. The most important among the list of 'musts' for mobilisation are the hip or pelvic joint, shoulder joint, thoracic and lumbar regions, knees and ankles, because they usually bear the brunt of most activities. Circling the shoulders, rotating the hips, flexing the ankles and pointing the toes, bending the knees, side bends and rotating the upper torso with the hips stationary, are all examples of mobilising moves.

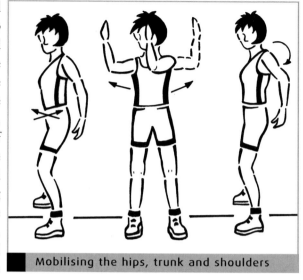

**Mobilising the hips, trunk and shoulders**

## Raising your pulse rate

The objective is to increase the heartbeat to some 50–60 per cent of the personal maximum, in order to increase the blood supply to working muscles and their connective tissues, including tendons and ligaments, so that they are warm and pliable. They will then be ready to take on a greater workload.

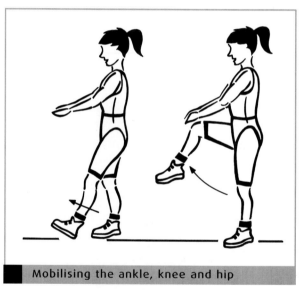

**Mobilising the ankle, knee and hip**

Rhythmic movements involving the large muscle groups, such as marching/brisk walking, side steps and step touch, that can be slowly increased in intensity, are widely used in aerobic classes. Generally, in exercise to music classes, this part of the warm-up is similar to the main aerobics component, except that it is slower, much lower in intensity and excludes explosive movements such as jumps and high kicks. Obviously the approach will vary according to the fitness of the participants. Again, some degree of judgement is needed.

# Preparatory stretches

These stretches should be done only after you are warm, otherwise they can be harmful. For example, if you are a runner or have arrived in the gym for a work-out on, say, the treadmill, do not stretch immediately. Take a few minutes to mobilise joints, loosen up muscles and increase blood flow. All muscles that are to be used in activities following the warm-up must be stretched. Usually this would always include the gastrocnemius (the main calf muscles), the soleus (inner calf), the hamstring and adductors. These are normally the muscles most used in practically any exercise regime. Runners would focus on the hamstring, shin and calves. Rowers would prepare with greater emphasis on the arms (deltoids, biceps and triceps), trapezius, pectorals and the quadriceps. Aerobic and body conditioning classes would also include the quadriceps, the erector spinae, the lumbar and the arms (deltoids and triceps).

Generally stretches are performed in a standing position in aerobic classes to maintain, as much as possible, the benefits of the raised heartbeat. Usually some pulse-raising movements are made between stretches in order to maintain the heartbeat. This helps participants to move smoothly to the aerobic component of the exercise. The figures below illustrate some of the main preparatory stretches.

Stretches are usually held for about 10–12 seconds, but there is no fixed rule. It can vary with the activity and level of training and flexibility of those involved. Sprinters might do their preparatory stretches on the ground because it provides the more intense stretch needed for the sprint. Doing a stretch supported by a wall or on the ground often helps to hold it with less pressure on the joints. Runners often hold stretches for 25–30 seconds, the length of time recommended for final stretches in aerobic classes rather than at the start. More examples of stretches are illustrated in Chapter 10, on flexibility training.

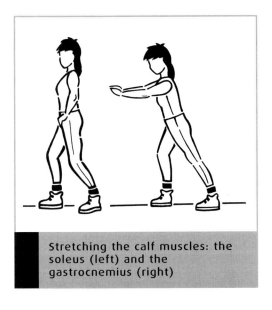

Stretching the calf muscles: the soleus (left) and the gastrocnemius (right)

Stretching the adductor muscles in the inner thigh (left) and the hamstring (right)

Stretching the deltoid (left) and the triceps (right)

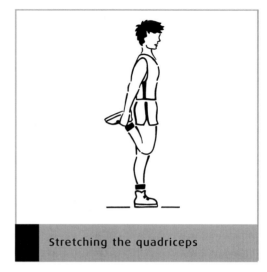

Stretching the quadriceps

# The benefits of a warm-up

Sport research has shown that a warm-up before the main exercise reduces substantially the incidence of sports injuries. By keeping muscles warm and joints well lubricated it reduces muscle tear and damage to joints. The cardio-respiratory system is allowed to build up gradually to the increased demand about to be made on it. This avoids the discomfort, including giddiness, palpitations and breathlessness, that can be provoked by a sudden increase in exertion. By sending preparatory signals to the brain that warn it of the type and range of activities the body is likely to be undertaking, it also improves the body's pattern of response and encourages good quality movement.

# Aerobic training: keeping on the curve

Aerobic activities include all physical exercises that are powered by the oxidation of food through a continuous cycle of ATP synthesis and energy release (see Chapter 3, Energy and energy systems). Aerobic activity can be carried out for a sustained period of time when the intensity of the exercise is reasonable. This means an intensity that is sufficient to make the work-out effective for improving the cardio-vascular and respiratory system, but not so hard that fatigue sets in and/or the anaerobic energy system takes over. The recommended training zone is generally between 60 and 80 per cent of the personal maximum heart beat (see Chapter 2, pp. 6–8).

The duration and frequency of exercise should be based on the FITTA principle, which stands for **F**requency, **I**ntensity, **T**ime, **T**ype and **A**dherence. Careful planning of these five elements is needed when embarking on activity because sporadic exertions bring little benefit. After two weeks of rest or inactivity, some 50 per cent of the fitness gained can be lost. Time must be set aside for regular exercise.

Regular aerobic activities contribute, over time, to important physiological changes in the body. Many of these changes relate to the cardio-vascular and respiratory systems. The heart increases in size and volume: the left ventricle, in particular, becomes stronger and more effective in pushing oxygenated blood into the aorta and on to the body. Each contraction propels a larger volume of blood than previously: both the stroke volume and maximum cardiac output increase. The improvement in the heart means that it does not work so hard in everyday life. Blood pressure improves both at rest and during activity. The same exercise routine carried out regularly over a period of time does not require the same effort.

Not only the heart improves: the number of blood capillaries increases in response to the larger volume of blood being handled. Men in training have a capillary density in their muscles as much as 40 per cent higher than those who lead a sedentary life. The larger number of capillaries mean that the oxygen released in the muscle increases. The body's other internal organs also benefit from the improved blood supply. The lungs become adapted to greater demands for oxygen and both the tidal volume and the oxygen intake increase. These improvements contribute significantly to reducing or ameliorating coronary heart diseases such as hypertension.

Muscles also benefit from aerobic activities. The muscle fibres change to contain more myoglobin, the oxygen-carrying pigment responsible for oxygen storage and release in muscle cells. Like haemoglobin in red blood cells, myoglobin contains iron and protein. There is a surge in the number of mitochondria, the tiny structures within the cell that are responsible for energy storage and release.

During training, total body mass and fat are reduced and lean body mass is increased. This helps raise the overall basal metabolic rate. As a result, aerobic activities, especially when complemented by healthy eating, help promote weight control or loss. Overall, you will feel and look better.

# Programming effective training: the aerobic curve

Careful planning is required to keep within the aerobic training zone. The activity must build up in intensity to reach it. The length of the build-up varies substantially depending on the chosen aerobic activity and personal fitness. It generally takes 2 to 5 minutes for the cardio-vascular/respiratory systems to respond to increased physical demand. Discomfort, even cramps, can occur if intense activity is rushed into. People who have not exercised before or who have had a long break from exercise, generally need more time for the build-up. More time may also be advisable if it is cold. Once perspiration begins the body is ready for more intensive activity which can be increased until the training zone is reached.

To remain within the plateau of the training zone, the intensity of the work-out has to be varied. In a dance or aerobic class, a combination of low and high impact moves is used to keep within the zone and to avoid involving the anaerobic energy system. Once the desired level of aerobic training has been completed, the intensity of the movements is gradually reduced. This build-down helps to bring the heart beat steadily back to its normal rate. This phase is essential to avoid the pooling of blood in the calf muscles.

Together, the build-up to the training zone, the maintenance of activity at this plateau and the subsequent build-down constitute the *aerobic curve*. The aerobic curve varies according to the needs and objectives of participants. In a simple aerobic curve, the aim is to work essentially towards a peak heart rate while remaining in the training zone. A fit person requires less time for the build-up and build-down and can spend more time in the training zone. The figure opposite provides an example of the proportion of time that could be spent by a beginner and an advance trainer in the different phases of aerobic training. The table provides estimates of the target heart rates within the effective training zone. This declines with age.

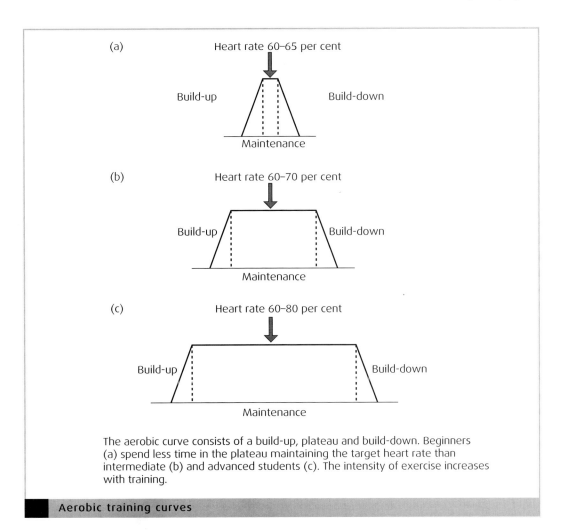

The aerobic curve consists of a build-up, plateau and build-down. Beginners (a) spend less time in the plateau maintaining the target heart rate than intermediate (b) and advanced students (c). The intensity of exercise increases with training.

**Aerobic training curves**

**Effective personal training zone**

| Age | Personal maximum heart rate | |
|---|---|---|
| years | 60 per cent | 80 per cent |
| 20 | 120 | 160 |
| 25 | 117 | 156 |
| 30 | 114 | 152 |
| 35 | 111 | 148 |
| 40 | 108 | 144 |
| 45 | 105 | 140 |
| 50 | 102 | 136 |
| 55 | 99 | 132 |
| 60 | 96 | 128 |

# Different kinds of aerobic training

## Running

A variety of techniques are used in training for running. Hill training sessions, for example, make the leg muscles contract more forcefully than normal. Uphill training increases the concentration of aerobic enzymes in the leg muscles which eventually adapts the muscles to work at high levels without fatigue. The run could be sequenced as follows: a warm-up jog (equivalent to your build-up), followed by a fast uphill jog, then a downhill jog to allow some recovery, followed again by an uphill stint. The sequence is repeated four to five times. The number of repetitions varies with a person's fitness, but generally the 'reps' should be increased with increased fitness. The uphill run could also be increased and the recovery downhill run reduced in order to increase the intensity of the work-out. The sequencing means that several aerobic peaks are involved.

The term *fartlek*, meaning 'speed play' in Swedish, underlines the basis for some of the training methods used by runners. This imitates race conditions where it is necessary to surge forward to break away from the other runners. Here too, sudden peaking is involved, but the duration of these sequences is not predetermined. For example the training might be to run until a bicycle is about to overtake, then to run faster to try to prevent it, and once having been overtaken, to slow down. Since when the next bicycle is going to pass cannot be anticipated, the spurt is not at regular intervals.

Long-distance running involves yet another technique. Training for marathons by running long distances regularly depletes muscle fibres of muscle glycogen and may even damage them because of the repeated accumulation of lactic acid. The general consensus among trainers is that the intensity of training, not the duration, is important. In other words, running slowly for a long distance is less effective as a preparation than running fast for a shorter distance. Based on a similar principle to fartlek, the recommendation is to inject short spurts of speed every few minutes into the run. This helps to activate the fast twitch muscles without causing lactic acid to accumulate. Increasing the aerobic potential of fast twitch muscle fibres helps in a long-distance run when the slow twitch muscles start to fatigue, generally after about 45 minutes. This form of training is beneficial because it teaches the body to burn fat and conserve glycogen. Here too, the aerobic curve is multi-peak, but with greater frequency.

Treadmills are useful aids to training because they remove the element of uncertainty in weather and terrain and can imitate uphill, flat and downhill conditions. Running on the treadmill is obviously different from running outside; it requires less energy for the same speed because the runner is unaffected by the elements, particularly the wind, and the unevenness of the ground. Training needs can be simulated to some extent on the treadmill by varying the angle and the speed.

# Exercise to music and aerobic classes

Exercise to music classes are generally considered to be aerobic, although in most cases they also have some anaerobic components. The classes are designed to embrace all five principles of fitness: cardio-vascular efficiency, strength, endurance, motor skills and flexibility. Usually they start with a warm-up, followed by aerobics, body conditioning (muscular strength and endurance) and stretch. Aerobics classes, by way of contrast, concentrate primarily on cardio-vascular efficiency and generally have little or no body conditioning or floor work. The following discussion focuses on the aerobic component of exercise to music classes and can also be used to design pure aerobic classes.

The most commonly used training structure in aerobic components or classes is a single peak aerobic curve where participants build up to a peak heart rate which is held for a period according to the fitness of the class or individual. Thereafter the intensity of the exercise is reduced until the heart beat returns more or less to the starting rate. The build-up begins with rhythmic hand and leg movements that are low in both intensity and impact. These movements are then gradually interspersed with higher impact/higher intensity ones; the tempo of the music rises and the beat becomes more motivating. The alternation of movements continues, all the time increasing the intensity of the exercise, until the ratio of high to low is much bigger. When the peak is reached, the ratio of high to low impact movements might be maintained for a while (see the figure on p. 65) and then comes the build-down. Gradually the arm movements are reduced and the music slows. The low impact/intensity moves increase until they are predominant. A double or multi-peak sequencing of aerobic training can also be followed using this pattern.

After deciding on the aerobic structure, the next step is to plan its execution. To do this we draw upon a bank of movements that have been devised for aerobics. Some of the most frequently used ones are illustrated below. The build-up would start with low impact moves which are generally gentler movements where one foot is on the ground. Examples include the brisk walk, grapevine, step tap, scoops and box steps. The vigour of these movements can be increased moderately with more intense low-impact moves such as side and back lunges (extending the leg to

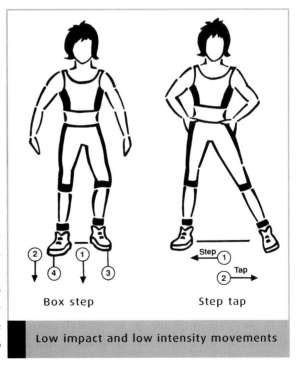

Box step          Step tap

**Low impact and low intensity movements**

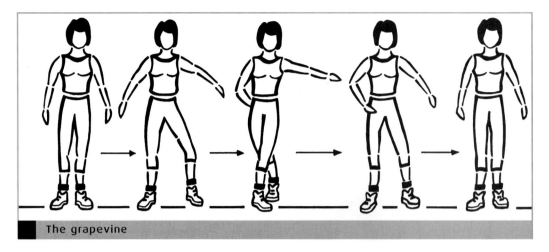

The grapevine

side and back), heel digs (flex the foot with the heel on ground) and low knee lifts. In the case of arms, gentler movements are those with shorter arm leverage such as biceps curls and the upright row. The higher you raise the arms, the greater the intensity of the workout because the heart has to work harder to pump blood to them. Big staccato movements such as punching out are also more energetic than smooth flowing ones such as arms swaying from side to side.

Side lunges, knee lifts and heel digs

As the intensity increases, all the above steps could be executed with a bounce, with one foot still on the ground, initially at low levels and possibly followed by higher foot lifts at increased speed. By this time the point in the curve would probably have been reached where high impact moves might be incorporated. High impact is when both feet are off the ground and could include jumping jacks, flick kicks, power jumps, power lunge, fast jog and knee lifts, accompanied by a jump that brings both feet off the floor.

It is important to alternate high and low impact moves to avoid excessive stress on the musculo-skeletal structure and possible injury. The high impact moves encourage an increase in the aerobic capacity of the fast twitch muscles thereby increasing endurance when they come to the aid of fatiguing slow twitch muscles. This is similar in effect to the training for long-distance running mentioned earlier.

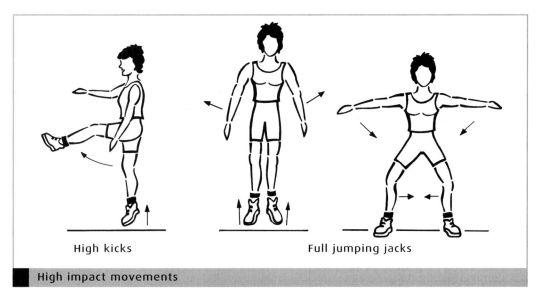

High kicks                    Full jumping jacks

**High impact movements**

The appropriate mix of low and high intensity and impact movements depends on the age, fitness level and objectives of the participants. In general, low-impact aerobics are recommended for beginners, overweight individuals, those with a low level of fitness, the elderly and individuals who have not exercised for a while. For these candidates, the progression along the aerobic curve would involve only low-impact movements. Intensity is increased by a moderate quickening and strengthening of leg and arm movements.

While low-impact aerobics can be used safely throughout the aerobic routine, the same cannot be said for high-impact. Attempting to train aerobically using only high-impact moves would almost certainly lead to exhaustion. Whatever the mix in terms of high and low, the movements must be varied to give interest. It must ensure all big muscle groups are worked and all round training achieved. Excessive repeats can result in boredom, exhaustion and even injuries. The participant will move out of the aerobic curve and the training zone. At the extreme, unbalanced muscular development occurs.

## Circuits and other aerobic activities

In a classroom environment, circuits are a popular form of aerobic training. People can do them at their own pace, and thus the training zone can be varied to suit the personal maximum. At the same time, stations in the circuit can be arranged to provide whatever peaking sequence is desired. It provides variety, reducing any likelihood of muscle over-use. However, to keep this an aerobic activity and to avoid a sudden drop in heart beats, it is not advisable to have stations such as abdominal crunches following vigorous activities such as lunges, high kicks and jumping jacks. The sudden switch to a prone position can lead to giddiness. There is a also a loss of aerobic efficiency.

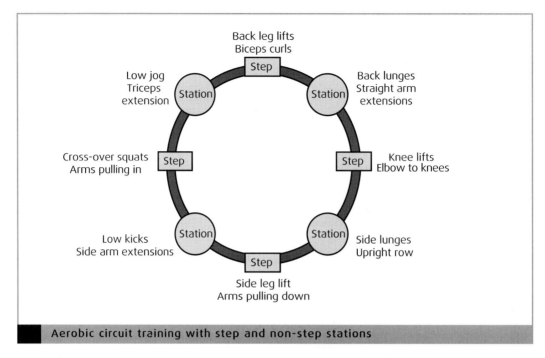

**Aerobic circuit training with step and non-step stations**

Aerobic training using circuits requires at least three minutes at each station using a moderate intensity of exercise. This is the minimum time needed to build up to a sufficiently high oxygen uptake. Up to 12 minutes might be needed at low-intensity levels. If the same big muscles groups are used in consecutive stations, the duration at each station should be at the minimum. The increased time that needs to be spent at each station in an aerobic circuit contrasts with the requirements of strength development.

Prolonged resistance training to build up strength of any single muscle group would result in an accumulation of lactic acid and fatigue. Rest intervals are vital for strength training and, since they allow the heart beat to slow, it is preferable to set strength training aside as a separate activity, for example at the end of the aerobic circuit session before the cool down and stretch. This is not to say that circuits should not be used for muscular strength and endurance training, but aerobic circuits are best kept separate from them.

Outdoor activities such as walking, cycling, cross-country skiing, rowing and swimming are also good aerobic activities. Just as with conventional aerobic training, the principle of alternating the pace of the activities should be applied where feasible.

# Avoiding over-training

Reference has already been made to the the importance of training regularly. While busy people can find this difficult, for others the problem is overzealousness. This can easily lead to over-training, with harmful rather than beneficial results.

Training is based on the principle of overload, giving the muscles more work than usual. It is, therefore, about physical stress and stimulus on the musculo-skeletal system to encourage improvement. If this is over-done regularly, the over-training syndrome sets in. Instead of maintaining the exhilaration that comes after a good work-out because of the healthy dose of endorphins that is released into the system, chronic fatigue sets in and remains throughout the day. Other symptoms include raised heart rate early in the morning, slow recovery of heart rate after training, muscle soreness, absence of menstruation, susceptibility to infection, weight loss and even diarrhoea and intestinal imbalance.

The body, exhausted from the incessant abuse, is giving out important signals that have to be recognised and treated. In the case of an athlete training for competition, these symptoms indicate that he or she has gone beyond their peak performance. More training does not necessarily mean better results because the dividing line between peak performance and over-training is very fine. For the overzealous, working out to lose weight, the feeling of sluggishness could easily inspire 'comfort' eating.

The over-training syndrome appears to affect athletes engaged in aerobic activities, especially long-distance runners, more than those involved in anaerobic sports. Training in anaerobic sports (which rely on lactate as an energy source) provides less opportunity because fatigue soon sets in, inhibiting further training.

The chronic over-training syndrome has to be treated with complete rest for as much as six weeks, during which time depression could set in because of the enforced inactivity. To avoid over-training, rest days must be incorporated into the exercise regime to allow muscles and body cells to recuperate. Other forms of milder activities could be undertaken during this period. To restore glycogen levels in the muscles an interval of some 24 hours between intensive training sessions is required.

# Body conditioning: training for strength and endurance

Training for strength and endurance results in significant beneficial changes in the body. The number of muscle fibres increases as does the proportion of fast twitch muscles. The net result is an increase in the force and power that muscles can exert as well an extension of the range and type of physical work that can be done. The presence of more muscle fibres increases the lean body mass and with it the basal metabolic rate. Strengthening the postural muscles provides more support to the skeletal frame and helps improve posture and body shape. Strengthening the muscles used in movement improves physical performance generally. Strength training helps individuals whose muscles have atrophied after long illnesses to regain the ability and confidence to move and work. Conditioned muscles look better, perform better and endure better.

The objectives of training for strength and endurance can go beyond muscle tone. Body builders, for example, train intensively using high external resistance (weights etc.) to increase muscle bulk. Sprinters and discus and javelin throwers also train for strength. Each of these pursuits benefits from its own particular training regime. This chapter, however, will focus on muscle tone rather than such specialist training regimes.

## Basic principles of muscle contraction

Muscles work through contraction in essentially one of three ways:

* *concentrically* – the muscle shortens bringing the two ends closer together

* *eccentrically* – the muscle lengthens under tension to its normal length

* *isometrically* or *statically* – the length of the muscle remains unchanged under tension as the muscle holds a position.

In a sit-up or abdominal crunches, for example, the rectus abdominus, which originates from the pubic bone and inserts into the ribs, contracts concentrically lifting the trunk upwards. When the trunk goes back to its normal position, the rectus abdominus is contracting eccentrically because it is returning to its normal length under tension (see figure on p. 74). In squats, the quadriceps contract eccentrically when going down and concentrically when

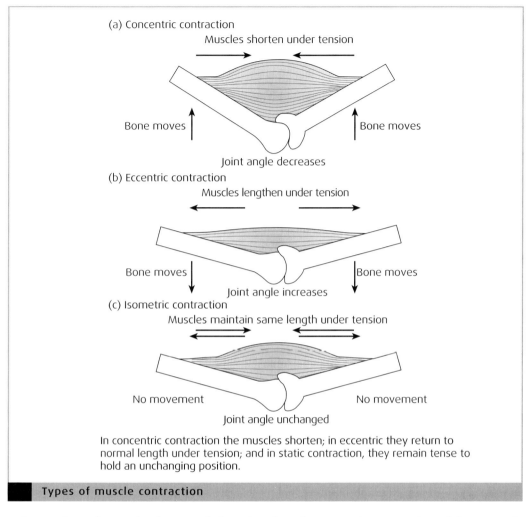

(a) Concentric contraction

Muscles shorten under tension

Bone moves

Bone moves

Joint angle decreases

(b) Eccentric contraction

Muscles lengthen under tension

Bone moves

Bone moves

Joint angle increases

(c) Isometric contraction

Muscles maintain same length under tension

No movement

No movement

Joint angle unchanged

In concentric contraction the muscles shorten; in eccentric they return to normal length under tension; and in static contraction, they remain tense to hold an unchanging position.

**Types of muscle contraction**

going up. In push-ups, the downward phase involves the eccentric contraction of the pectorals while the upward phase involves a concentric contraction. In brief, concentric contractions occur when the direction of movement is opposite from the pull of gravity, while eccentric contractions occur in the direction of gravity.

Concentric and eccentric contractions come under *isotonic training* which aims to allow the muscle to develop tension in opposing movement. In practice, the tension varies depending on the angle of the lever at the joint and the speed of the contraction or movement. In eccentric contraction, the downward phase of the movement, the muscle has to work with gravity and must act as a brake to stop the limb or the part being moved from falling suddenly. This creates greater resistance for the muscle at work. If the eccentric phase is lengthened by slowing down the downward motion, the muscle is put to greater effort and tension. In a progressive training programme, therefore, the ratio of concentric and eccentric contractions is varied and their length of implementation lengthened to provide the over-load needed to improve strength.

Static contractions, that is allowing the muscle to develop tension without varying the length of the muscle, are used in *isometric training* regimes. Although loosely referred to as static contractions, the prime mover muscle does shorten internally, but because it is offset by a contraction of the antagonist (opposing) muscle, the muscle length appears unchanged. In most cases, these contractions are generally effected by holding a position.

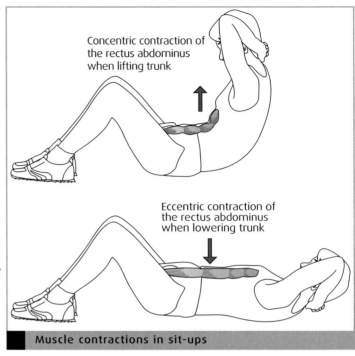

Concentric contraction of the rectus abdominus when lifting trunk

Eccentric contraction of the rectus abdominus when lowering trunk

**Muscle contractions in sit-ups**

Isometric training is useful when there is insufficient space for sweeping movements. More importantly, it is useful for developing strength at specific spots (muscle around the joint where it is targeted) for specific activities which require a position to be sustained for a long time. This would include activities such as downhill skiing, gymnastics, t'ai chi and yoga. Since it involves less motion, isometric training avoids sudden changes in the angle of execution, reducing the incidence and possibilities of injuries to the joints.

For those starting exercise with problems in their joints, such as the knee, static contractions of muscles, in this instance the quadriceps, offer a good introduction to exercise. These advantages or benefits bring with them some disadvantages. The impact of isometric training is limited to specific target areas. Because isometric contractions do not involve much movement, there is no improvement in motor skills and coordination. Finally, static contractions result in reduced blood flow to the heart during such exertion and higher systolic and diastolic pressures than other strength training methods.[13] Because of its benefits, isometric exercise has a role to play and remains widely used in the fitness industry, especially with the rise of holistic regimes, and for exercising after injuries. It is important, however, to use isometric training in moderation and in conjunction with isotonic training. It is not recommended for those with heart problems.

Modern technology has focused on these two broad categories of muscle training with the development of equipment that changes the position of the exercise and speed of contraction and different forms of weight to provide added resistance. Faced by a bewildering choice, how should one choose?

Moderation, consistency and a firm commitment to the five goals of fitness should, again, serve as the guiding principles. It is important to master the correct techniques and positions for isotonic and isometric contractions using the body as the main resistance before moving on to the use of weights and equipment. If the body is held correctly, it offers an ideal medium for providing the resistance required at least initially.

Whether weights are needed depends on the objectives: do you wish to tone and firm up and maintain this condition or do you wish to build greater muscle definition or bulk? Although men are more likely than women to build muscle bulk because of the size of their muscle fibres (both slow and fast twitch) and greater concentrations of the hormone testosterone, women themselves differ in their propensity to build muscle. Whereas female ectomorphs tend not to build up bulky muscle mass, endomorphs and mesomorphs are more prone to the hypertrophy of muscles (see p. 41). Therefore, if you fall within the mesomorph or endomorph categories and don't want to increase your muscle bulk, increasing the number of repetitions might be preferable to increasing resistance by using weights. By contrast, ecotomorphs could embark on body-building programmes to increase strength using weights without necessarily building bulky muscles.

Whatever the objectives, good body alignment is needed to have an effective and safe strength training. If the body position is incorrectly held, the use of external resistance could exacerbate the injuries that can result. For example, lifting the leg outward and sideways to work the gluteals and the leg abductors (tensor fascia lata), can easily transfer the stress to the small of the back, and if external resistance were to be added through the use of ankle weights, the stress would be even more severe.

It is vital to work opposing muscle groups (see box below). If the quadriceps are strengthened, for example, the hamstring should be strengthened as well. Otherwise,

| Selected major opposing muscle groups | | |
|---|---|---|
| Lower limbs | quadriceps | hamstring |
| | tibialis anterior | gastocnemius/soleus |
| | adductor longus, magnus and brevis | gluteas medius and minimus, tensor fascia lataus |
| | iliopsoas/hip flexor | gluteus maximus |
| Upper limbs | flexors of wrists and fingers | extensors of wrists and fingers |
| | biceps | triceps |
| | deltoid | latissimus dorsi |
| Torso | pectoralis | rhomboids/trapezius |
| | rectus abdominus | erector spinae |

unbalanced muscle strength will lead to poor posture and unequal stress on the body's musculo-skeletal structure. The most widespread example is the problem of shin splints – a fine stress fracture which results in pain at the front and sides of the lower leg. This is common among runners because of the imbalance between the strong gastrocnemius and soleus muscles (the calves) and the weak tibialis anterior muscles in the shin. An excessive amount of jumping, skipping and similar high impact moves in class exercises can also result in this because the powerful contractions of the calf muscles result in their over-development. The gastrocnemius and soleus become tight, causing stress in the opposing muscle, the tibialis anterior. The build-up of pressure in the muscle, a condition known as compartment syndrome, causes pain.

The FITTA (frequency, intensity, time, type and adherence) principle described in aerobic training applies also in training for endurance, strength and body conditioning. While the training should be regular and sufficiently frequent to have an impact (three to four times a week), there must be sufficient rest between training sessions and between muscles worked. The intensity of the training has to be moderated to ensure that muscles are over-loaded but not excessively so. Over-vigorous training can injure muscle attachments and joints because muscles respond to training much faster than the ligaments and tendons to which they are attached. If intensity is excessive, fatigue sets in, resulting in poor performance, incorrect positions and injuries.

The type of exercise and the time devoted to it need careful planning, taking into account objectives, fitness and age. It is important to stay with an exercise regime and to acquire correct techniques in terms of body alignment and breathing. Switching from one type of strength and endurance training to another will not serve much purpose. To achieve the desired results, consistency is required. Progress can take the form of increasing the resistance, repetitions, varying the speed of contractions, increasing the duration of the work-out and shortening the rests between the different sets of exercise.

# Training using body resistance: the fusion recipe

In Chapter 5, I reviewed the various 'holistic' regimes, including yoga, t'ai chi, Pilates and Alexander technique, that have grown in popularity in recent years. A common theme runs through all of these, namely that they have grown in popularity partly because of the search for safer methods of exercising and the search by many people for greater tranquillity in life. We also saw, however, that in practice not all that is considered holistic (a loose use of the word because they are not holistic in the sense of being complete fitness programmes) is necessarily safe.

Nevertheless, all of these regimes have elements that are especially beneficial for achieving health and fitness. Examples include the emphasis on correct body alignment, an awareness of breathing and its use to promote relaxation, and greater stability and control of the body. I have integrated these basic tenets of the Eastern arts that provide the tranquillity and sought-for safety in work-outs into the main stream exercise regimes of the West. This, however, is not the complete story. In building up the fusion recipe I have also reviewed other practices such as Lotte Berk exercises and callanetics. They too have had an influence on the exercises contained in the following chapters. So while you will find similarities between the fusion recipe and all the practices mentioned, you will also see significant differences, both in terms of concept and practice.

## Correct body alignment

The emphasis placed by fusion exercises on body alignment is aimed at bringing mainstream Western exercises in line with some of the more attractive aspects of Eastern practices. This is not to say that Western sports science does not know about body alignment, but knowing and implementing it are two different things. Haste and the tendency in modern life to 'get on with it' often mean that people rush to undertake an exercise movement without taking the time to assume the correct body posture. Rarely in the past did we see a body-conditioning class spend time in aligning the body or getting into the correct starting position. In the fusion recipe for fitness and health, alignment of the body and breathing techniques are the cornerstone of any movements. The focus is to get the body into an alignment where the normal curvature of the spine is maintained (see Chapter 3) without the rigid tensing of the muscular system to hold the body. It is important to note that this does not necessarily mean a perfect upright posture with shoulders braced back, neck stiff and chin tilted forward, such as is generally associated with, say, a soldier standing to attention or even the rigid stance that we were made to adopt in PE lessons when I was a young girl. Normal actually means the ability to maintain balance in the body with the head relaxed on top of the neck, neither too far forward or back, so that the rest of the body does not need to compensate for any potential imbalance. Here, I am also influenced by the Alexander technique of body awareness, but taking it well beyond day-to-day activities into the arena of exercise regimes.

In the fusion approach every exercise starts by checking on the posture and position of the body. Starting without ensuring that your body is correctly aligned can lead to injuries, but spending a little time to get into the proper alignment optimises the results that you can obtain from the exercises.

You should ensure that your weight is evenly distributed, that you are not standing more on one leg than the other nor pushing too far forward or leaning too far back. Check also that your neck is relaxed and free, that the head sits comfortably on it, and that shoulders are relaxed with the shoulder blades down and not rounded forward. The crown of your head should be aligned with your feet: if the head is too far forward, the buttocks will be pushed back to maintain balance, and vice versa. Above all, ensure that the hip, or pelvic area, is wide and stable and the back is not rounded or the small of the back pushed forward and the buttocks back. This applies equally whether you are standing, kneeling or lying on your back. Think of your spine as building blocks stacked on top of each other, perfectly balanced without the need to be held rigidly in place by muscles.

When you are lying on your back, check that you are not slanted or rolled over to one side or the other, that both shoulders are on the floor and that the weight of the body is evenly distributed with both sides of the buttocks resting evenly on the floor. Your neck should be long at the back: if the head is tilted up, the neck hyperextends and movements can result in stress to the back of the neck. Test if you have the correct position by gently raising your head using both hands to support the base of the skull and then bring the chin slightly in towards the chest, freeing the neck. Then gently place the head down again and turn gently from side to side. You should be able to turn from side to side freely. With practice, you will assume the correct position automatically.

If you are lying on you side, make sure that your legs are stacked on top of each other and that your hip joints are also aligned on top of each other.

If you are on all fours, ensure that the weight of the body is evenly distributed; check by observing if you are pressing more on one hand than the other; check that the hip joint is aligned above your knees; and check also that your back is in a neutral position and not sagging.

## Core stability

When you begin an exercise movement, several things happen. As I have explained in earlier chapters, you have the main muscle moving to effect the work-out (prime mover), the supporting muscle working to assist the movement (antagonist muscle) and muscles contracting to stabilise the joints (synergist muscles) to ensure the principal movements are made efficiently and effectively. Without the coordinated and synchronised movements of the synergist muscles, the work-out would not be effective and, even worse, injuries could occur. When you pull one limb of a puppet, all the other bits of the body start moving around because there is nothing to make it stable. We are not like that because muscles automatically act synergistically to stabilise the body during movement. Even so, the body works better if you get into a 'correct' body position that facilitates this stabilisation.

Consider a situation where sit-ups are performed with the legs extended straight in front. This unstable position causes the iliopsoas muscle (see opposite) to contract synergistically to stabilise the lower trunk, pulling the lower back off the floor, which in turn results in injury and stress to the back. This is a good example of an exercise gone wrong because the stability of the body was not ensured at the outset. How can we ensure stability of the body so as to allow the strengthening of the intended muscle group freely, effectively and safely?

Stability means control. Several key stabilising muscles need to be involved. Among the most important is the transverse abdominus (see p. 87). Others include the illipsoas, which consists of two muscles, the iliacus and the psoas, the multifidus, the pelvic floor muscles, the adductor brevis, the rectus abdominus, the obliques, the diaphragm and the erector spinae (see also Chapter 9).

The most important muscle is the transverse abdominal muscle, because this acts as a corset for the trunk, holding it in position so that the limbs can move from a stable base without distortion or injury to the body, principally protecting the spine and the hip. Engaging the iliopsoas or hip flexor provides stability whenever movements involve the lower limbs or trunk. As explained earlier (see Chapter 5), this is very much in line with the principles of t'ai chi where the 'tan tien' (the point three fingers' width below the navel) is regarded as the central core of the body, and limb movements are mere extensions of it. In all probability, when t'ai chi originated in ancient China, little would be known of muscle structure, hence the almost magical explanation and translation of 'heavenly gate' for what in practice is a very sound principle for movements. If you stabilise the central core of your body, you move and perform better. This is the tenet from which fusion exercises take its cue.

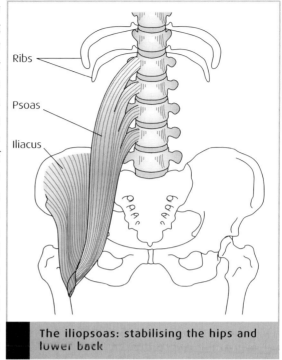

**The iliopsoas: stabilising the hips and lower back**

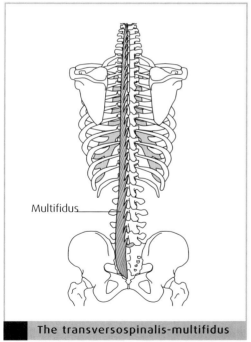

**The transversospinalis-multifidus**

How do we engage these stabilising muscles? As in most of the Eastern martial practices, including t'ai chi, fusion exercises focus on breathing techniques to engage the transverse abdominal muscles as a stabilising force (see Chapter 9). You will see, over and over again in my descriptions of movements in the following chapters, the instruction to inhale letting the belly expand and, more importantly, to exhale letting the navel move towards the spine. When breathing out to draw the navel towards the spine, think of an imaginery point lying three fingers' width below the navel and aim to draw that point and the abdominal area below, inwards. This engages the transverse abdominal muscles more effectively and allows the rib cage to remain wide and stable for normal breathing. If you allow the navel to move towards the spine when breathing out, but at the same time constrict the upper abdominal muscles, breathing is hampered and the transverse abdominal muscles are not effectively engaged. As you breathe out, sending the navel towards the spine, the diaphragm relaxes and draws with it the transverse abdominal muscles because the two are interconnected. This exhalation creates a hollowing of the abdomen. Almost simultaneously the iliopsoas is also engaged, as the pelvis tilts gently forward to help stabilise the pelvic girdle. This, in turn, stabilises the trunk and spine as well as the lower limbs. This series of stabilising movements, initiated by breathing, provides the stable base with which to work.

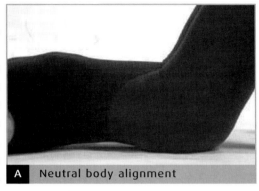

A  Neutral body alignment

You can increase stability even more, if need be, by drawing the adductor brevis, the short inner thigh muscles spanning the ischial tuberosity, pubic ramus and the femur at the top end of the thigh, inward as though you were doing a pelvic floor exercise (for more, see the following chapter and p. 94). This latter is the key to the breathing techniques used in Qi

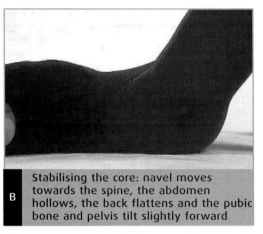

B  Stabilising the core: navel moves towards the spine, the abdomen hollows, the back flattens and the pubic bone and pelvis tilt slightly forward

Qong for the regulation of energy flows. I have also incorporated this in the fusion exercises for stretching and relaxation, as you will see in Chapter 10. This is especially beneficial when breathing exercises for relaxation are carried out from a sitting (normally cross-legged or in half and full lotus) position because it provides greater anchorage to the ground, freeing the lungs encased in the rib cage to respond to the calming effect of the breathing exercise. An additional bonus, of course, is the beneficial impact on the pelvic floor.

My mother used to draw heavily on breathing technique as an expert markswoman. I recall when I was a child that she would spend hours standing in position gripping a hand weight and breathing into the position to stabilise her aim for free and .38 pistol shooting. Often, my brothers and I tried in vain to push her. So proud was she of her stability that well into her 60s she was still able to challenge her grandchildren to dislodge her from her stance. It certainly brought its rewards. Among her many achievements, she was a Gold Medallist in the Asian Festival of Sports of 1975. Now in her 70s, she remains a staunch proponent of t'ai chi and Qi Qong exercises.

Other muscles can be brought into play to stabilise the body. If the exercise involves the upper limbs, the trapezius might also be involved. Arm exercises with rigidly held shoulders are likely to transfer the stress to the neck and the rhomboids – the muscle in the middle of the upper back along the spinal column. Breathing in to raise the shoulder (scapula) up and exhaling to bring it down will engage the trapezius muscles to stabilise the upper back, returning the scapula into its normal alignment. This allows the arms to work freely. Exercises involving the lower limbs hinge primarily on the stability of the core pelvic girdle described above, and the alignment of the knee over the ankle.

In all the exercises in the chapters that follow, I place great emphasis on maintaining normal spinal curvature during movement, i.e. during the execution of the exercise, in order to avoid stress on the small of the back. In some exercises, however, the starting position might not involve this 'neutral' curvature. When lying down on the back, a normal spinal curvature generally means that the small of the back is raised slightly off the floor, but this position does not sustain and support the back when the legs are moved, even if the transverse abdominal muscle is engaged. This is especially the case when the stomach muscles are too weak to maintain that so-called corset control. To provide additional support a very slight pelvic tilt is

## How does Fusion Fitness differ from Pilates?

Because both disciplines talk about core stability, I have often been asked the difference between the two. The many versions of Pilates make a direct comparison difficult, but the following points are, I believe, relevant in any discussion of fusion fitness and Pilates.

In a typical fusion fitness class, cardiovascular exercises (focused on improving the heart, lung and respiratory and blood circulatory system) and motor skill development remain as essential components, alongside strength, endurance and flexibility training. Mat-based Pilates has little or no cardio-vascular component or dynamic motor skill development. Both disciplines place great emphasis on core stability and on the role of the transverse abdominal muscles in providing it, but fusion exercises make greater use of the pelvic roll to maintain core stability. As explained in the main text, the involvement of the iliopsoas is particularly beneficial when the abdominal muscles are too weak to maintain the core position unaided. In addition, Pilates exercises start with a neutral spinal curvature while the emphasis of fusion exercise is on maintaining normal spinal curvature during movements.

The portfolio of exercises used in fusion fitness classes is generally different from those in Pilates, although there are, as in all disciplines, some

similarities. In strength and endurance training, fusion exercises rely on the principle of overload based on a progressive build-up of body resistance to the work-out as the participant gains in strength. Both isotonic and isometric training techniques are used, but with a greater emphasis on isotonic exercises. Fusion exercises also have little in common with apparatus-based Pilates.

In structure, fusion classes remain essentially the same as those taught in exercise to music classes. The principle of pursuing all five fitness components remains intact. The fusion recipe, however, brings together all the features that make the holistic regimes effective and sought after and incorporates them within the mainstream of exercise classes while avoiding those movements and positions that I believe to be less safe.

My pursuit of 'fusion' is largely because I see little purpose in compartmentalising the good features of any particular regime, obliging participants to attend separate sessions of different disciplines. Time is precious and the full panoply of exercise regimes may not be available. Integration and not separatism should be the aim so that the widest possible range of participants can draw upon the best of oriental and occidental fitness regimes within a single session.

introduced. The introduction of a small pelvic tilt at the start of the exercise enhances the stability of the pelvic girdle, especially in exercises for the buttock and upper thigh muscles. This increases the effectiveness of the exercise, providing greater resistance to the work-out.

While the tilt flattens the lower back slightly at the start of the exercise, normal curvature is resumed once movement commences, leaving the stabilising muscles to maintain control of the position. In this, fusion exercises converge with the oriental martial technique of maintaining a stable stance rather than more modern practices such as Pilates, which starts with a neutral normal spinal curvature (see box on p. 81).

The benefits of maintaining a stable base during movement are significant. Working with a stable base reduces the likelihood of injury, including stress on joints, and especially injury to the back. It improves the performance and effectiveness of the work-out because it reduces the involvement of other supporting muscles, allowing the workload of the exercise to fall squarely on the muscle that is being targeted. For example, in raising the leg sideways with a stable base, you are using the outer thigh and buttock muscles (abductors and gluteals) and not the hips (iliopsoas). Significant improvement in posture and bearing will result. Appearance and confidence will improve and, more importantly, problems generally associated with poor posture such as back pain, headaches and poor breathing and movements will diminish. Engagement of the transverse abdominal muscle will also contribute significantly to a flatter tummy.

## Getting it together the Fusion Fitness way

Moving from the Eastern techniques related to breath control, body alignment and core stability (with the addition of the slight pelvic roll for increased stability), I then reviewed the musculo-skeletal structure of the human body, as well as its mechanics. I drew up a series of exercises using the principles of isotonic and isometric contractions that would condition the muscles and improve their strength and performance and, in the process, appearance of the body. I drew upon the existing bank of exercises, modifying them with the principles outlined above. Using this fusion recipe I also developed new exercises to meet some of the more specific problem areas that men and women have.

I hope that the following chapters will help tackle the common problems of flabby tummies, legs and under-arms, love-handles and sagging bottoms. I have achieved considerable success with my own students who range in age from their late teens to 70 years old or more. But, one word of advice. It is vital to acquire the techniques of body alignment, breathing and stability control before rushing to do large number of reps, or repetitions, and sets of these exercises. Spend time acquiring these techniques by stopping when you lose control over body alignment to start again. With patience, you will find it well worth the time. Enjoy the results.

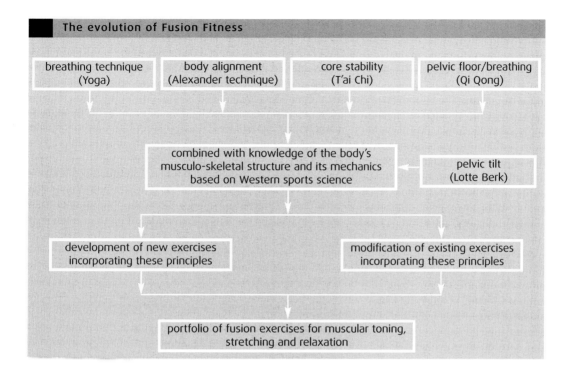

**The evolution of Fusion Fitness**

breathing technique
(Yoga)

body alignment
(Alexander technique)

core stability
(T'ai Chi)

pelvic floor/breathing
(Qi Qong)

combined with knowledge of the body's
musculo-skeletal structure and its mechanics
based on Western sports science

pelvic tilt
(Lotte Berk)

development of new exercises
incorporating these principles

modification of existing exercises
incorporating these principles

portfolio of fusion exercises for muscular toning,
stretching and relaxation

# Fusion exercises: putting theory into practice

In this chapter, I describe the principal muscles in the body followed by step-by-step procedures to increase their strength and endurance. The exercises include ones that I have developed and used in my classes after considerable research, practice and observation of the results. I have also adapted existing techniques to make them safer and more effective, in the process reviving ones that, while popular, were deemed potentially unsafe. In doing these exercises, care should be taken to start in the correct position and breathe properly.

At the start of a training programme, when some muscles are weak, stronger ones tend to take over and people adjust their position in order to accommodate this imbalance. In doing so they are likely to lose the correct body alignment. If at any point you feel you are losing the correct position, stop, rest and begin again. It is more important to master the technique than to exercise immediately but wrongly. Poor habits are difficult to correct.

I have developed sequences for getting into the correct position for each exercise. I have repeated them for easy reference, but of course once mastered they should automatically become part of what you do. Even when practising on my own, I go through the sequence for getting the body into position.

This applies also to breathing. In general, you exhale to tuck the tummy in (navel to the back of the spine) to get into position. You breathe normally thereafter. Also, in general, you breathe out while exerting effort as in the contraction of a muscle, e.g. lifting the leg off the floor, raising the trunk, squeezing the knees together, bending the knees and lowering the trunk in squats. You breathe in to release the position and, therefore, using the first example, you breathe in as you lower the leg after lifting it. The reason you breathe out as you exert effort is that this allows the central core of the body to remain stable and in correct alignment during exertion. Breathing out, as explained earlier in Chapter 8 and further elaborated in the section on abdominal muscles that follows, allows you to engage the transverse abdominal muscle, the body's so-called corset. You breathe in to refuel your energy and to release the muscle.

This technique is especially important in strong exertions, such as lifting a heavy weight and in work-outs that require high intensity and low reps. However, in many low to moderate intensity exercises where the objective is both to tone and to build up endurance (as in most floor work in exercise to music classes), breathing out during moderate exertion of effort is important but probably less critical than maintaining a breathing rhythm that ensures a good and regular supply of oxygen. Once you start with correct body alignment, the chance of going out of alignment during low to moderate exertion is less than in strong exertion. In some exercise sequences, where you work both eccentrically and concentrically, for example when you lift for a count of two and go down for two, or lift for one and go down for three, it might not always be possible to apply this blanket approach of breathing out in exertion. If such a blanket approach were to be adopted, the resulting breathing would be rapid and shallow. Therefore, although I have added reminders to breathe out as you lift and to breathe in as you lower in the exercises that follow (appropriate because they are all in the simple format of lift for one and down for one), once you change to more complex formats of contractions at varying speed, the better solution is to breathe normally. To ensure continued good posture, check the body alignment frequently, stopping whenever you feel that you are coming out of position. Resume the exercise when you feel rested.

Irrespective of the intensity of the exertion, it is essential to breathe correctly when getting into position at the start of the exercise in order to stabilize the central core of the body. It is also useful to remember that although great stress is placed on breathing, it is perfectly natural; we have not invented breathing with the diaphragm. So do not get overly stressed over the breathing instructions that follow and **do not hold your breath**. Once you have mastered the basic principles mentioned above, the sequence of breathing during the exercise will come naturally.

To build up endurance, repeat each movement until the muscles are working slightly beyond their normal capacity (see Chapter 2 on the principle of 'over-load'). There will be a slight accumulation of lactic acid, but as muscles become conditioned, they will be able to do more because of an increase in the oxidative capacity of both fast and slow twitch muscles and greater tolerance to lactic acid. To build up strength, increase the body resistance by varying the contraction. I have avoided specifying the number of reps for each of the exercises that follow. The number will vary with the age and level of fitness of participants, the objective of the class, the way in which the different exercises are sequenced and even the speed of the music. The slower the music, the harder you would have to work when training for strength development. Instructors must use their discretion. In a class situation the participant must also rely on his/her own judgement and take a rest when needed. In a mixed-ability class, and most classes fall into this category, it is almost impossible to have the right number of reps for everyone, so instructors should advise class participants to rest whenever they feel tired, and resume exercises when they feel ready.

In a class where participants are of the same ability, a safe rule of thumb is to start with one set of 8 reps for beginners, and to build this up. For those who are very strong 4 sets of 8 reps or slightly more could be attempted. There is no hard and fast rule, except that the participant should aim for an over-load, but **not** work through pain.

I suggest variations in the exercises that follow. With experience, you will probably be able to devise more. Apply the FITTA principle to progress even further when you are strong. Increase the number of reps of each movement or the number of sets. Increase the intensity of the movements: work more slowly, pausing at each movement; increase the ratio of eccentric to concentric contractions; reduce the rest period between sets of exercise; and increase the time spent on the exercise.

In setting out the exercises for the different muscle groups, I have provided a variety of exercises for each muscle to give a choice of options and positions. Although the exercises cater to the same muscle group, they vary in their impact on the different muscles within the group. Do not do all of them in one session, however, because this would probably be too much. Appendix 4 provides examples of training programmes which you might find useful.

Now, if you have music, turn it on but choose music that has slow controlled beats. The slower the music, the harder the work-out. Music helps keep you going!

# Torso and legs

## Abdominal muscles

There are four abdominal muscles: the rectus abdominus, transverse abdominus, obliquus externus (external obliques) and obliquus internus (internal obliques).

The rectus abdominus is a long strip of muscle which originates from the pubic bone and inserts into the fifth, sixth and seventh ribs and xiphoid process — the lower end of the sternum. This muscle, broader at the top and narrower towards the pubic end, is divided by the linea alba. Its contraction lifts the upper torso. The external obliques are the largest muscles running on each side of the body from the eight lower ribs down in an oblique line to the iliac crest. The internal obliques lie largely beneath this but they are attached to the iliac crest and run obliquely up. The uppermost fibres insert into the seventh to the ninth costal cartilages

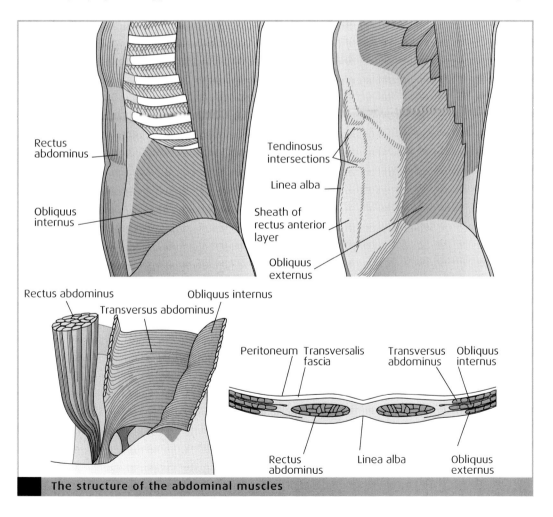

The structure of the abdominal muscles

but the lower fibres are joined with the aponeurosis of the transverse abdominus to the pubic crest. An aponeurosis is a sheet of tough fibrous tissue which acts like a tendon, attaching muscle to the bone. The transverse abdominus, the innermost stomach muscle, arises at the fascia in the lumbar region of the spine (between the iliac crest and the twelfth rib) and the lower six intercostal cartilages where it interdigitates with the diaphragm. The transverse abdominus runs transversely like a corset for the body, one part blending with the internal obliques to insert into the pubic crest and the rest passing into the rectus abdominus.

## The conventional body crunch

The most common method of exercising the abdominal muscles is the crunch. This primarily works the rectus abdominus.

- Lie on your back with knees bent and feet hip distance apart. Place your hands with elbows out wide on each side of the head.

**A** 

- Raise the trunk off the floor by no more than 30 degrees using the tummy muscles and then lower again. Breathe out as you come up and breathe in as you go down. You should feel a tension in the abdominal muscle stretching from below the sternum and downward. Be careful not to push the stomach muscles out when raising the trunk.

- Repeat the movement. The number of repetitions will vary with the individual; you could start with a set of eight and work upwards over time to as many as can be sustained.

- Variations in the speed and sequencing of the contractions, such as going up in two counts and down for two, could be introduced to intensify the work-out.

The upward movement is a concentric contraction with the rectus abdominus shortening. It is this shortening that pulls the trunk up. In the downward phase the contraction is eccentric with the rectus abdominus returning to its normal length under tension. Keep your eyes directed toward the ceiling. A gap should be kept between the chin and neck. Do not let the head hang back but give it good support with the hands. It is important to use the hands only for support: they should not be used to pull or jerk the head forward – a common error when doing this exercise. An alternative position for beginners is to fold the arms across the chest and look down the length of the body when crunching up, instead of supporting the head. In this position, the neck supports the head and avoids the tendency to jerk the head forward. A disadvantage is that neck ache can arise because the neck muscles are contracting isometrically to hold the position.

So far I have illustrated the conventional crunch in the manner in which it is normally taught. This exercise can be made safer using the fusion approach to stabilise the core area (abdomen, hips and lower back). Before raising the trunk, exhale to let the navel move towards the spine and the spine move towards the floor. All the other steps described above remain the same. Note that the extent to which exhaling allows the small of the back to rest on the floor depends on the spinal curvature of the person concerned. In most cases, with a normal spinal curvature, this exhalation process brings the small of the back in contact with the floor. If the small of the back is still off the floor it may be more comfortable to place a small towel, folded flat, under the small of the back. The towel is not to hold up the back so that the abnormal curvature is maintained, but to support it after exhalation. I have repeated this recommendation in the following exercises as a reminder.

The body crunch works mainly the rectus abdominus which is important as an opposing muscle group to the spinal muscle, the erector spinae, and can contribute to better posture. Intense training on this muscle will give a 'six-pack' – well-developed ridges of muscles running down from below the chest to the pubis.

# Moving beyond conventional crunches

For women, the problem of bulging and flabby tummy muscles is often different from that of men. The womb lies in front of the digestive system. Normally relatively small, it increases in size during the menstrual cycle and, of course, pregnancy. The increase is so great in pregnancy that the linea alba, the narrow gap that runs between the two vertical columns of the rectus abdominus separates, creating a space between the two ridges of the muscle.

The transverse abdominus, the abdominal muscle that acts as a corset to hold the internal organs back, also loosens. Firming this muscle puts the body's natural corset back in its place. Sadly, the muscle is neglected in the conventional body crunches. In fact, most people doing conventional body crunches push the stomach muscle out as they strain to raise the trunk, and breathe in instead of out during the process. This does little for the transverse abdominus, although the rectus abdominus is being worked. The result can be a strong overlay of rectus abdominus muscles over bulgy lower tummy muscles, which are difficult to get rid of once developed.

In response to this problem I have developed two exercises which I call the transverse and reverse abdominal squeezes. I place great emphasis on breathing with the diaphragm to work the muscles: the transverse abdominus, the innermost abdominal muscle, interdigitates with the diaphragm, and assists in expelling air out of the lungs.

## Transverse abdominal squeeze

**A** •  Lie on your back with the feet firmly placed hip distance apart just as for the body crunch.

•  Take a deep breath and exhale fully letting the navel sink towards the spine and let the small of the back sink toward the floor. You should now have an engaged transverse abdominus. Individuals who suffer from

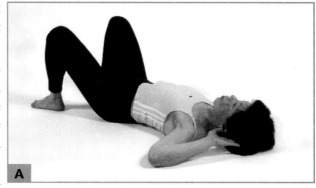

lordosis or an abnormally curved spine could place a towel, folded flat, under the small of the back, if the back remains off the floor.

**B** •  You can either work from this position or, if you are an advanced student, in the next out breath raise both shoulders off the floor while supporting the head with hands on either side of it.

**C** •  Breathing normally, lift first one foot up turning the knee out and then the other foot, also turning the **D** knee out. Click the heels together. You now have both legs raised with the knees out and heels together, a bit like a frog! Do not try to raise both feet at the same time because you could lose the muscle tension that you have developed when engaging the transverse abdominus. Remember, this is the deepest layer of the abdominal muscle.

•  With the heels together, squeeze the knees in to touch each other. As you squeeze the knees together breathe out and tuck in the navel further. You will feel a tightening or contraction of the lower abdominal muscles – your 'corset'.

•  While breathing in release to let the knees fall apart; the heels remain together while breathing in. Repeat, squeezing the knees in and releasing, until you feel the overload. The performance should be slow and controlled, with even breathing.

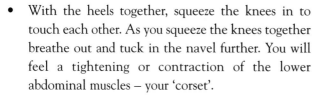

Once the technique is mastered you can advance from the basic position of the transverse abdominal squeeze to increase the intensity of the work-out and work the surrounding muscles. You can do this, for example, by running the reverse abdominal squeeze outlined below as a second stage in your abdominal work-out without any break. Alternatively, if it is too much, rest and start afresh with the reverse abdominal squeeze as a separate exercise.

## Reverse abdominal squeeze

This exercise works both the rectus abdominus and the transverse abdominus.

- Start from the same floor position as the transverse abdominal squeeze, with legs bent and off the floor.

**A**
- This time, once you have brought the knees together, keep them in this position and contract, again breathing out as you do so, and letting the navel sink in. As you do this you will feel a tightening or contraction of the lower abdominal muscles. The pubic bone will tilt up slightly and the bent knees are brought in slightly towards the chest as a result of the contraction of the rectus abdominus.

**A**

- Release the contraction and breathe in, letting the navel resume its original position. The release will move the knees slightly back allowing them to return to their original position.

- Repeat for as many times as is comfortable. Add variation by contracting for two counts and releasing for two.

In this exercise, the rectus abdominus muscles in the direction of the pubic bone are working actively. This is in contrast to the conventional body crunch, where the rectus abdominus in this area remains still (the point of origin) and the active end is towards the upper trunk as you raise the upper torso. This is why there is some debate regarding the points of origin and insertion of the rectus abdominus. In pelvic tilts and the reverse abdominal squeeze, for example, the pubic bone is actually moving and the more stable point is where the rectus abdominus is attached to the ribs. As a result, in some books, the ribs are given as the point of origin for the rectus abdominus, which differs from the more traditional definition (see p. 22). In this exercise the iliopsoas muscle works as a synergist to keep the position of the pelvis/hip stable.

Because the movements of the knee and pubic bone are very small, controlled and, more importantly, a consequence of the abdominal contraction, I describe the exercise as a 'squeeze'. This distinguishes it from the conventional reverse curl, in which the knees are brought in towards the chest and the hips are lifted up. This is a reverse curl because it is in an opposite movement to the trunk curling up in the conventional crunch. The traditional reverse curl has only a limited impact on the abdominal muscles because it works mainly on the iliopsoas. Also, a common error when people do the traditional reverse curl is the tendency to have jerky (rocking) movements as the knees are brought towards the chest. This pulls the spine because the iliopsoas muscle is not working synergistically.

Although the rectus abdominus is the prime mover in the reverse squeeze, the transverse abdominus muscle is being worked simultaneously because of the way I have sequenced the exercise. When working on the transverse squeeze, the transverse abdominus muscle is engaged before progressing to the reverse squeeze. Since the transverse abdominus inserts into the pubis via the rectus abdominus, engaging the rectus abdominus at the second stage and maintaining the breathing rhythm and technique keeps the transverse abdominus engaged.

## Reverse abdominal squeeze, legs straight

Once the technique is comfortably mastered, you can progress further by straightening both legs, keeping the knees soft or slightly bent. You could sequence the exercise as a third stage moving on to it without a break or you can take a breather before going through the blueprint of getting into the correct position, but keeping the legs straight. This is a more intense work-out for the lower abdominal area because of the greater resistance provided by the straight legs.

**A** • Keeping the legs extended towards the ceiling, contract the lower abdominal muscles by breathing out and letting the navel sink into the back of the spine. This time the contraction of the lower abdominal muscles will result in a slight upward push of both feet; the pubic bone will also tilt upwards.

• Pause and then release. Vary the time that the contraction is held and repeat for as many as can be sustained.

A

## Moon walk I

- Progress even further by moving alternate legs in a walking motion with feet extended towards ceiling.

A

- Breathe out to contract the abdominal muscles, navel to the back of the spine, with each step and breathe in to release, before switching to the other foot. The stronger you are, the bigger the steps that can be taken, but all the motion should be slow and controlled.

- Do not swing your legs. Concentrate and focus on the abdominal muscles. The hip and back position should be absolutely stable: this is achieved by maintaining the breathing rhythm. Big steps increase the likelihood of the small of the back coming off the floor because they affect the ability of the ilipsoas muscle to hold the hips in a stable position. Should this happen, come off the position immediately, bring both knees to the chest, hold and rest. Once comfortable, start again. There should not be any stress on the back at all.

- Repeat as many times as can be sustained.

## Moon walk II

A

- The next progression is to push each shoulder alternately to the diagonally opposite leg which is in motion, supporting the head with the hands and keeping the elbows wide and open. This exercise works the obliques as well. Care should be taken not to pull the elbow towards the opposite leg. A violent and jerky move could injure the back or neck.

This series of movements works all four abdominal muscle groups. As mentioned earlier, they can be done separately, as in a beginner's class, with a rest in-between and continued checks on the position or you can run through all or a selection of them in a continuous sequence. Much will depend upon the fitness of the class.

# Pelvic floor exercise

One final element can be added – pelvic floor exercises. Pelvic floors are vital for men and women, especially the latter because of the tearing of muscles during childbirth, to avoid future problems of incontinence.

- Lie face up with knees bent and feet firmly on the floor.

- Breathe out to contract deeply and low in the pelvic area and as you contract, the pubic bone tilts up slightly. You should imagine that you are about to pee, but you are contracting to hold back, squeezing all the muscles around the pelvic floor and bringing them upwards.

- Then release, breathing in.

The movement can be incorporated into the abdominal contraction illustrated above. Hence, in the transverse abdominal squeeze, combine the squeezing of the knees together with the pelvic floor contraction.

## The obliques: working the waist

To counter excess weight around the waist, I suggest additional exercises for the obliques. A conditioned rectus abdominus and transverse abdominus helps, but both internal and external obliques should be toned. The exercises for the obliques, based on conventional methods, have been modified to ensure the spine is in a stable position.

### Side reaches

- Lie on your back with knees bent, feet hip-distance apart and slightly away from the bottom.

- Take a deep breath and exhale, letting your navel sink towards the spine, and rest the small of your back on the floor.

**A** 
- Breathe in again and this time as you breathe out raise the trunk and the shoulders come off the floor.

**B** 
- Breathing normally, support the head with one hand, face towards the ceiling, and reach down to one side with the other hand as though you are trying to touch the side of your foot. It is

important to keep both shoulders equidistant off the floor and not be lopsided. Breathe out as you reach down and breathe in as you return to neutral.

- Repeat until you feel the overload and then change side.

## Shoulder to knee

- Lie in the same position. Take a deep breath and exhale, letting your navel sink towards the back of the spine, and rest the small of your back on the floor.

**A** •  On the next out breath raise the shoulders, supporting your head with both hands and keeping the elbows pointing outward. This is your starting position.

**B** •  In a controlled, smooth way, push one shoulder towards the opposite knee, letting the other shoulder rest on the floor to give the upper trunk support and

stability. Breathe out as you push towards the opposite knee and breathe in as you return to neutral. Keep your body fully square facing the ceiling. Be careful not to round the back or pull the elbows forward.

I prefer to work one side at a time. Moving from side to side is not as safe because the changes can become jerky, increasing the chance of damaging the back muscles. If you wish to work alternate sides always come back to the centre. For example, in the elbow out, hand by the side of the head position, come up to the centre, then to the left, back to centre and then to right. The angle of the swing is less, allowing improved control.

## Z-position

**A** •  Lie on your back with knees together and feet on the ground, but slightly further away from the bottom than in the side reach.

**B** •  Take a deep breath, exhale and lower both knees to one side, preferably to rest on the floor. If the position is difficult or uncomfortable, and for those with back problems, rest your knees on a rolled towel so that there is no pressure on the back. Placing the feet further away from the bottom than in the other two oblique exercises also helps reduce the angle of the drop when you bring the knees down. Try to keep your knees together and the upper trunk squarely facing the ceiling. Do not pull to one side.

**C** •  Place your hands on each side of the head and raise and lower your trunk, breathing out as you come up and in as you go down. Both the external and internal obliques will be engaged. Keeping the top knee down also works the adductors (inner thigh muscle) of the top leg. Repeat until you feel the overload.

•  Change sides and repeat the same sequence.

•  Introduce variations such as coming up for two and down for two, up for one and down for three (lengthening the time of the eccentric phase). Vary the speed of the work-out.

•  You can increase the overload, by raising the trunk up and then reaching upwards with alternate hands as though pulling on a rope. This increases the intensity on the obliques and also works the lattisimus dorsi. Do not let the tummy bulge up in any of these movements.

# Back muscles: erector spinae

The erector spinae is a complex muscle which arises from the sacro-iliac crest, the lower thoracic spine and spinous process. It forms a strong muscle mass which continues upwards to divide into three columns of muscle, inserting into the upper ribs, spinous process and the cervical spine. The muscle contracts to bend the body backwards or sidewards and also helps rotate the spine. This is the opposing muscle group to the abdominal muscles. The erector spinae is assisted by the transverso-spinalis-multifidus (see p. 79). The multifidus is a series of paired small muscles extending the full length of the spine, each spanning two or three vertebrae. It is responsible for the lateral flexion, rotation, extension and hyperextension of the spine. It also helps in stabilising the spine by keeping the vertebrae aligned.

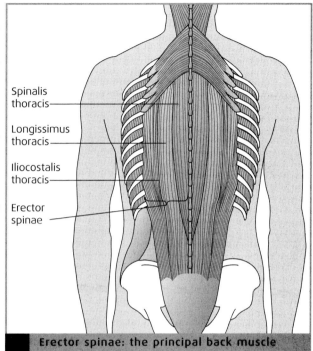

Spinalis thoracis

Longissimus thoracis

Iliocostalis thoracis

Erector spinae

**Erector spinae: the principal back muscle**

## Back extension to strengthen the back muscles

- To strengthen the erector spinae, lie face down on the floor with both arms stretched out in front, or place your hands by the side of the head. The legs are extended out behind and resting on the floor.

- Take a deep breath and exhale keeping the hips firmly on the floor, weight evenly distributed.

**A** • Keeping both legs still, lift the trunk off the floor in a slow controlled motion, breathing out as you rise and breathing in as you descend.

- Repeat as many times as is comfortable.

A

Gently tilting the pelvis forward prevents pinching of the small of the back and keeps the hip joint stable. The head comes slightly off the floor when the trunk is lifted up, but do not over extend the neck. The face should be directed towards the floor. It is best to pause between sets of repeats in order to avoid fatigue and poor quality moves. This is true for all the muscle exercises, but particularly in the case of the erector spinae: the position is not a comfortable one because the movements exert pressure on the abdomen.

## The buttock and outer thigh muscle: Abductors

The muscles that make up the buttock consist of the gluteal maximus, gluteal medius and gluteal minimus. The gluteal maximus is responsible for extension of the leg to the back (back leg lifts). The gluteal medius and minimus, together with the outer thigh muscle, tensor fascia latae, are responsible for carrying the leg backwards and outward. Beneath the gluteals are the muscles responsible for lateral rotation of the hip. Of these, the quadratus femoris lies at the lowest end of the buttocks.

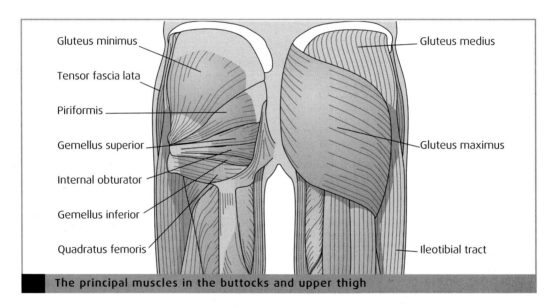

**The principal muscles in the buttocks and upper thigh**

## Firming the buttocks: Gluteus maximus

The conventional way of conditioning the bottom is to focus on the gluteus maximus, the biggest and most powerful muscle in the buttocks. I have adapted a widely used method of working this muscle by incorporating features on body alignment that maximise its effectiveness and make it safer.

## Back leg lift

A  • Kneel, making sure that the hips are aligned above the knees. Breathing normally, rest your elbows on the floor and align them directly below the shoulder. Make sure that the weight of the body is evenly distributed and you are not leaning heavily to one side or the other. Your spine is now in a normal alignment.

B  • Exhale to tuck in the tummy, round the back slightly towards the ceiling and tilt the pelvis slightly forward to give extra body resistance to the work-out and ensure that the small of the back does not sag.

C  • Extend one leg behind and lift the extended leg, just off the floor. This is your start position.

D  • In a slow and controlled way, lift the leg higher, pause and then lower to starting position. The lift should be sufficient to tighten the buttocks muscles, but not so high as to cause sagging or pinching of the small of the back. Breathe out as you lift the leg and breathe in as you lower it.

• Repeat as many times as comfortable. Vary the speed of the contraction.

The upward motion of the leg reflects the concentric contraction of the gluteus maximus because the gluteal has its point of origin in the ilium and sacrum and inserts into the femur. The downward motion is the eccentric contraction of the muscle.

You will note that as you extend the leg behind and lift the foot off the floor, the back returns to its normal position. If the back was not rounded and the pelvis tilted forward at the start, the chances of the back sagging are increased during motion. Pelvic tilts at the

start of movements that require the use of abductor muscles (gluteals and the tensor fascia lata) help retain the normal curvature of the spine during the movement.

## Side leg lift

A • An alternative position involves lying on your side with your legs stacked on top of each other and the body aligned. Exhale, sending the navel towards the back of the spine, and gently tilt the hips forward to increase resistance and stabilise the hip joint. Some people find it easier to fold the bottom leg to obtain greater stability, but the top leg will still have to be aligned with the bottom.

B • Lift and lower the top leg in a slow and controlled manner. Breathe out as you lift and in as you lower. Again, the upward motion is a concentric contraction and the downward phase the eccentric contraction of the gluteals. The tensor fascia lata is also involved – contracting to bring the leg away from the body in the uplift.

## Erasing the sag: sequential contractions

Strengthening the gluteals will help improve muscle tone in the buttocks. This is not disputed. However, except where a very sedentary lifestyle is led, the gluteals are among the most active muscles in the body because they are actively engaged in activities that involve moving the legs. Why then do the bottoms of people who are not overweight and reasonably active sag or bulge outward where the thigh joins the hip? The explanation lies at least in part in the condition of relatively neglected lateral hip rotating muscles such as the quadratus femoris, that extend around the bottom of the buttock and the tensor fascia lata (see muscle diagram on p. 98). The following exercises focus on the muscles around this region, especially the quadratus femoris, to help tone and support the bottom. (Other muscles around this region include the gemellus inferior situated above the quadratus femoris.) This is one of the most effective methods for toning the bottom and losing the sag and it is well worth getting the technique right.

## Straight back leg extension

A
- Lie on your left side with the right leg stacked on top of the left and keep the body aligned. The legs should be straight, but relaxed.

B
- Turn the body, without changing its alignment, to face the floor. Rest both elbows in front of you with the palms pointed towards each other and the elbow pointed out. You should be comfortable in this position.

- Rest the face and torso on the floor, but keep the left hip just off it. The left knee faces down and the left leg is straight but relaxed. The right side of the body is resting comfortably on the floor.

- Inhale and exhale to let the navel sink towards the spine to hold in the tummy then tilt the hip gently forward to add body resistance to the work-out; this will also help stabilise the pelvic joint and prevent the small of the back from sagging.

C
- Lift and lower the left leg in a slow and controlled way, breathing out as you lift and in as you lower. The lift should not be excessive.

- Vary the speed of contractions as you progress, instead of up for one count and down for the same, go up in two and down for two etc. This movement works the gluteals, mainly the gluteal maximus.

## Right angle lift

- Now pause when the leg is lifted and, keeping the leg in position, turn the body so that the left hip is now again stacked on top of the right hip and facing front. You may wish to come up on to your left elbow and support your head by placing a hand at the back of it.

**A**
- Bend the top leg at a right angle, keeping the calf parallel to the floor.

- Lift and lower the top leg in a slow and controlled way, again, breathing out as you lift and in as you lower. You should feel immediately an impact on the outer part of the leg where it meets the line of the bottom. Again vary the speed of contraction as you progress. The tensor fascia lata is now working with the three gluteals.

## Acute angle moving in

**A**
- At the end of the lift, pause and turn the knee out towards the ceiling with the toes pointing down – a lateral rotation of the femur to engage the quadratus femoris.

- Maintain the body alignment – tummy tight, hips stable – and move the leg down towards the back. Tilting the hip gently forward keeps the hip joint stable and prevents the work-out from turning into a hip flexor movement.

Obviously to exercise the left buttock the series is started lying on your right side.

In all three positions, the body should be balanced and movements controlled. You should not feel any discomfort. The work-out is focused just beneath the bottom, towards the outer part of the thigh. The gluteals, tensor fascia lata and the quadratus femoris are all involved. You should feel the impact, even 24 hours later!

Other techniques exist to firm the buttocks, among them the buttock lift. This exercise was popular for a long time in the 1960s and 1970s, but it fell out of favour, like many of the exercises used in that period, because it was considered too extreme. The adverse effects were considered to exceed the benefits. The most serious complaint was the stress that the exercise exerted on the small of the back. The modified version that follows has been adjusted to eliminate this and other problems presented by the traditional buttock lift.

## Modified buttock lift

- Lie on your back with your knees bent and feet hip distance apart and placed slightly away from the bottom. The upper trunk should feel comfortable and relaxed.

- Breathe in and exhale, bringing the navel towards the spine. This allows the abdomen to flatten and the pelvis to stabilise.

A
- In the next out-breath, lift the buttocks to slightly more than fist height off the floor. This is the starting position. Be careful not to lift the buttocks up by pushing into the small of the back.

- Squeeze the buttocks up and then release by gently lowering them to their starting position. Again breathe out as you lift and in as you lower. The movements are slow and controlled, the back should not arch up and there should be no stress on the back.

- Repeat until you feel the over-load.

Further progressions can be made to this position so that you are working the tensor fascia lata (outer thigh) and the adductors (inner thigh).

B
- At the end of the up-lift, pause to check that the back is correctly aligned (i.e. it is not pinching) and then squeeze the knees in to touch, breathing out as you do so. The feet remain hip distance apart.

C
- Release, breathing in, and take the knees apart.

- Repeat as many as you can sustain. You will also find a tightening of the inner thigh muscles and upper end of the outer thigh just below the bottom.

You can progress even further:

D
- Walk your feet until they are together.

- With knees closed, squeeze the buttocks up, pause and release down. Again, breathe out as you squeeze up and in to release.

- Repeat.

The intensity of the work-out on the gluteals, tensor fascia lata and adductors is noticeable to say the least. I have grown to enjoy the sensation and particularly its effect!

## Inner thigh muscles: adductors

Adductors, located in the inner thigh, are responsible for moving the leg inward, hip flexion and lateral rotation of the hip. They consist of four muscles: the pectineus, adductor brevis, adductor longus and adductor magnus. They originate from the pubic bone and lower part of the hip bone and insert into the femur.

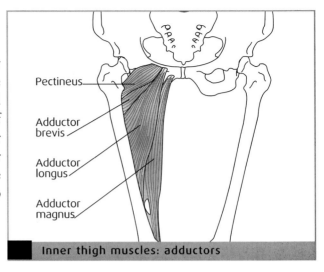

Pectineus

Adductor brevis

Adductor longus

Adductor magnus

**Inner thigh muscles: adductors**

### Inner thigh see-saw: toning the inner thigh

- Lie on your side with legs extended, one on top of the other, making sure that the body is completely aligned. The upper trunk can rest on the floor or it may be more comfortable to support the head.

**A**
- Keeping the lower leg extended, bend the top leg and bring it over until the knee touches on the floor. Those with back problems might need to have a rolled towel on which to rest this knee. The extended leg should be straight, with the knee soft.

A

**B**
- Lift and lower the extended leg. Lift as high as can be comfortably sustained. The movement should be slow and controlled. The intensity can be increased by reducing the speed of the movements, especially when lowering the leg. Pausing at the end of the lift also increases the intensity. Again, breathe out as you lift and in as you lower. Don't touch the floor with your foot when you come down – keep the stomach muscles in good control!

B

I have added further to the intensity of this exercise in more advanced classes by adding a variation which involves use of the obliques.

c
- As the extended lower leg is lifted, reach towards the lifted foot with the upper arm, effecting an oblique crunch. Breathe out as you reach out towards the lifted leg.

- When the leg goes down, release the crunch, breathing in as you do so. Allow the arm to return to its starting position.

- Repeat as many times as can be sustained. Add variation by changing the speed of the movements, for example, going up for two, down for two, up for one and down for three, and vice versa.

## Quadriceps

This group of muscles is situated in the front thigh. It consists of: the rectus femoris, the largest and most powerful in the group; the vastus lateralis; vastus medialis; and vastus intermedius. The rectus femoris originates from the front point of the ilium while the others originate in the upper portion of the femur. All of the muscles insert into the tibia via the patellar ligament. The rectus femoris contracts, flexing the thigh at the hip to lift up the leg. The iliopsoas (hip flexor muscle) is also involved in the process. All four quadriceps muscles work the knee joint and are responsible for movements involving knee extension, such as straightening the lower leg.

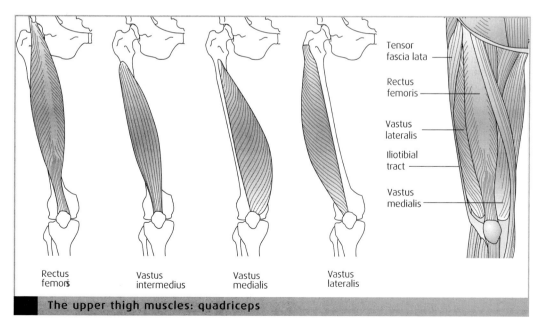

Rectus femoris

Vastus intermedius

Vastus medialis

Vastus lateralis

Tensor fascia lata

Rectus femoris

Vastus lateralis

Iliotibial tract

Vastus medialis

**The upper thigh muscles: quadriceps**

The most common way to exercise the quadriceps is through squats. Note however, that in all the exercises for the quadriceps that follow, the iliopsoas is involved.

## Conventional squats

**A** • Stand with your legs hip distance apart, feet facing front.

**B** • Keeping the stomach muscles tight and back straight, crouch down until your bottom is about 45 degrees above the knee (not lower than the knee).

• Straighten your legs slowly to raise the trunk again. I find greater resistance to the workout on the quadriceps is obtained if you tilt the pelvis slightly forward (but keeping the tummy tucked in) as though you were squeezing up, when straightening the legs. This helps to stabilise the hips as well. You breathe out as you lower and in as you straighten up.

• Repeat until you feel the overload.

A number of variations on the squat exist, including:

**A** • ski squats, where the bottom is pushed back and the body is inclined forward.

**B** • travel squats, where you squat to one side and drag the leg back to the centre which
**C** exercises the adductors, the inner thigh.

## Pedal and stride

Pedal and stride exercises offer an alternative way of strengthening the quadriceps:

- Lie on your back on the floor, with knees bent and both feet on the floor.

- Breathe in and exhale to let the navel sink toward the back of the spine.

**A** • Keeping the tummy muscles controlled, in the next out-breath raise one leg off the ground. The knee of the raised leg should be slightly bent. This is your starting position.

**B** • In a slow and controlled manner, lift the leg higher, pause, and lower, taking care that your foot does not come down to the floor. Breathe out as you lift and in as you lower.

- Repeat as many times as is comfortable. The working leg remains bent, keeping the angle of the bend unchanged when lifting and lowering. A further variation of this exercise would be to bend and straighten the leg.

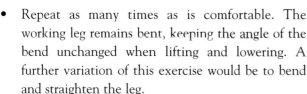

If you are a more advanced student, you might wish to skip this stage and start with the following.

- Lift up your upper trunk, supporting it with your elbows resting on the floor and aligned below the shoulder. Shoulders are relaxed. The knees are bent and both feet are on the floor. Make sure that you face front and your head is not tilted back.

- Breathe in and exhale to let your navel sink toward the spine. Retain control of the stomach muscles.

- In the next out-breath, raise one leg off the floor, with the knee slightly bent. This is your starting position.

**C** • Raise and lower the leg, without changing the angle of the bent knee, in a slow and controlled manner. Breathe out as you lift and in as you lower. Add variation by changing the speed and counts going up and down. Further variation would be to bring the knee in towards the chest and then fully extend the leg, leading with the heel.

- Repeat until you feel the overload on the quadriceps.

By now, you should feel a significant load on the muscle and you might need a break. If you are very strong and wish to progress even more, go to the next step, which is a very advanced position and should be approached only if your abdominal muscles are very strong.

- Bring the trunk up even further to almost a sitting position and carry out the same moves to stabilise the hip and engage the transverse abdominal muscles. Breathe in and exhale to let the navel sink towards the spine.

D - Lift and lower the leg, as before, with as many repeats as you can sustain.

The position develops resistance as the angle between the leg and the trunk becomes more acute, increasing the leverage and making it harder to lift the leg. To do this exercise without stressing the back requires great strength and control in the abdominal muscles because they have to hold the trunk in position, in order not to stress the spine. Position D is not recommended for beginners nor intermediate students or those who have not mastered the abdominal exercises described above.

## The barre

This exercise is invaluable because it contributes to a strong and toned upper leg or quadricep muscles, which both looks good and helps avoid knee problems. Borrowed from ballet practices, it requires the use of the barre or at least something stable, strong, and at least above waist height for support. It involves very controlled and strong movements and is not for the weak hearted! You can, however, work at your level and build up strength to move to the most advanced stage.

A - Stand sideways slightly away from the barre or wall, and rest the nearest hand on it for support.

B - Bring the knee of the outer leg up towards the chest, supporting it with the free hand clasped around the back of the thigh. Check that you are completely stable.

- Bend the body towards the lifted leg, keeping the knee of the standing leg soft. This increases the intensity of the exercise but reduces the stress on the supporting leg. This is your starting position.

**C** • Now extend the raised leg to the side at an angle of about 45 degrees, pointing the toes as high as is comfortable. The extended leg should be straight. Pause, then bend the leg to release. Movements are slow and controlled. The hips are kept absolutely still.

• Repeat as many times as can be sustained.

To start with, it is preferable to keep the number of reps in each set small, so that you can have a breather between sets. Vary the angle and size of the bends to get a change in resistance. You can execute the same moves with the leg extended in front rather than to the side, which will change the emphasis on the work-load of the different quadricep muscles.

This exercise is deceptively hard. When I first did it, I realised that I was not as strong as I thought. The ache that followed was incredible as I did the sets at a height that was obviously beyond me at that time. It is important not to have the leg so high that you cannot sustain the movement or you feel excessive strain. The higher the leg, the greater the resistance applied to the quadriceps and the more difficult the exercise. Work towards greater height, but do not start with it. Pointing the toes when you stretch the legs out will also work the arch of the foot, which is often neglected. This is a wonderful upper leg shaper and well worth the effort.

## Hamstring

This group of muscles, consisting of the semitendinosus, semimembranosus and biceps femoris, is located at the back of the leg. The point of origin is the ischial tuberosity (bottom of the pelvis, the ischium) and the back of the femur, and it inserts into the tibia. The hamstring contracts to flex the knee, bringing the heel towards the bottom and lengthening the muscles at the front of the thigh.

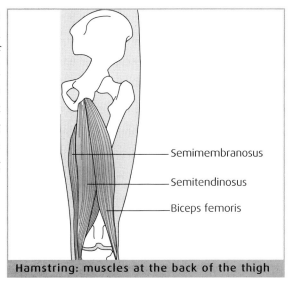

Semimembranosus

Semitendinosus

Biceps femoris

**Hamstring: muscles at the back of the thigh**

## Leg curl

One of the most common floor exercises for this muscle group is the leg curl.

**A**
- Kneel, with your elbows resting on the floor. Make sure that the hips are aligned above the knee and the elbows are aligned below the shoulders. Keep your weight evenly distributed.

- In the next out-breath pull the tummy in to help straighten the back and keep it from sagging. This position also enhances the body resistance when working the hamstring.

**B**
- Breathe in, and as you exhale, bring one knee off the floor, so that the foot faces the ceiling.

**C**
- Breathe normally to straighten and bend the leg in a slow and controlled way. It is important not to push the knee/leg too high up because this will cause the small of the back to sag and exert excessive pressure on the hip joint.

- Repeat to achieve the overload and then change sides.

Variations include straightening in two phases and bending in two phases.

# Calf and shin muscles: gastrocnemius, soleus and tibialis anterior

The gastrocnemius is the powerful calf muscle, which originates at the back of the femur, just above the knee, and inserts via a tendon into the achilles calcaneous. It is supported by the soleus, which originates in the tibia, just below the knee, and inserts via a tendon also into the achilles calcaneous. Both muscles contract to flex the heel, causing the toes to point, referred to as plantar flexion. The opposing muscle group is the tibialis anterior, located in front of the leg. Originating from the front of the tibia, just below the knee, it inserts into the inner edge of the foot. Contraction causes the foot to flex upwards, referred to as dorsiflexion.

Working these muscles involves moves that result in plantar and dorsi flexion. For example, raising and lowering the heel works the calf muscles. Flexing the foot works the tibialis anterior. The calves are worked intensively in daily activities such as walking, running and going up or down stairs. Most aerobic routines involve them. In step classes, they are the most worked of all the muscles. Therefore, I have included only a few exercises for them.

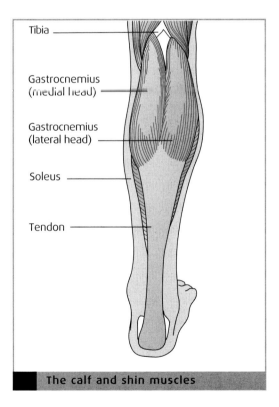

Tibia

Gastrocnemius (medial head)

Gastrocnemius (lateral head)

Soleus

Tendon

**The calf and shin muscles**

**A**

**B**

111

# TORSO AND ARMS

## Chest muscles: pectoralis major and minor

Pectoralis is the Latin name for breast. There are two groups of pectoral muscles: the pectoralis major and the pectoralis minor. The pectoralis major is a large fan shaped muscle which covers most of the chest and is responsible for the movement of the arms inward and across the body. It originates from the clavicle and sternum and the adjacent parts of the second to the sixth ribs and inserts into the humerus. The pectoralis minor is a smaller muscle beneath the pectoralis major. It originates from the third to the fifth ribs and inserts into the scapula (shoulder blade), which it moves down and forward.

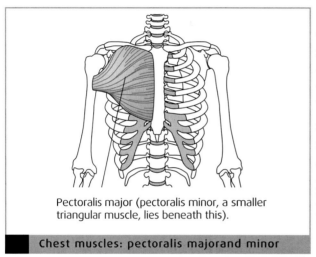

Pectoralis major (pectoralis minor, a smaller triangular muscle, lies beneath this).

**Chest muscles: pectoralis majorand minor**

The pectoral muscles are a major source of muscular strength and feature widely in strength and endurance training, especially for men. They are important for women because they provide vital support for breasts. The most common method for training this muscle for endurance and strength is the floor press-up. I provide three versions here devised according to different levels of strength.

### Press-ups

**A** • Kneel and place both hands on the floor with the knees aligned below the hips. The hands are kept fairly wide apart to maximise the impact on the pectoralis and for balance.

A

**B** • Hold the tummy in so that the back does not sag, then bend your arms to lower the chest to just above the floor.

• Raise the torso by straightening the arms.

**C** • To increase the intensity of the work-out, extend the legs further behind so that more weight and resistance is shifted to the chest, and execute the same moves.

**Box press-up**

**D** • To increase the body resistance even more, extend both legs fully.

Progression is achieved by varying the speed of the contraction. The muscle meets greater resistance if the chest is lowered slowly with a pause at each phase of descent.

**Half-extension**

Many variations of the press-up exist, but they are not usually recommended for the average person because they are potentially dangerous. They include combining floor press-ups with ballistic moves such as taking both hands off the floor to clap between press-ups or the inverted press-ups where the hands are turned inward with the fingers touching. Floor press-ups also strengthen the triceps, biceps and deltoids.

**Full-extension**

## The chest press

The chest press provides a convenient way of exercising the pectoral muscles:

**A**
**B** • Grasp the opposite wrist with the hand and push inward to the medial line of the chest or, alternatively, push the heel of the palms together and then release.

• Repeat until you feel the overload.

The chest press is very useful for women seeking to tone the chest muscle because it can be done practically anywhere at any time. It focuses on the area just below the

shoulder joint, which is important for supporting the breast and does not put stress on shoulder joints or require strength. It is unlikely to increase strength but done regularly, the exercise helps tone the pectoralis. For greater muscular strength, weight training, combined with the full floor press-ups, is generally used.

## Upper back muscles: trapezius and rhomboids

These are opposing muscles to the pectoral muscles. The trapezius, a large diamond-shaped muscle at the back, stretches from the base of the skull and the shoulders down to the lower part of the thoracic spine. Its point of origin is from the 7th cervical joint to the 12th thoracic vertebra. It inserts into the clavicle and the scapula. The trapezius helps support the neck and is responsible for the raising and adduction of the shoulders as well as the lateral flexion of the neck and its rotation. The rhomboids, a smaller muscle, also arises from the 7th cervical vertebra and the upper five thoracic vertebrae. It inserts into the scapula and contracts to pull (adduct) towards the spine, and also rotates the scapula. The trapezius and rhomboids tend to feel tight and strained in desk-bound people.

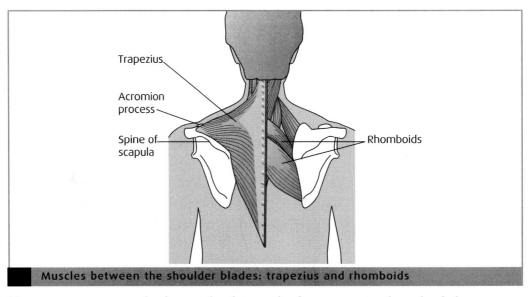

Muscles between the shoulder blades: trapezius and rhomboids

Here are some exercises for the muscles that can be done conveniently at the desk:

- Slowly circle the arms or shoulders.
- Raise both shoulders towards the ears and lower. Repeat several times until you feel an easing of tension in the shoulders and upper back.
- Gently squeeze the shoulder blades together.

The trapezius and rhomboid muscles are also involved in push-ups. When the chest is lowered, the shoulder blades are pushed inward.

# Back muscle: latissimus dorsi

This flat, almost triangular muscle starts from the lower spinous process (the sixth lower thoracic spine and the fifth lumbar vertebrae) and the crest of the ilium, and converges into the humerus (upper arm bone) just below the shoulders. It is primarily responsible for moving the arm downward and backward.

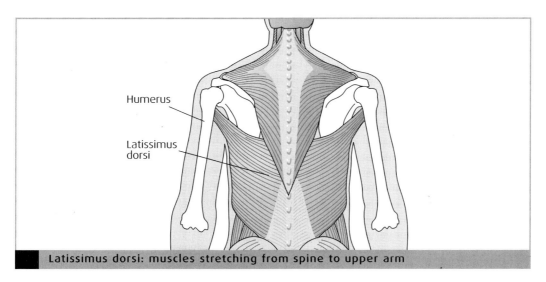

Humerus

Latissimus
dorsi

Latissimus dorsi: muscles stretching from spine to upper arm

Exercises for the latissimus dorsi include pulling down and rowing movements. A common exercise is as follows:

*   Take hold of a bar, holding it above the head, spacing the hands well apart.
*   Lower the bar, keeping it behind the head until it is just above the shoulder. Pause, then raise the bar again to its original position.
*   Repeat as many times as can be sustained in a slow and controlled manner.

This exercise also works the rhomboids and trapezius. Weights or dumbbells could also be used instead of the bar.

# Arm muscles: deltoids, biceps and triceps

These muscles are situated in the upper arm. The deltoid is the rounded muscle in the outer upper arm. It originates from the scapula and clavicle, and inserts into the humerus. When it contracts, it moves the arm upwards. The biceps is the muscle in the upper arm responsible for bending the arm towards the body, for example, when lifting an object. It also helps rotate the forearm. It originates from the scapula and inserts into the radius. Finally, the triceps is at the back of the upper arm. It originates from the scapula and humerus, and inserts into the ulna. It contracts to straighten the arm and is the opposing muscle group to the biceps.

In the ageing process or during weight gain, the triceps tends to be the worst affected, becoming flabby and loose skin. The problem is most widespread in women, partly because most women do little heavy manual work but also for genetic reasons. In view of this, I have provided a larger range of triceps exercises than for the deltoids or the biceps.

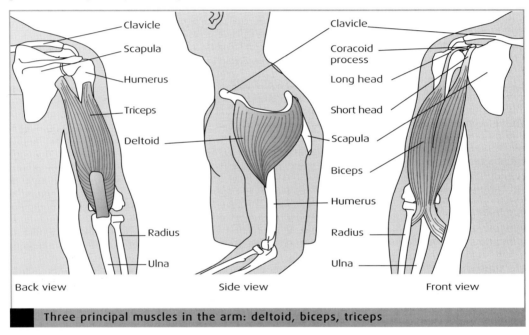

**Three principal muscles in the arm: deltoid, biceps, triceps**

Floor press-ups also involve the triceps, biceps and deltoids. Increasing the body resistance by going into half or full press-ups increases the intensity of the work-out on them. Other milder exercises for these three muscles using own body resistance include upright row for the deltoid (A), triceps extension (B) and biceps curl (C). You may wish to use weights for these exercises.

## Triceps extension on the floor

This is a more advanced version of the triceps extension, which is widely used.

A
- Sit on the floor with your legs bent and hands firmly down on either side of the body, but behind the buttocks, with the fingers facing forward.

- Take a deep breath and exhale letting the navel sink toward the back of the spine.

B
- Holding the tummy in, lower the body towards the back by bending the arms, exhaling as you do so.

- Inhale to return to a sitting position, straightening the arms.

C
- To give even greater resistance, in the same position, lift the buttocks off the floor, straightening the arms, breathing in as you do so. This contracts the triceps concentrically.

D
- To release, bend the arms at the elbow and lower the buttocks, breathing out. This contracts the triceps eccentrically.

Good tummy control is needed in order to protect the back and ensure that the work-out is focused on the back upper arm muscles. Individuals with poor stomach control or weak shoulders should **not** attempt to lift the buttocks off the floor (C and D) because this increases the force on the joints. Be careful not to jolt the shoulders.

An alternative but advanced work-out for the triceps, which I find very useful and involves no weight or stress to the shoulders, is as follows:

## Back arm lifts

- Stand with your feet hip distance apart. Exhale to tuck the tummy in and lean slightly forward.

**A** • Breathing normally, extend both arms out to the back and as high as is comfortable. Keep the arms and elbows tight against the body.

**B** • With your fists lightly clenched to face downward to the floor, bend the wrists (which also bends the elbows slightly) and extend and lift your arms up towards the back. Breathe out as you lift and in as you release.

- Repeat until you feel the overload on the triceps.

## Scissoring the arms

**C** • To increase the intensity of the work-out, unclench the fist at the end of the lift and rotate the arms so that your fingers point upwards to the ceiling and the elbows are facing down.

**D** • Scissor the arms in big movements. Breathe normally and maintain tight tummy control throughout.

You should feel the work-out on the triceps quite strongly. Regular use of this exercise will result in a marked improvement in the tone of the triceps within three weeks. For serious muscular strength and endurance training aimed at building muscle bulk, these exercises can be performed using weights.

# Training for flexibility: taking away stress and strain

# 10

Flexible people can bend, reach and turn without strain or force. Their muscles are pliable and supple. Their joints are similarly mobile. Even these fortunate individuals, who probably owe their condition to regular exercise, must confront the decline in flexibility that can come with ageing. The postural muscles which support the body tend to shorten with time. This gives rise to the stooped posture of many elderly people. The muscles responsible for maintaining and generating movement can also weaken. Joints become stiff. This loss of flexibility, associated with age, can be made worse by the continuous muscle contraction associated with frequent high-intensity exercises. Sports such as running, jumping and sprinting can contribute to the onset of tight muscles.

The tendency for flexibility to decline with age does not mean that the loss of flexibility is inevitable. It is widespread, largely because very few people stretch as part of their daily routine. Some do not even stretch at the end of a hard work-out. As a result the contracted muscles remain tight and over time become permanently so. Yet a few minutes of stretching every day will help to maintain muscle suppleness and joint mobility as well as relieve the tension and stress that can accumulate in the shoulders. You only have to watch household pets or even birds in the garden as they go through their regular stretching routines to know that this is the natural way to prepare for movement and to set the body healthily at rest after activity.

## The benefits of stretching

Stretching improves posture, reduces back problems and enhances the quality and grace of movements. This is easily illustrated. If you stretch up towards the ceiling after a long day spent in front of the desk, you feel a wonderful lengthening of the back muscles and a release of tension. With the stretch, the vertebrae in the spinal column get a chance for space and movement, which they have been denied during the long hours of enforced sitting. This is recognised by many companies, who now include as part of their induction courses a section on health and safety where, among other things, they emphasise the need for a comfortable working position and regular breaks away from the desk to relax and stretch.

In sports, stretching helps to improve performance because it enables joints and muscles to be taken to their full range. A runner with tight shin muscles will find it hard to run uphill or sprint. Dancers cannot perform with tight hamstrings. People who play tennis, football or similar sports that require rapid changes in direction must maintain the flexibility of the adductors. The iliopsoas muscles, which are crucial for rapid changes of direction by the lower body, also need to be strong and supple.

Muscle tightness can cause serious sports injury. Stretching muscles before and after they have been worked contributes substantially to reducing injuries such as muscle tear and damage to ligaments and tendons. The impact of tight muscles is often cumulative. For the knee cap to work well, the quadriceps that hold it in position must be balanced so that it is correctly aligned. If they are not, it can be pulled out of alignment. If the hamstring is tense this will stop the leg from being straightened. This excessive flexion of the knee, in turn, causes the knee cap to press in harder on the femur. This pressure can result in inflammation and pain. The increase in the flexion of the knee caused by tight hamstrings will also lead to higher impact on the ankle as the foot lands on the ground. A tight illiotibial band (see opposite), which results from over-use, can lead to pain in the lower thigh or outer side of the knee. (For more detail, see Chapter 10 which considers sports injuries.)

Stretching each muscle after it has been involved in activity helps maintain its length and flexibility and prevent the onset of injuries. It also helps to improve coordination between opposing muscle groups. It counteracts the tendency for muscles to bulk following intensive training. It is especially relevant for those who do not wish to have big muscles. Finally, stretching reduces muscle soreness as the muscle returns to normal length and the build-up of lactic acid is dispersed.

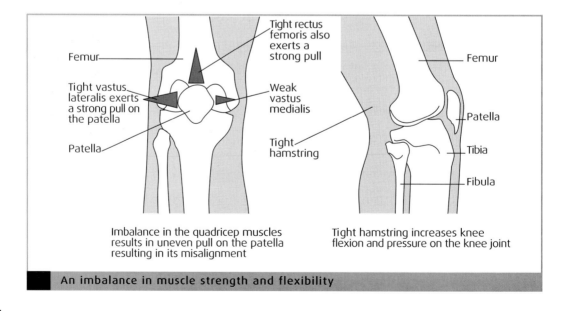

Imbalance in the quadricep muscles results in uneven pull on the patella resulting in its misalignment

Tight hamstring increases knee flexion and pressure on the knee joint

**An imbalance in muscle strength and flexibility**

# Types of stretching

In Chapter 6 I touched upon the importance of stretching prior to and following exercise. For flexibility training these stretches have to be complemented by a fuller, more thorough stretching of muscles on the completion of the activity. The extent and nature of the stretches depends on the objective. If it is simply to return the muscle to its length before the start of the activity, then a short maintenance stretch might suffice. This could be similar to the preparatory stretches described in Chapter 6, and are held for around 10 to 12 seconds.

If the objective is to develop the flexibility of the muscle, then the stretches will have to be held for substantially longer. Generally referred to as *developmental stretches*, there is no fixed rule on how long the stretch has to be held. Instead a rule of thumb applies: hold until the muscle relaxes, then develop the stretch further and hold again for say 25 to 30 seconds, or as long as is comfortable. There should be no force. The first phase takes time because, as explained in Chapter 3, the muscle spindles react to the initial stretch by tightening the muscles, the so-called *stretch reflex*. The faster and more abruptly a stretch is effected, the more the muscles respond by contracting rather than releasing. Hence, it is vital to go into a stretch in a slow and controlled way, paying special attention to the stability of the joints involved.

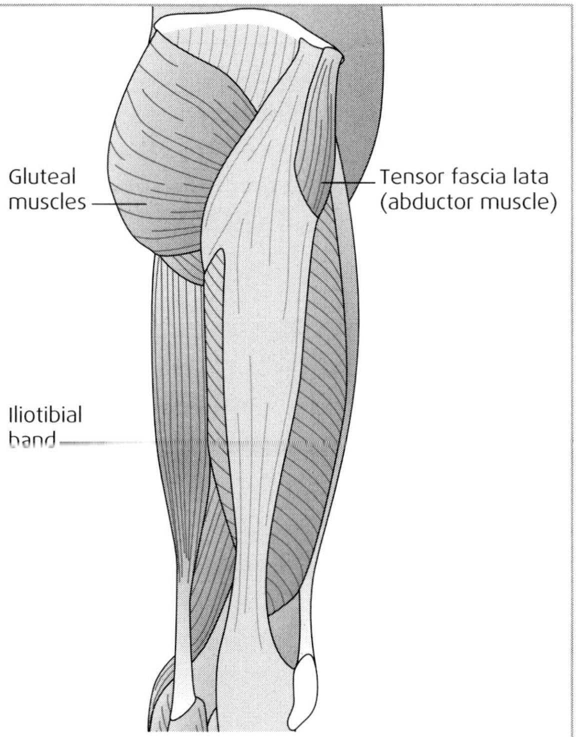

Gluteal muscles

Tensor fascia lata (abductor muscle)

Iliotibial band

Gentle stretching of the gluteal muscles helps to lengthen and loosen the iliotibial band

A shortened iliotibial band caused by poor training and overuse can lead to inflammation and pain when exercising

There are four groups of stretching techniques:

- ballistic stretching
- static stretching
- active stretching
- stretching against external resistance or proprioceptive neuromuscular facilitation (PNF).

*Ballistic stretching* involves lengthening the muscle to the maximum that can be reached and then bouncing to take the stretch even further. Bouncing at the end of the stretch causes the muscles to tighten in response. The greater the force of the bounce, the tighter the muscles become and the enforced strain can result in muscle tear and damage.

As a result, ballistic stretches, commonly used in the past, are now largely frowned upon, except in training for competitive gymnastics. A typical ballistic stretch is as follows:

**Ballistic stretch: inner thigh (adductors)**

- Place the feet wide apart with knees turned out to either side.

- Lower the bottom until the muscles in the inner thigh feel stretched to their maximum.

- Bounce to lower the bottom further and increase the stretch.

In this example, the knee and hip joints are also destabilised and subjected to pressure.

*Static stretching* is the opposite of ballistic stretching. It is the gradual lengthening of the muscle until a stretch is felt. The stretch is held and then released and no bouncing or force is involved. This is a safe and gentle way to lengthen the muscle, using mainly gravity and the support of the body. For example, to stretch the hamstring:

- Lie on your back with the knees up, feet down on the floor.

**A** ▎ • Bring one knee up towards the chest and straighten it upwards, supporting with both hands. Keep your bottom on the floor and the extended leg straight.

The stretch is felt at the back of the thigh (hamstring) from the bottom down to the back of the knee of the straightened leg. The muscles, both the quadriceps and the tibialis anterior, are relaxed.

A

Many people do not feel sufficiently stretched by static stretches. To develop the stretch further, the opposing muscle group is sometimes brought into use. Continuing with the static stretch for the hamstring, this becomes an *active stretch* if the foot of the extended **B** leg is flexed. The back of the leg, including the hamstring and the gastrocnemius, is lengthened even more. However, because the tibialis anterior is actively

engaged in flexing the foot and is shortened, the position should not be held for longer than 10–15 seconds. This avoids prolonged contraction and stress of the opposing muscle group. Gentle repetition of active stretches is preferable. Active stretches, with repetitive flex and release, are an integral part of a warm-up in most exercise to music classes, and are considered best suited for stretching muscle groups that cross major joints such as the hips, knees, ankles and shoulders.

One of the safest muscle stretches uses external assistance or *PNF*. This is the alternate static stretching and isometric contraction of a muscle against an object or partner. The isometric contraction should not be held for longer than six seconds. Using the example of a hamstring stretch, the extended leg of the participant lying down is supported by a partner who holds the leg. Stretch statically against the partner who should provide only mild assistance in the stretch (e.g. helping to gently ease the leg towards the participant) and then contract isometrically against the partner who provides the resistance against the contraction. Release

after 6 seconds and repeat the stretch and contraction. However this approach is only safe if the partner is competent. There has to be complete trust between the participants, and it is preferable for many of the exercises that they are of similar height and strength.

Working with an inanimate object such as a barre can overcome some of these potential difficulties. By placing the leg on the barre and leaning forward, the hamstring can be stretched statically without using the opposing muscle group, but with support. Make sure the barre is at the correct height. If it is too low, it exerts stress on the back – too high and it can stress the hip joint, knee and the leg.

All the different groups of stretching techniques, therefore, have some, not unsurmountable, disadvantages.

**Stretching the hamstring with help**

# Training exercises for flexibility

Stretches require a good understanding of one's body and sound technique, otherwise they may be executed badly and cause injuries. It is important to know your body's capacity and to set sensible targets. You should stretch to your personal maximum and avoid competing with others. Unfortunately, stretching tends to encourage competitiveness in a class in part because the act of stretching is slow and gives participants time to compare and contest with each other. The reverse, of course, also occurs. Some people are so self-conscious that they avoid stretching if they possibly can. It is important to be aware of the differences that exist between people and accept them. Then set your own objectives for flexibility training.

Objectives vary between individuals: for some it could be to maintain the muscle length, for others to develop flexibility within their natural range, while a few might wish to push further. You should note that extreme stretching positions are not suitable for everyone and can be dangerous unless participants are well trained and already have a supple body. Remember that extending flexibility beyond the full natural range of movement is not necessary for normal activity. It is a personal choice.

It is extremely difficult to determine what is 'natural' and what is not because of the wide differences in people's flexibility and build. Even cultural differences can come into play. Kneeling and sitting on the heel might be considered as extreme flexion by some, for example, but in the Far East it is part of the normal range of movements. In Japan, you kneel to eat. Squatting down is also often considered extreme flexion, but again in the Far East it is a common position in daily activities, including both working and eating. Kneeling and bowing down to the floor is a prayer position for Moslems, just as sitting cross-legged is in Buddhism.

Personal judgement is needed. I tend to disagree with the current trend in sports science to consider any position that requires 'extreme flexion' to be unsafe. Nevertheless, there are instances, as I explain below, when extreme flexion *is* dangerous. Generally speaking, if you experience pain and discomfort, it is not for you. In this context, stretching is not advisable for any one who has an injured joint, however 'safe' the position. Wait until you are fully recovered.

Always stretch when the muscles are warm and not before. Stretching involves the opening of joints to a greater angle than in regular activity. This has to be done slowly and without force. Ball and socket joints are especially unstable. Excessive straightening of hinge joints, such as the knee, can also cause stress and damage. Practice breathing slowly and evenly to relax the muscles because quick and excitable breathing tenses up the muscles. It is also important to bring the synergistic muscles into play to help stabilise joints and support the stretches. The instructions below are as important as the figures because they take you stage by stage through the stretch. Give yourself ample space in which to work and do not hurry the exercises. (Appendix 4 provides suggestions on how to sequence the different stretch exercises.)

I have divided the stretches into those for the torso, upper limbs and lower limbs. In the step by step instructions I have emphasised the technique of breathing with the diaphragm to improve balance, control and muscle relaxation. The instruction to inhale means breathing in deeply to let the diaphragm and the abdomen move, allowing the maximum expansion of the lungs; exhale means breathing out to let the stomach muscles return closer to the back of the spine. In stretching, exhalation should be slow and controlled and not as strong as in muscular strength training exercises. **Breathe normally when you are holding a stretch.**

# The Torso

## Back muscles: erector spinae, the transversospinalis–multifidus, trapezius and latissimus dorsi

### Feline stretch (the erector spinae)

**A**
- Kneel on the floor making sure that the hips are aligned above the knee.

- Place both hands on the floor, directly below the shoulders.

- Keeping the face down, take a deep breath.

**B**
- Exhale, tucking the tummy in, and at the same time tuck in your chin and round the buttocks under. Exhaling enables you to round the back more in a stretch and also helps support the trunk.

- Hold the stretch for 10 to 12 seconds.

- Gently return the back and neck to their original position. During the movement take care not to hyper-extend the neck or let the spine sag in an inverted arch.

- Repeat the stretch two to three times, holding slightly longer in each session.

The feline stretch also lengthens the trapezius muscles between the shoulder blades (see p. 114). You should notice an easing of the muscles running from the neck down the back and between the shoulder blades, and a greater relief of tension than if you were to effect just a single long stretch.

### Prayer position (the latissimus dorsi)

**A** • Kneel and sit back on your heels and stretch both arms out in front. Keep the face and trunk close to the floor and tuck the buttocks well under. This is a good stretch for the latissimus dorsi and back (see p. 115).

### Half serpent (erector spinae, transversospinalis-multifidus and latissimus dorsi)

The half serpent mobilises the vertebrae and lengthens the back muscles. This is an advanced position and should be attempted only afer the feline and prayer positions have been mastered.

- Start from the prayer position.

- Take a deep breath and then exhale, keeping the tummy tucked in.

**A**
**B**
- Breathing normally, glide forward with the chin and chest close to the floor until the head is between the palms of the hands.

- Inhale and come up in a feline stretch, arms fully extended (see A, p. 125).

- Exhale, tuck your head down, keep the back rounded and bottom tucked under (see B, p. 125). Hold.

- Release and sit back on your heels. The movement should be slow and controlled with even breathing.

- Repeat two to three times.

This a wonderful safe stretch that helps mobilise the joints between the vertebrae. You should feel slight movements in them as you glide forward. With practice your movements should become graceful and you should feel a strengthening and lengthening of the spinal muscles. Your ability to turn and twist will improve.

## Full serpent (erector spinae and latissimus dorsi)

This advanced position is not suitable for people with weak back or tummy muscles. Based on yoga, it can be a dangerous stretch if you let the small of the back pinch inwards. The following step by step procedure avoids this.

- Kneel and sit back on your heels stretching both arms out in front, as in the prayer position. Keep your face and trunk close to the floor and tuck your buttocks well under. Keep the tummy tight.

A
- Breathing normally, glide forward, keeping the chin and chest close to the floor until your head moves past your hands and the body is almost completely prone.

- In the next out-breath, tilt the pelvis slightly forward so that the pubic bone touches the floor. The pelvic tilt stops the small of the back from sagging and pinching in.

B
- Breathe in and exhale to lift the body, resting on your elbows.

- Hold.

- Release, breathing out and gliding back to a heel sitting position.

An alternative advanced finish, called the *full cobra*, is recommended only if you have mastered full pelvic and transverse abdominal control. Well executed, however, it is a good back extension exercise which helps maintain lower back mobility. Instead of raising the body and resting on the elbows, rest on your hands with arms extended fully. Before coming up ensure that the hands are resting on the floor alongside the chest with fingers

A
pointed forward. Also make sure that you are facing forward. Do not tilt your head backwards because this will hyper-extend the neck. You should not feel any stress in your lower back if the tummy is tightly controlled and the pubic bone is firmly on the floor. The hamstring will tighten where it meets the buttock.

# Abdominal muscles: the rectus abdominus, transverse abdominus and obliques

### The yawn (abdominal muscles)

This is an overall stretch for major muscle groups including those in the arms, torso and legs.

- Lie on your back and bring both arms above the head.

**A** • Inhale deeply and stretch out your arms and legs in opposite directions as though you are going to yawn, until you feel a stretch in the rectus abdominus, the central panel in the stomach area between the sternum down to the pubic bone.

- Hold, breathing normally.
- Exhale and release.

### The Z-stretch (obliques)

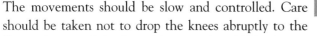

**A** • Lie on your back, drawing up your knees and keeping your feet on the floor.

**B** • Exhale and gently lower both knees, keeping them close together, to one side of the floor. At the same time, rotate the trunk toward the opposite side.

- The arms can be extended out in both directions, keeping the shoulders on the floor. Alternatively, bring both arms to point in the opposite direction to the knees. The first arm position is more difficult and advanced.

- Hold the position, breathing evenly during the hold.

- Exhale and release by bringing the knees to the centre. Repeat on the opposite side.

The movements should be slow and controlled. Care should be taken not to drop the knees abruptly to the floor. Those with back problems or the elderly should use a rolled towel or flat cushion to support the knees when they are brought down to the side, so that the angle of the knee drop and therefore stretch of the obliques is reduced. This stretch incorporates a moderate spinal twist which is also beneficial for the back.

# Chest/back muscles: pectoralis, trapezius and latissimus dorsi

### The roll-back (pectoralis)

Stretching the rectus abdominus in the 'yawn' would have allowed for a slight stretching of the pectoralis, because the arms were stretched upwards. This is an additional, more specific stretch for the pectoralis, which can be done either standing up or seated cross-legged.

**A**
- Bring both arms to the back and clasp the hands together, and inhale.
- Hold.
- Exhale to release, bringing both hands to their normal position.

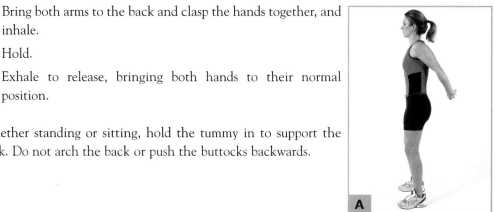

Whether standing or sitting, hold the tummy in to support the back. Do not arch the back or push the buttocks backwards.

### The roll-forward (trapezius and latissimus dorsi)

- Stand or sit cross-legged, keeping the body tall.
- Inhale and then exhale to let the navel sink toward the spine.

**A**
**B**
- Breathing normally, bring both arms forward, slightly above shoulder height, to clasp your hands. The shoulders are rounded forward in this motion until a stretch is felt in the muscles between the shoulder blade (trapezius) and those running below the arms to the spine (the latissimus dorsi). Keep the head inclined slightly forward. This helps lengthen the whole of the spinal column.

- Hold and then release.

This is a wonderful stretch for releasing tension in the trapezius and even the rhomboids. Both muscles act as a brace, holding the shoulders, and become tense if a lot of time is spent sitting at a desk.

**The forearm twist (trapezius, latissimus dorsi and deltoids)**

- Stand or sit cross-legged, keeping the body tall.
- Place your hands on the opposite shoulders so that one elbow is resting in the crook of the other arm.

A
- Straighten the forearms with the palms of the hands facing each other and then put the palms as closely together as possible keeping the elbows in place.
- Inhale, raising the forearms so that the elbows are about level with your mouth or until you feel a stretch in the muscles between the shoulder blades.
- Exhale, bringing the forearms down again to around chest level so that the upper arms are parallel to the floor. The stretch in the trapezius muscle should intensify.
- Hold, breathing normally, and then release.

A

# Arms

## Biceps, triceps and deltoids

Stretching these muscles has already been covered in Chapter 6 (see p. 62). The same exercises, but held longer, can be used for the final stretch.

# Buttocks and legs

## Abductors, gluteals and tensor fascia lata

### Bum stretch (gluteals and tensor fascia lata)

- Lie on your back with your knees drawn up and feet firmly placed on the floor. Breathe normally.

**A**

- Bring one foot up to rest the ankle on the opposite knee. The knee of the lifted leg will be turned out to the side.

**B**

- In the next out breath, raise the other leg off the floor, bringing the supporting knee towards you, until a stretch is felt on the gluteals and the outer upper thigh area (tensor fascia latae) of the opposite leg (see p. 98).

- Hold, breathing normally, and then gently release.

- Repeat using the opposite leg.

It is important to exhale when you raise your legs towards you so that the hip joints are stabilised by the transverse abdominus, which contracts to hold the lower torso in place. The movements should be slow and controlled.

### Hold the horns (gluteals, tensor fascia lata)

This is an alternative hip stretch.

A
- Lie on your back with both legs up. Both legs are bent.

B
- Exhale to cross the knees.
- Hold the position, supporting the ankles with the hands and breathing evenly.

C
- Inhale and as you exhale gently ease the knees closer towards the chest, maintaining support of the ankles. Hold for slightly longer.
- Repeat by crossing on the other side.

You should feel a stretch of the gluteals and tensor fascia lata on the top leg.

A

B

C

# Adductors

This group of muscles (see p. 104 for diagram) has to be stretched well, largely because they are prone to adaptive shortening. At the end of a work-out a developmental stretch should be applied, holding the muscles longer and stretching them more intensely. This stretch can be done in several ways.

## Groin stretch (adductors)

A
- Sit up tall and bring the soles of your feet together. The knees are turned out in opposite directions.

- Breathe in, drawing the feet close towards the groin and then exhale gently, easing the knees towards the floor until a stretch is felt in the inner thigh.

- Hold, breathing normally, and then release.

There should be no force exerted on the hip joint. The shoulders should be relaxed and the back straight.

## Wide angle stretch (adductors)

- Sit up tall and spread your legs as wide as possible. Take care to ensure that the knees are not turned in but face upward.

- Breathe in and then exhale to hold the tummy in, and stabilise the hip joint.

A
- In the next out-breath, gently lower the body to the front until a stretch is felt in the inner thigh. Breathe evenly. No force should be applied.

- When the tension of this initial stretch eases, develop the stretch by reaching out further and hold for another 20 to 25 seconds. Exhale as you reach out, but

breathe evenly during the stretch. At no point should you hold your breath. The trunk of people who are very flexible could touch the floor and the stretch could be developed into a back stretch. More will be said about this in the following section (see p. 136).

# Thigh and shin muscles

## Quadriceps and tibialis anterior

**Thigh and shin muscle stretch (quadriceps and tibialis anterior)**

- Lie face down with your legs extended backward.
- Keep the knees together and in the next out-breath tilt the pelvis forward until the pubic bone is on the floor.

A
- Breathing normally, bring one foot towards the buttocks and support the foot with the hand. Pointing the toes will increase the stretch in the quadriceps and stretch the muscle in the shin (the tibialis anterior).
- Hold and then release.

This stretch can also be done standing up or lying on the side.

## Hamstring

Examples of how to stretch the hamstring have already been provided earlier in this chapter and in the section on preparatory stretches. The hamstring needs developmental stretches at the end of activities because it is prone to adaptive shortening. Any of the methods illustrated previously (see exercises on pp. 122–3) could be used. However, hold the initial stretch until the tension eases and then take the stretch slightly further without force, holding for 20–25 seconds more. An additional, advanced hamstring stretch is as follows.

**Forward bend stretch: hamstring**

A
- Sit up tall with both legs extended in front.
- Inhale, lifting the upper torso up.

**B** • Exhale, letting the navel sink toward the spine and keeping the tummy tucked in tight, lean forward, reaching for your toes until you feel a stretch in the hamstring. Breathe normally. If the feet are flexed, you will also stretch the gastrocnemius (calves). The flexion of the feet should be supported by the hands.

**C** • Hold until the tightness eases and then try to reach further towards the toes to develop the stretch.

The extent to which the upper trunk can move forward varies widely. The trunk of very flexible people may well touch the legs, allowing the hands to grasp the feet. This finishing position is considered extreme flexion, but for the very supple the hamstrings cannot be stretched thoroughly without it. There should be no pain in the hamstrings or stress in the back if full abdominal control is mastered.

Instead of stretching both legs at the same time, you can stretch each in turn by bending the resting leg and placing its heel close to the groin or knee of the straightened leg.

## Calf muscle: gastrocnemius

Examples of how to stretch the gastocnemius, the calf muscle, have already been given when discussing active and externally assisted stretching of the hamstrings and the forward bend stretch. The gastocnemius is another muscle that should be held for longer where possible because it is subject to continuous activity and contraction. Stretching this muscle will help reduce soreness and muscle bulk. If the gastrocnemius is stretched by actively flexing the foot, then instead of developing the stretch through 'long holds', repeat the stretch. Otherwise, as explained previously, the opposing muscle group – the tibialis anterior in this case – will be stressed because it is this muscle which helps flex the foot.

# Progression in training

### Full wide angle stretch (adductors, erector spinae and latissimus dorsi)

Once muscles gain, or regain, their suppleness, the stretch positions described above can be taken further. Take for example the wide angle stretch of the adductors. The angle can be widened by taking the legs out further. The intensity of the stretch can be increased by reaching out further to the front and making greater use of the floor by stretching the adductors against it. The aim is to lengthen the body forward while avoiding a downward curve that would exert pressure on the cervical spine. The neck needs to be kept relaxed. Strong abdominal muscle control prevents the hips from rolling forward. The exercise incorporates a stretch on the erector spinae and the lattisimus dorsi. The length of time for which the stretch is held can also be increased slightly.

This is a progression in flexibility training that keeps the basic stretch position unchanged, but modifies the intensity and angle of stretch. Eventually, you might be able to reach out until your chest is on the floor, but then again you might not! It presents a goal to work towards, but it is *not* an end in itself. For those who can bring their chest to the floor without any strain, holding the body midway, rather than stretching forward, provides a contrary exercise involving as it does isometric contraction to hold the trunk up. This is where the physiological and physical differences between people *must* be recognised and stretches adapted to suit the individual.

Caution: only for the very supple and strong

### Stretching in flight (hamstring and gastrocnemius)

An advanced stretch used for both the hamstring and the gastrocnemius.

- Sit up tall.

- Inhale, lifting the torso, and then exhale, tucking the navel toward the spine. Breathe evenly.

**A**
**B**

- Keeping your back straight, bring the knee of one leg towards you and then slowly extend or straighten the leg towards the ceiling, exhaling in the process.

A

B

- Hold the leg with both hands to support it. You should feel a strong stretch at the back of the leg running from the hamstring down to the calves.

- Let the stretch settle before gently bending the knee to bring it even closer and then straighten the leg again. You should feel a stronger stretch.

- Release and repeat on the other leg.

The closer you can bring each leg towards you and the straighter the leg, the stronger the stretch. But do not use force. For many the leg will be extended to the front rather than upward. Apart from its direct impact on the hamstring and gastrocnemius, this stretch helps improve coordination and balance.

## Full flight

This stretch should be attempted only if you have good abdominal muscle control and a sound grasp of the technique for stabilising the hip joint. People who are very strong can stretch both legs simultaneously, supported with both hands. **Caution: only for the very supple and strong.**

A • Sit up tall.

B • Inhale and draw in both knees close to the chest.

C • Exhale, straightening both legs out and point them towards the ceiling. Support both legs with the hands, breathing normally.

A

Breathe evenly while holding the stretch but do not lean heavily backwards or round the back because this will pass the stress to the small of the back. Do not attempt this advanced stretch if you have back problems. If at any point, you are not comfortable, abandon the stretch.

The progression in flexibility training can also involve adopting even more extreme stretch positions. The plough position, as we saw in Chapter 5, is used to lengthen the erector spinae. It is not recommended for general use and has in fact been deemed dangerous. I must confess that I do practise the plough occasionally, a stretch with which I have had a love–hate relationship for

B

C

some 20 years, having been taught it long before I realised the dangers associated with its practice. Like an alcoholic returning to the bottle, I return to doing it as a test of my flexibility. Unless you have practised it since you were young or have previous training in dance, ballet or gymnastics, the plough carries risks that might not be worth taking – many other stretches exist that are equally effective for the erector spinae. The general recommendation for flexibility training is to opt for alternative safer methods.

Over-stretching ligaments can result in instability in the joints. Ligaments, once stretched, remain stretched because they are tough fibrous tissues. It is for this reason that expectant mothers are advised not to take advantage of the hormone relaxin in their system, which provides increased flexibility, to stretch more. When the hormone level declines, the hip joint in particular becomes unstable if over-stretched. The damage may not be apparent when young, but comes to light when muscles weaken with age. The problems related to stretches are dealt with in more detail in Chapter 11.

# Relaxation

We have now come to the end of the work-out. This is the time to complete the cycle of exercises by allowing the muscles to relax and the body to savour the release in tension that comes after the stretch.

I always like to work with music. This time choose music that is calm and soothing and let it wash over you.

## Lying down

You can lie down with your feet drawn up or fully extended in front of you, i.e. in whichever position you feel most comfortable, palms turned up to face the ceiling. Make sure that your body is aligned. Now close your eyes and breathe evenly and slowly, turning your head from side to side to release the tension in your neck. Relax the forehead, relax the jaw and let the body feel heavy on the floor. Release the shoulders and feel their weight on the floor. Let the weight of the body go. Breathe evenly and lie quietly.

When you are ready, stretch both arms up on the floor, in the opposite direction to your feet. Hold the stretch and then release. Repeat. Stay quiet for a couple more minutes and then gently roll-up.

## Adaptation of Qi Gong breathing technique

I find this extremely calming. I have adapted the technique to make it a pelvic floor exercise as well as a relaxation technique. Hence, this is not exactly how a Qi Gong kung fu (master of Qi Gong) would perform the exercise which in the original version relates breathing to acupressure points for self-healing.

Sit cross-legged, palms of the hand turned up on each knee and with the thumb touching the third finger to make a circle. Your head should face down. Check that the body is balanced with the weight of the body evenly distributed on both sides of the bottom. Close your eyes. Start by breathing evenly.

Now imagine that you have a little steel marble at the base of your body and that your body is like a magnetic field. You are going to breathe in, first contracting the pelvic floor, to draw the marble up the front of your body and all along up the body, to your chin, nose, forehead and up to the top of the skull. Then breathe out, long and slowly, letting the marble roll gently back down the back.

Breathe in slowly by curling the tongue up the palate of your mouth moving your head up until the eyes, if they were open, are reverted at an angle up to the ceiling (you should not tilt your head back fully). Breathe out unfurling the tongue slowly and gently lowering the head until it is again in the starting position.

Repeat this breathing process at least 10 times and feel the tension release in your body. Then revert back to even breathing. When you are ready, gently open your eyes and roll-up.

# Sports and exercise injuries: training to avoid them

# 11

All activities carry some risk, even crossing the road. Sports and exercise are no exception. It is estimated that over 10 million sports injuries occur each year. Many of them are a result of accidents, but a significant proportion are from repetitive stresses and strains on joints, muscles, tendons and ligaments. These can occur because of over-use or over-training, wrong techniques, poor equipment or even unbalanced muscle development. This chapter reviews some of the more common injuries, their causes and how they might best be avoided.

## Common sports injuries

Sports injuries come in a variety of forms, depending on the cause of the damage:

- *Sprains* are caused by sudden twists or wrenches of the joints, especially of the ankles, knees or wrists.

- *Strains* result from force, over-use and over-stretching muscles or tendons.

- *Contusions* are caused by a severe blow or force as when kicked or punched.

- *Fractures* of bones are either simple, compound or stress/hairline fractures. In simple and compound fractures, the breakage is usually complete and part of the bone may even stick through the skin. In stress and hairline fractures, a fine crack can run partially or completely through the bone. Simple and compound fractures are normally caused by the impact of sudden force, whereas hairline fractures are generally associated with over-use and stress.

*Injury to joints* is one of the most common sports injuries. This is largely because joints bear the brunt of the force applied by muscle contractions against resistance. Although the surfaces of joints are cushioned by cartilage, their resilience deteriorates with continuous use. Wear and tear or damage to the cartilage cause the opposing surfaces of the joints to roughen and grate against each other, making the joint prone to arthritis and bursitis. Arthritis, inflammation of a joint, results in pain, stiffness and swelling. In bursitis, the bursa, a fluid filled sac that surrounds the joint, becomes inflamed resulting in pain.

Joints, when subjected to large force, can also be twisted out of position. People who play sports that involve sudden changes in direction and acceleration such as football, squash and tennis are prone to knee injuries.

Incorrect training, resulting in or encouraging imbalanced quadricep development, can cause a misalignment of the patella or knee cap on the femur, sometimes referred to as 'runner's knee'. Wrong technique in leg extension exercises, especially if external weights are used or if exercises are carried out incorrectly using a machine, is another cause of knee injuries.

*Bone injuries* include stress fractures such as shin splints. Over-use and over-training are usually the main causes, aided and abetted by weight-bearing activities such as running on hard surfaces wearing footwear that does not provide adequate cushioning to the force sustained by the lower leg, especially the tibia and toes. Poor biomechanics (flat or highly-arched feet and abnormal gaits) and styles of running can also cause them. Repeated stress on the foot can result in a benign growth of bone, called a spur, which can be intensely painful. For example, continued stress on the heel bone can result in calcification of the ligaments originating from it, and a spur is formed at the insertion of the achilles tendon.

*Muscle injuries* are common. They range from bruises, resulting from external forces which rupture small blood vessels, to cramps and spasms as a result of inadequate warm-up, dehydration or fatigue. Injuries can also result from a rekindling of previous damage such as strains or muscle tear, by over-training or over-stretching. A sudden contraction of the hamstring, especially following inadequate warm-up and preparatory stretching, can result in a torn or pulled muscle. A pulled muscle can also be caused by imbalances in muscle strength, for example very strong quadriceps and relatively weak hamstrings. Muscle injuries can also arise when movement is constrained by a tightness in the joints. The inability of the hip joint to open up to its full range of movement can tear the adductor muscles when unexpected wide movements are made with the leg.

*Tendon injuries*, in contrast to muscle injuries, are relatively rare, although they can be very serious and painful. Tendons can be ruptured or become inflamed as with tendinitis. Over-use, exercise on uneven terrain and tight tendons are possible causes for the rupture of the achilles tendon. The achilles tendon is a strong fibrous tissue that connects the gastrocnemius, the muscle in the lower leg, to the heel bone. Abrupt footwork and repeated stress can cause the tendon to snap (see p. 142). Stretching the calf muscles and achilles tendon helps prevent this.

Poor training and biomechanics can cause inflammation of the iliotibial band, the group of fibrous tissues that connects the gluteal muscles and the tensor fascia lata muscle to the tibia, just below the knee. This is manifested in a pain in the lower outer thigh or the side of the knee. A common cause is running only on one side of cambered roads. The slope means that the pelvis is always tilted to one side, causing consistent stress to the iliotibial band. Unbalanced muscles, such as tight gluteals or quadriceps, can make the situation worse (see pp. 120–1).

*Ligaments* can be injured but the symptoms are often manifested in the form of joint pains or joint instability because ligaments join bone to bone. Ligaments do not heal easily. One extreme example of a ligament injury is when it becomes over-stressed and snaps. The anterior cruciate ligaments (see below) are located in the centre of the knee, running from the back of the femur to the front of the tibia. They function as a stabiliser, holding the tibia and femur in place. If excessive force is applied when the knee is bent, the ligament can be injured. In extreme cases, the ligament may tear and snap. The result is a fall and extreme pain and swelling around the knee.

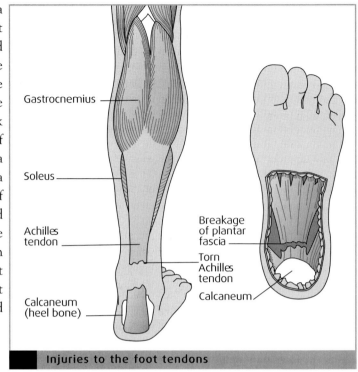

Gastrocnemius

Soleus

Achilles tendon

Calcaneum (heel bone)

Breakage of plantar fascia

Torn Achilles tendon

Calcaneum

**Injuries to the foot tendons**

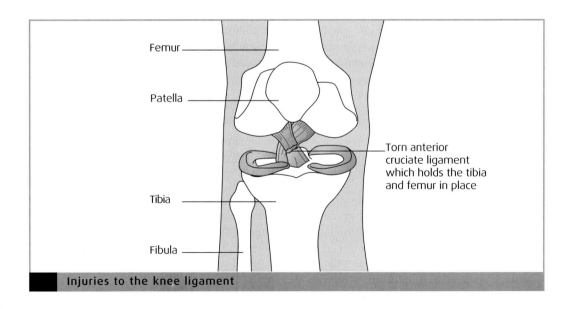

Femur

Patella

Tibia

Fibula

Torn anterior cruciate ligament which holds the tibia and femur in place

**Injuries to the knee ligament**

### Selected major sports and exercise injuries[14]

| Location | Problem | Symptoms | Cause | Prevention |
|---|---|---|---|---|
| Joints | Arthritis (most forms are not direct result of sport injuries, e.g. rheumatoid, seronegative, infective, ankylosing spondylitis, gout) | Inflammation, pain, stiffness | Cartilage damage (causes not related to sports injury are not covered here) | None, but keeping joints mobile and adopting a cautious approach to loaded and repetitive movements help minimise cartilage damage |
| | Synovitis | Inflammation of the synovial membrane, local swelling, tenderness and pain | Local trauma, arthritis, over-use, infection | Cautious approach to loaded and repetitive movements |
| | Baker's cyst | Painless fluid filled swelling behind knee | Torn cartilage, weakness of knee capsule, arthritis | Cautious approach to loaded and repetitive movement |
| | Runner's knee or chondromalacia patellae | Acute knee pain | Quadriceps imbalance, sustained damage, poor biomechanics | Improve muscle balance and strength, proper footwear |
| | Bursitis: e.g. housemaid's knee (prepatellar bursitis), clergyman's knee (tibial tubercle bursitis), tennis elbow (olecranon bursitis), frozen shoulder (can result from deltoid bursitis) | Pain and tenderness, inflammation and swelling from accumulation of fluid | Over-use, direct force, arthritis | Good warm-up and preparatory stretch to help prepare joint |
| | Ankle sprain | Pain, bruising, swelling | Twisting of ankle | Improve joint mobility and strength, use proper footwear |
| | Back pains | Pain and reduced mobility | Weak abdominal muscles, poor posture, poor training, overweight | Improve abdominal muscle strength, stretching, use proper footwear |

## Selected major sports and exercise injuries – continued

| Location | Problem | Symptoms | Cause | Prevention |
|---|---|---|---|---|
| Bones | Stress fracture e.g. shin splints | Pain | Over-use, over-pronation, ill-fitting shoes | Moderate training programme; gradual increase in intensity of effort |
| | Spurs | Benign growth in bone, pain and inflammation | Repeated stress | Moderate training programme, gradual increase in intensity of effort |
| Muscle | Hamstring pull | Pain, muscle spasm, loss of strength | Sudden contraction of hamstring, over-use of muscle, weak hamstrings relative to quadriceps | Warm-up and stretch before and after activity |
| | Quadriceps strain/tear | Sudden pain especially going down, swelling and tenderness | Sudden contraction of quadriceps, over-use of muscle | Warm-up and stretch before and after activity |
| | Gastrocnemius strain | Pain especially in descent, difficulty in supporting body weight | Over-use and overload of muscle | Warm-up and stretch before and after activity |
| | Adductor strain/ tear | Pain | Over-stretch, limited hip mobility | Warm-up and stretch before and after activity |
| Tendons | Tendinitis e.g. achilles tendinitis | Painful swelling in tendon, sometimes restricted use of muscle to which tendon is connected | Injury; repeated stress and overload, poor biomechanics | Moderate training programme; appropriate footwear in case of achilles tendon |
| | Rupture, e.g. achilles tendon rupture | Sudden pain, shock and swelling; inability to support muscle and weight, immobilisation | Violent stretching, aggressive stop and start foot-work; repeated stress | Moderate training programme, use proper footwear in case of achilles tendon |
| | Iliotibial band friction | Pain in outer knee or lower thigh | Incorrect training, poor biomechanics | Balanced muscle development and training; stretching |

| | Selected major sports and exercise injuries – continued | | | |
| --- | --- | --- | --- | --- |
| Location | Problem | Symptoms | Cause | Prevention |
| Ligaments | Rupture or tear e.g. anterior cruciate ligament | Knee joint suddenly fails | Excessive force and stress on knee in bent position | Correct training technique and position; avoid excessive flexion and force on joints |

# Safe training

In any discussion of sports injuries, repeated stress and over-training emerge as major factors in sports injuries. Poor biomechanics, poor training methods, the wrong use of equipment, including inappropriate footwear, and muscular imbalance are among the others. The principles of good training simply address these major areas, most of which have already been covered elsewhere in the book.

Moderation is essential in exercise. The body has to have adequate rest in order to recover from exertion and to perform well. Exhaustion results in poor coordination, poor performance and injuries. The principle of overload is to build up greater endurance and strength by progressively giving the body more than its normal workload. This prompts the skeletal muscles, both fast and slow twitch, to adapt and develop. They can only do so, however, if the muscles are not injured or over-used. Rest days are essential. It takes some 24 hours to restore glycogen levels, the primary source of energy for working muscles (see Chapter 3).

It is important to ensure that the movements that constitute the exercise or sport are executed well. Special attention needs to be paid to joints because they take the bulk of the force. Keeping the knees soft in landing after a jump is essential to reduce impact on the knees. Athletes need to be aware of how they walk and run to ensure that their feet land correctly. In running, the heel strikes the ground, the arch flattens to absorb some of the impact and then the foot rolls inward allowing the ball of the foot to touch the ground while the heel lifts up. This rolling inward motion, called pronation, allows the push to move forward and helps absorb the shock of landing. Flat feet tend to over-pronate with an excessive roll inward, causing injuries to the lower leg. High arches in the feet tend to lead to under-pronation so that the ankle takes the shock. Correct footwear can reduce these problems. It is important not to land on the toes or the ball of the foot when running.

The hip joint and the small of the back, especially the fifth lumbar, are subjected to considerable pressure and stress in some floor exercises. In abdominal curl-ups for example, it is important to ensure that the small of the back is supported and not arched. Stabilise the hips by drawing the knees up and engaging the iliopsoas muscle to act as a synergist muscle. Correct breathing and engagement of the transverse abdominus, which I have repeatedly stressed, contribute greatly to a safer and more effective work-out.

Excessive flexion is another problem. For example, when bending the forward leg to stretch the leg extended behind, it is important to align the knee of the front leg above the ankle. If the knee goes beyond the ankle, the entire weight is shifted to the front and excessive pressure is exerted on the knee and ankle. The figures below provide examples of poor movements and positions that can injure joints.

In floor press-ups (top of bottom illustration), poor alignment of arms and inadequate stomach control can cause lower back and shoulder injuries. In V sit-ups (bottom illustration), excessive leverage when raising the trunk stresses the lower back. Frequently, people raise their body by pushing out the stomach muscles which over time leads to the development of bulging stomach muscles.

It is important to warm-up and stretch before and after the completion of an activity. Stretching before the activity helps improve performance as it loosens the muscles and helps stretch the connective fibrous tissues. Reduced tightness reduces the incidence of muscle strain and tear.

Balanced muscle development is extremely important because any imbalance can injure the weaker opposing muscle group. Shin splints are often caused by a weak tibialis anterior relative to the strong gastrocnemius; hamstring pulls result from over strong quadriceps; and weak abdominal muscles pass all the effort of body support to the back, stressing the erector spinae. Cross-training is useful in improving balanced muscle development, especially if a sport discipline focuses on particular muscle groups or only on a limited range of the five principles of fitness (see Chapter 2).

For muscular strength and endurance training, the movements should be slow and controlled. Avoid

**Extreme knee flexion**

**Deep knee squats**

**Poorly executed V sit-ups and full length press-ups**

large, vigorous movements. When stretching, avoid ballistic stretches. The body should be taken to its natural joint range, but extreme movements that cause discomfort and pain should be avoided.

## Treatment for sports injuries

The recommended first aid for all injuries, including strains, sprains, and fractures is R.I.C.E. This stands for **R**est, application of **I**ce, **C**ompression and **E**levation of the injured part above the level of the heart. Rest or ceasing the activity helps prevent further injuries; ice helps reduce bleeding; compression reduces swelling; and elevation helps increase the drainage of fluid from the injured part. Do not, however, try to treat yourself. Contact a doctor immediately or as soon as possible. A correct diagnosis is essential for prescribing treatment.

## Nutrition: the other side of the exercise equation

# 12

Achieving the right balance between energy intake and expenditure is of prime importance in weight control. To get the balance correct we might calculate our basic metabolic rate and then add on an estimate of the amount of energy we expend on day to day life plus an allowance for any extra physical activities or sports (see Chapter 4). But what we eat cannot be limited to calculations of energy: it affects our health and our body functions and is tied up with our cultural and social interactions, such as the enjoyment to be derived from good food and good company. We are, in every respect, what we eat.

Restricting the discussion to human physiology, we need to balance our nutritional needs as well as our energy requirements. There is a tendency to discount this, particularly among women, and to place undue emphasis on body weight and the notion of slimming. This preoccupation has resulted in wave after wave of diets ranging from high protein to high fibre, fruit and vegetable to no or low fat diets and even detox diets where the emphasis seems to be more on starving than eating. Most of these diets will help to reduce weight but may have repercussions on health if followed for long. Unless good eating habits are developed, the loss in weight is likely to be followed by gains with a vengeance once the diet is abandoned. Health is not about thinness. It is about being fit, which means having sufficient energy and nutrition for physical activities, *and* a healthy body. So let's put aside fashion and fads and get back to basics.

## Balancing food requirements

The dietary balance recommended by the World Health Organization for an average person is 55 to 75 per cent carbohydrates, 15 to 30 per cent fat and 10 to 15 per cent protein. In addition we need vitamins, minerals and water. It is important to note, however, that these are general recommendations. They do not represent targets for individual people, which would vary depending on body proportions, weight, height, age, gender and activity/work. They also vary according to country because the recommended actions are often adjusted to reflect national population consumption characteristics (see Chapter 4 and p. 45). In the UK, for example, the Committee on Medical Aspects (COMA) for Food and Nutrition Policy recommends that 50 per cent of the total energy intake should be in carbohydrates, 15 per cent in protein and 35

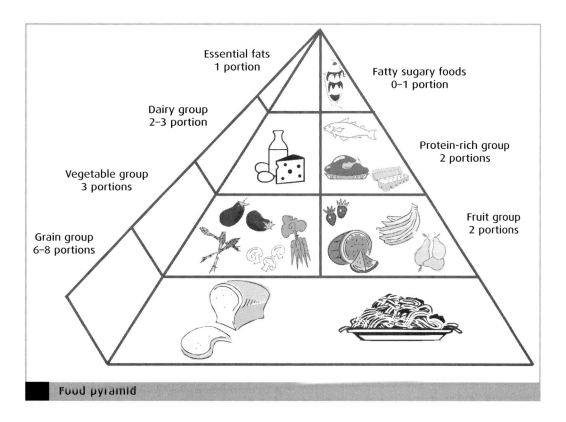

Food pyramid

per cent in fat when no alcohol is consumed. If alcohol is consumed, it is suggested by COMA that it should provide no more than 5 per cent of the total calorie intake.

# Carbohydrates

Carbohydrates consist of starches (complex carbohydrates or polysaccharides) and sugars (simple carbohydrates or monosaccharides and disaccharides). They provide the energy. All carbohydrates have the same amount of energy – 4 Calories per gram. However, cellulose, the polysaccharide that makes up the bulk of plant cell walls, has no calorie content because it is not digested. Instead it contributes to dietary fibre, which is important for maintaining regular bowel habits. But not all fibres are insoluble. Soluble fibre constituents, e.g. pectin, are absorbed by the body and are found in fruits, vegetables and pulses. Their consumption helps reduce cholesterol in blood.

Most of our intake of carbohydrate comes from starch in, for example, cereals, flour, bread, potatoes, couscous, rice and pasta. Ideally starch should provide at least 90 per cent of the total daily carbohydrate intake. These polysaccharides break up during the process of digestion and are converted by digestive enzymes into the monosaccharide, glucose. The glucose is absorbed into the blood for immediate use or is stored either as body fat or glycogen in muscle cells and in the liver. The glycogen stored in muscle cells converts to glucose for energy release. The glycogen stored in the liver releases glucose to maintain blood sugar levels, ensuring an adequate supply of energy to the brain and nervous system.

The remainder of the carbohydrate intake (between 5 and 10 per cent of total calorie intake) should be from sugars in the form of sucrose, lactose and maltose. During digestion, these simple carbohydrates are broken down and absorbed into the blood stream for immediate use or storage. Most of the sugar in our diet is in the form of sucrose, nearly all of which comes from commercially produced white sugar. Refined sugar is considered to be of poor nutritional value because it contains only energy. By contrast, most foods high in complex carbohydrates (polysaccharides) also contain minerals, iron and vitamins. In terms of weight, the amount of carbohydrate that should be consumed by a woman with a WHO recommended total dietary intake of 2200 Calories and a 55 per cent carbohydrate intake is around 300 g per day.

| Selected foods rich in carbohydrates | |
|---|---|
| Cereal sources | Vegetable sources |
| Wheat | Roots and tubers |
| Bread (brown, white, wholemeal, granary, ciabatta, casareccio, chapatti, nan, pita, chanai) | Potatoes, sweet potatoes, cassava, yams, parsnips, beetroot, tapioca, Jerusalem artichokes |
| Pasta (spaghetti, macaroni, penne, tagliatelle, linguine, lasagne) and noodles | |
| Wheatgerm (couscous, semolina) | Legumes |
| | Beans (kidney beans, broad beans, flageolet, butter beans) lentils (red and green), chickpeas, peas, sugar snap peas, mange tout peas |
| Rice | |
| Cooked rice (steamed, boiled, fried, paella, risotto, pilaf, biryani, rice congee) | Fruit sources |
| Rice products (vermicelli, rice pancakes, rice dumplings/buns, rice cakes) | Dried fruits (raisins, currants, sultanas, dates, prunes) |
| | Fresh fruits (apples, bananas, pears, plums, figs, dates, papayas) |
| Maize or Corn | |
| Corn bread (fajita, tortillas and enchilada), polenta | Nuts |
| Oat/millet/sorghum | Chestnuts* |
| Porridge, gruel | |
| Mix of cereals | *Only chestnut is listed here. Unlike other nuts, which are high in fat and protein, chestnuts are high in carbohydrate and low in protein and fat. On a weight-to-weight basis, four times more peanuts would be needed to provide the amount of carbohydrate available in the equivalent weight of chestnuts. |
| Breakfast cereals (muesli, cornflakes, rice crispies, mixed cereal bars) | |

# Fats and fatty acids

The fat in food provides the largest amount of energy – 9 Calories per gram. Fat refers to separated fat such as butter, visible fat in meats and invisible fat contained in many foods. For example, about 50 per cent of a peanut is fat; 30 per cent of chocolate and cheddar cheese is fat; 8 per cent of raw liver is fat and 12 per cent of lean beef is fat.

Fats are chemical compounds that contain fatty acids. There are two broad types of fatty acid: saturated fatty acids and unsaturated fatty acids, which are in turn divided into monounsaturated and polyunsaturated fatty acids. Animal fats or fats that are solid at room temperature generally contain more saturated fatty acids. Examples include butter, cheese, lard, palm oil, coconut oil, cream, peanut butter, chocolate and beef, lamb and pork fat. Unsaturated fats are liquid at room temperature and are contained in plant and fish oils. Examples include olive oil, fish oils (mackerel, sardines and salmon), almonds, avocados and selected vegetable cooking oils. However, modern food processing has broken down this division between hard and liquid fats making it more difficult to distinguish physically saturated from unsaturated fats. Vegetable and fish oils can also be solidified by the addition of hydrogen producing in the process trans fatty acids. Margarine, for example, is produced by the hydrogenation of vegetable oils. Trans fats, produced by hydrogenation, are not the same as natural trans fats found in some foods of animal origin. Some research suggests the possibility of a link between a high consumption of artificial trans fats and heart disease, but this is still a matter of scientific debate.

Fats consumed in food are broken down in the body into triglycerides which are released into the bloodstream and are either used immediately for energy or stored as fat in the adipose tissues of the body. The liver also produces triglycerides from carbohydrates and protein. Triglyceride is the main type of fat transported in the body. The adipose tissues can be drawn upon to supply energy between meals. Aside from fat stores, the adipose tissues provide insulation that helps maintain body temperature, maintain reserves of fat-soluble vitamins (see p. 170) and help cushion body organs such as the heart, reproductive system and kidneys.

Not all fatty acids need to be provided through the diet. Most of them can be synthesised within the body, but two polyunsaturated fatty acids, linoleic and alpha linoleic acids, must be provided in the diet. Because they cannot be produced within the body, they are referred to as essential fatty acids (EFAs). Linoleic acid (an omega-6 fatty acid) occurs in large amounts in plants and vegetable oils and in small amounts in some animal fats. Alpha linoleic acid (an omega-3 fatty acid) is found in most vegetable and fish oils. Vegetable oils with high concentrations of linoleic acids include safflower, sunflower, soya, cotton seed and corn oils.

The essential fatty acids have numerous functions in the body. For example, they are involved in the functioning of cell membranes and the production of hormones as well as the synthesis of other fatty acids. Their importance makes very low fat diets inadvisable unless medically prescribed. Such a diet also has the inherent danger of depleting the body of fat-soluble vitamins A and D.

# Cholesterol

In any consideration of fat and health, a major preoccupation is the role of cholesterol which, like fat, is classified as a lipid. A high level of cholesterol in the blood is associated with a high risk of coronary heart disease (see opposite). Unfortunately, focus on this medical aspect has given cholesterol the reputation of being a harmful substance and led to a great deal of mis-understanding.

Cholesterol is produced in the body as part of its normal metabolism and is continuously being synthesised and broken down. The body can produce most of the cholesterol that it needs; the liver alone can produce up to 1 g per day. Cholesterol provides rigidity to cell membranes, serving a similar purpose in animal cells to that of cellulose in plant cells, and is an important component of the myelin sheath which surrounds nerve fibres. It is needed to produce hormones such as those involved in the control of inflammation, maintaining blood pressure, and contracting the uterus during labour. Cholesterol is also vital to the development of the brain and vascular system of the foetus. Therefore, far from being harmful, it is essential for development and health.

## Foods and their cholesterol content

| | |
|---|---|
| high | Egg yolks, offal (brains, heart, liver, kidney), cheese, cream, butter, lard, palm oil, coconut oil, fatty meats, prawns, sardines, chocolate, rich biscuits, pastries and cakes |
| moderate | Beef, chicken, lamb, pork, rabbit, turkey, cod, lobster, mackerel, oysters |
| low | Cottage cheese, skimmed milk, margarine, salmon, low fat yoghurt |
| none | All plant foods: vegetables, cereals, fruits, plant oils (except coconut and palm oil) |

## Foods that lower blood cholesterol

| | |
|---|---|
| cereal based foods | wholemeal bread, granary bread, rye crispbread, oat porridge and breakfast cereals containing cooked bran; oat bran |
| fruits | apples, avocados, bananas, pears, oranges, dried fruits (prunes, figs, apricots) |
| vegetables | salad, garlic, onions, beans, celery, sweetcorn |
| polyunsaturated oils | corn oil, sunflower oil, soya oil, peanut oil, safflower oil |
| monounsaturated fats | olive oil, avocados |

| cholesterol level (millimols per litre) | risk factor |
|---|---|
| less than 5.2 mmol/l | low |
| 5.2–6.5 mmol/l | average |
| 6.5–7.8 mmol/l | moderate |
| greater than 7.8 mmol/l | high |

**Blood cholesterol levels and the associated risk**

Associated risks of high cholesterol: hypertension, coronary heart disease, angina, atherosclerosis, thrombosis

Cholesterol is moved around the body in the blood attached to proteins in the form of large molecules called lipoproteins. Cholesterol carried in low density lipoproteins is called LDL-cholesterol while that carried in high density lipoproteins is called HDL-cholesterol.

The low density lipoproteins carry cholesterol out to body tissues where it is used for various metabolic functions, including cell repair and the production of hormones, but in the process it deposits some of the cholesterol in the cell walls (especially damaged artery linings), where it can build up as plaque. The resulting chronic 'furring' of the arteries, called atherosclerosis, interferes with the blood flow causing stress to the heart and the blood circulatory system. Hence, a high level of LDL-cholesterol in the blood indicates a greater risk of heart disease. In view of this, LDL-cholesterol is often called 'bad' cholesterol.

The high density lipoprotein, in contrast, removes excess cholesterol from the body cells to the liver where it is broken down to form bile. The bile passes into the gastrointestinal tract where the cholesterol-rich bile salts emulsify fats in the food, helping the enzyme lipase to break them down for absorption through the intestinal lining. The bile with its waste products is eventually excreted in the faeces (see p. 154). A high level of HDL-cholesterol, therefore, helps reduce the risk of coronary heart disease. For this reason, it is often called 'good' cholesterol.

This loose reference to 'bad' and 'good' cholesterol has contributed to the misconception that people can improve the cholesterol composition in their blood by eating more good and less bad cholesterol, but research has failed to demonstrate a clear link between the consumption of cholesterol and cholesterol levels in the blood. In fact, whether cholesterol is good or bad is not determined by the cholesterol in the food but by the lipoprotein carrier in the blood. There is strong evidence, however, that the consumption of saturated fat increases blood cholesterol levels. Since most of the cholesterol in the blood is LDL-cholesterol, the higher the level of cholesterol in the blood, the greater the risk of higher levels of LDL-cholesterol. However, because of the different properties of HDL-cholesterol and LDL-cholesterol, it is important to look at their relative proportions in the blood when evaluating personal cholesterol levels as well as measuring the total blood cholesterol. Most authorities

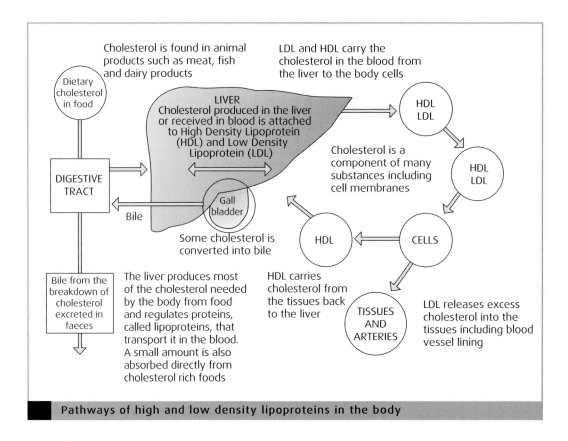

**Pathways of high and low density lipoproteins in the body**

on heart disease, such as the British Heart Foundation, consider it is much more important to limit foods rich in saturated fats than to cut down on food rich in cholesterol.

In brief, the overall consensus is that fat should be part of a balanced diet, but the consumption of saturated fat should be reduced in favour of polyunsaturated and monounsaturated fats, particularly by individuals suffering from heart diseases or excessively high levels of blood cholesterol.[15] Fish oils are recommended because they contain large amounts of omega-3 fatty acids and are a valuable source of iron and the fat soluble vitamins A, D and E. Sunflower and corn oils as well as other vegetable oils, which are good sources of the omega-6 fatty acid, are also recommended. Unlike saturated fats, these polyunsaturated fats do not encourage the deposition of cholesterol on the linings of arteries and some studies have shown that they can reduce cholesterol levels. Monounsaturated fats, found for example in olive oil and canola oil, have a similar beneficial effect. They have also been reported to lower the level of LDL-cholesterol without affecting that of the beneficial HDL-cholesterol.

Meeting these objectives can be a problem. Saturated fat has become an intrinsic ingredient in many foods. The high fat content of modern day foods combined with the invisibility of fat makes it difficult to moderate fat intake. A recommended fat consumption within a range of

15 and 30 per cent of total calorie intake seems high, but in practice it is difficult to keep within this limit. Take as an example the average recommended allowance for a woman of 2200 Calories per day. This means that between 330 and 660 Calories could come from fat, equivalent to between 37 and 74 g of fat. Think of the fat that is in a biscuit, a slice of cake, the oil we use, the milk that goes into tea and coffee: the limit is soon reached.

# Proteins and amino acids

Proteins are essential in our dietary intake because they provide the raw materials for growth and repair, and the production of hormones and enzymes for the regulation of cell function. Proteins also provide an emergency source of energy if carbohydrates are in short supply. The name protein is derived from a Greek word meaning 'first' or 'of primary importance'. The fact that they were favoured such a title suggests that their pivotal role in the scheme of life was long suspected.

To understand the importance of proteins you need do no more than consider the variety of roles they play in the body. Nearly all parts of the body – bones, skin, muscles – contain collagen, which is a protein. Nails and hair contain the protein keratin, while tendons and arteries contain elastin, another protein. Muscles contain the contractile proteins actin and myosin. In blood, haemoglobin and myoglobin are proteins, as are lipoproteins. Enzymes, the biological catalysts that make possible the complicated biological reactions at body temperature are proteins. Proteins also play a prominent part in the body's response to infection and speed recovery. The list is almost endless.

When proteins in food are digested they are broken down into the constituent amino acids, which can then be reassembled to provide the proteins needed by the body. The body can also synthesise some amino acids, but not all of them. For adults, eight amino acids, the so-called *essential amino acids*, must be provided in the diet either from plants able to synthesise them or in the form of animal protein. These essential amino acids are isoleucine, leucine, lysine, methionine, phenylalanine, threonine, tryptophan and valine. Children require two additional essential amino acids, arginine and histidine for growth. Animal protein contains all the essential amino acids, but plants vary in their content, so vegetarians will require a balanced vegetable 'cocktail' to meet requirements. Deficiency in protein intake can result in disorders such as stunted growth in children, poor muscle development, thin and fragile hair, poor skin quality and, in cases of severe protein malnutrition in children, kwashiorkor.

Kwashiorkor comes from the Ga dialect of west Africa and means literally 'first-second', its connotation being 'the disease of the first child when the second is expected'. It is traditionally associated with the early weaning of babies onto a starchy diet when pregnancies are closely spaced. A child suffering from kwashiorkor fails to gain weight, is peevish and has a poor appetite. Vomiting and diarrhoea are common and mental and physical development may be impaired. A misleading symptom is the swelling of the body (partly because of the enlargement of the liver) and limbs. Left untreated, children with advanced kwashiorkor die.

Fortunately, this form of malnutrition is rare in Western society. Excessive consumption of protein is more likely to be the problem in countries like the UK and US. Proteins can indeed be as fattening as carbohydrates. Excess amounts can be converted into fat or glucose and stored if the protein is not used immediately for energy. Proteins supply 4 Calories per gram, the same amount as an equivalent weight of carbohydrates. Again, the emphasis is on moderation in consumption.

Meat, fish, eggs, liver and kidneys are all good sources of protein, as are legumes or pulses. While meat, fish and eggs are easily digested, pulses such as beans, peas and lentils are less so. The lower digestibility of pulses makes them less effective as a protein source in areas or countries where the total intake of protein is low because of poverty. This is also a factor to be taken into account in vegetarian diets.

The association of animal protein with animal fat and the advice to reduce the intake of saturated fats have led many people in recent times to avoid meat. However, this does not mean that meat should be avoided. Red meat provides all the essential amino acids and is also a good source of iron, zinc and vitamins, especially B12 and retinol (see p. 170 and 172). The way forward is to eat meat and not fat. Lean meats include poultry and game. It helps to remove skin or any visible excess fat before cooking meat. Eating fish at least twice a week reduces consumption of saturated fats while providing important minerals and vitamins.

## Improving protein intake from animal and plant sources

Twenty different amino acids are found in animals and plants. Most of them can be made within the human body, but eight essential amino acids (ten in children) can be provided only from food. Animal proteins contain all the essential amino acids, but eating meat every day may not be an economic option and is often not the most healthy option because of the high saturated fat content of some meats. The alternative is to eat vegetables, but individual plant foods proteins do not contain all the essential amino acids. However, if a 'cocktail' of plant foods is consumed the deficiency of one can be compensated by another to meet the dietary requirement. A diet rich in pulses and cereals achieves this requirement, through a mutual effect. Pulses lack the essential amino acid methionine, but are good providers of lysine; cereals in contrast are relatively poor sources of lysine but contain abundant methionine. The only problem then is that the amount of plant food that has to be consumed can create difficulties for very young children.

### Guidelines to protein intake

*Animal sources* (contain all essential amino acids)
- eat fish very often, or at least twice a week
- eat lean meat often (poach, boil or steam)
- eat medium fat meat quite often (grill, stew)
- avoid or eat only occasionally meat with high fat content such as sausages, mince, salami, paté, pies and bacon

*Plant sources*
To ensure adequate essential amino acids, eat:
- pulses: peas, chickpeas, lentils, beans such as soy beans, mung beans, kidney, broad beans

*with*
- cereals: rice, wheat, corn, rye, oats, barley, millet, buckwheat

Eating a wide variety of different proteins and in moderate proportions is the best insurance for a balanced and complete diet.

How much protein do we need to consume? As with other major constituents of the diet, the recommended intake of protein varies between countries, gender and age group. Differing lifestyles can also have a major influence. Generally, it is set higher than the minimum requirement because a very low protein diet carries a risk of vitamin B and iron deficiencies. The guideline is that between 10 and 15 per cent of the total daily recommended energy intake should be through proteins. On this basis, for an average woman aged between 25 and 50 with a total recommended daily allowance of 2200 Calories, this would be between 55 and 83 g. In the UK, the recommended daily intake of protein for this age group is 72 g. This estimate is derived from the recommendation that 15 per cent of the estimated average requirement of energy (EAR) of 1940 Calories (see Chapter 4) should come from protein. This is a higher recommendation than in the past. In 1969, the UK's recommended daily protein requirement was 55 g.[16] In the US, a different method is used for estimating 'recommended protein allowance'. The latter is calculated by multiplying the weight of a person by a factor of 0.8 which, for a woman with a weight of say 63 kg, would give a daily protein consumption requirement of only 50 g.

# Present dietary patterns

**Note: all recommended intakes in the following tables are population averages and not intended for individuals.**

With increased affluence and the availability of convenience foods, the average diet in the West deviates sharply from the ideal. In the UK, for example, carbohydrates make up around 42 per cent of the total calorie intake, fat accounts for 38 per cent, protein 15 per cent and alcohol 5 per cent. With the exception of protein consumption, this is very different from WHO recommendations mentioned earlier. It also deviates from the recommendations of the UK nutrition authorities (COMA) and, more importantly, the 'wrong' types of carbohydrate and fat seem to be consumed. The carbohydrate consumed in the UK consists of a large proportion of sugar. Complex carbohydrate represents only 60 per cent of the total carbohydrate consumed, significantly different from a preferred 90–95 per cent, while sugar accounts for a substantial 40 per cent of the total, compared to the recommended less than 10 per cent (see p. 150). The main sources of sugar in the British diet are confectionery and preserves. These account for 29 per cent of the sugar eaten. Cereal products, including cakes, biscuits and puddings represent 23 per cent of the total sugar consumed. In contrast, fruits and vegetables combined provide only 14 per cent of the sugar intake (see p. 158).

## Average UK dietary pattern compared with intake recommended by UK and WHO[17]

| | % of total calories | | |
| --- | --- | --- | --- |
| | UK average | UK recommended | WHO |
| carbohydrates | 42 | 47–50 | 55–75 |
| fats | 38 | 33–35 | 15–30 |
| protein | 15 | 15 | 10–15 |
| alcohol | 5 | <5 | — |

## Average UK consumption of carbohydrates compared with intake recommended by UK and WHO[18]

| | % of total calories | | |
| --- | --- | --- | --- |
| | UK average | UK recommended | WHO |
| complex carbohydrates | 60 | 78 | 90–95 |
| sugar | 40 | 22 | 5–10 |

## Main sources of sugar in the British diet[19]

| | % of total |
| --- | --- |
| sugar confectionary, preserves | 29 |
| cereal products, incl. cakes, biscuits, puddings | 23 |
| soft drinks | 17 |
| milk and milk products | 13 |
| fruit and fruit products | 8 |
| vegetables | 6 |
| others | 4 |

Fibre consumption averages around 12 g per day compared to the WHO recommendation of 27–40 g, or the 18 g recommended by the UK. Fibre is important for the maintenance of a healthy gastro-intestinal tract, but it should not, however, be consumed in excess of the maximum because this can result in a loss of nutrients. Bran, for example, contains phytates which reduce the absorption of iron, zinc and calcium.

The consumption of fat in the UK not only exceeds the recommended total but consists predominantly of saturated fats. The biggest source of fat in the British diet is meat and meat

... diet[20]

| | % of total |
|---|---|
| | 26 |
| | 18 |
| | 15 |
| ...s | 12 |
| | 11 |
| | 6 |
| | 4 |
| | 3 |
| | 5 |

... s of fat[21]

| | % | |
|---|---|---|
| | total fat consumed | total energy intake* |
| total fat | 100 | 30 |
| saturated fats | 33 | 10 |
| monounsaturated fats | 40 | 12 |
| polyunsaturated fats | 20 | 6 |
| trans fat | 6.6 | 2 |

*This distribution assumes that 5 per cent of energy is from alcohol

products. Together, they account for 26 per cent of the total fat consumed. The smallest source comes from fish which provides only 3 per cent of the total recommended calorie intake. Combining the fat from meat and meat products, milk and milk products, butter and eggs (see above) gives a level of saturated fat consumption that is well above the recommended level. The table immediately above provides a breakdown of how the fat intake should be distributed.

In contrast to fat and carbohydrate, the consumption of protein in the UK is broadly within recommended levels. Although at the higher end of the range (15 per cent), it is believed that maintaining protein intake at this level does no harm. There could, however, be some advantages in changing the composition of the protein intake. Over half of the protein comes from meat and dairy products while fish accounts for only 6 per cent. Eating lean meats and larger quantities of fish, as well as pulses, would help improve dietary intake by reducing the consumption of saturated fats. In recent years the consumption of lean meats, especially poultry, fish and low-fat dairy products, has grown substantially, particularly in the aftermath of the Bovine Spongiform Encephalopathy (BSE) crisis in the beef industry. Unfortunately, the high cost of fish, the ever increasing availability of convenience foods and the entrenched tradition of eating animal products such as bacon, eggs and sausages, encourage the continued consumption of foods rich in saturated fats.

Dietary patterns in other affluent countries show similar trends. In the US, animal protein provides 67 per cent of total protein intake compared to 51 per cent in the early 1900s. Of the 93 g of protein consumed per person per day, 42 g come from meat (including poultry and fish) and 21 g from dairy products.

In a nutshell, using WHO's recommendations and assuming a total recommended daily intake of 2200 Calories, the daily diet of an average woman between 25 and 50 years of age should consist of about 300 g of carbohydrates (55 per cent), 37 to 74 g of fat (15 to 30 per cent) and 55 to 83 g of protein (10 to 15 per cent). For a man within the same age group with a total recommended daily intake of 2900 Calories, the diet should consist of about 400 g of carbohydrate, 48–96 g of fat and 73–109 g of protein.

Remember that these are estimates derived from population averages. Adjustments need to be made for individuals according to weight, height and lifestyle, and especially the level of physical activity. In fact, the calculation and development of individual diets is probably best left to a dietician. If there is a need to reduce weight, then the total calorie intake would have to be lowered by reducing the carbohydrate, fat and protein content of the diet. If more of one food within a particular category is eaten, an adjustment of other foods in the same category would be required to balance the diet. Other variations may stem from cooking methods.

To improve our diets several points emerge clearly. There is a need to cut back on the consumption of cakes, biscuits and puddings which are the sources of most of the sugar and fat that is non-essential. Where possible low-fat products and monounsaturated and polyunsaturated fats should be used in place of saturated fats. Complex carbohydrates should account for the bulk of the food eaten.

Food is not just about weight control, it is also about good health. Rather than count grams and calories, you should go by the basic principles of healthy eating:

- Do not eat more than you need to maintain a healthy weight

- Eat a wide variety of foods

- Eat plenty of fruits and vegetables

- Eat plenty of foods rich in starch and fibre

- Avoid foods that contain a lot of fat

- Avoid sugary foods and drinks

## Dietary intake for sports

The amount and type of food eaten during training, as well as the timing of a pre-competition meal, exert a major influence on athletic performance. The energy requirement of sports people depends on the activity. Activities such as bowling and golf could consume anything

## Total energy intake in intensive training for competitive sports[22]

| Sport | Average body weight (kg) | Estimated daily intake (Calories) |
| --- | --- | --- |
| bicycle racing | 68 | 5995 |
| boxing (middle weight) | 63.5 | 4675 |
| cross country skiing | 67.5 | 6105 |
| fencing | 73 | 5000 |
| field hockey (men) | 75 | 5720 |
| football | 74 | 5885 |
| gymnastics | 67 | 5000 |
| marathon racing | 68 | 5940 |
| sailing | 74 | 5170 |
| sprinting (track) | 69 | 4675 |
| vaulting pole | 73 | 4620 |

from 250 to 350 Calories per hour, but strenuous ones such as running, football, skiing and swimming burn off 350 Calories or more per hour. For any activity, the exertion by individuals will vary, so these must be considered approximate figures used to illustrate the differences in energy expenditure, and are not meant to be definitive. Total energy requirements of athletes in intensive training are usually significantly higher than for the average person. The total calorie intake for training in competitive sports generally exceeds 4500 Calories per day and can be over 6000 Calories (see above) depending on the number of hours of training and the intensity of the sport.

The intake of carbohydrates for athletes should be at least 60 per cent of total calorie intake, rising in some sports such as cycling to 75 per cent of total calorie intake. Larger amounts of sugar can be taken because of the need for quick access to glucose. Carbohydrates which provide this facility are normally high in the glycaemic index – an indicator of the increase in blood glucose levels after food is eaten (see p. 162). Foods high in the index provide the most glucose. They are favoured by athletes because they offer fast replenishment of energy for working muscles whereas complex carbohydrates must first be broken down to sugars before they can enter the blood for transport to muscles.

Generally foods with a higher glycaemic rating are best eaten before the athletic event/exercise, those with a moderate to high rating afterwards and those with a low to moderate rating even later. It is not advisable, however, to consume sugar *immediately* before an event. This may increase the level of insulin in the blood and hinder the breakdown of glycogen for empowering muscle contractions. During a race, however, especially in endurance sports such as the marathon, sugared drinks can prove advantageous because they help to conserve muscle glycogen.

| Glycaemic index for selected foods[23] | |
|---|---|
| types of foods | Glycaemic index |
| glucose | 100 |
| cereals | 92 |
| cornflakes | 80 |
| white rice | 72 |
| potatoes | 70 |
| white bread | 69 |
| raisins | 64 |
| white spaghetti | 50 |
| oatmeal | 49 |
| peas | 47 |
| wholemeal spaghetti | 42 |
| apples | 36 |
| milk | 34 |
| lentils | 29 |
| soybeans | 15 |

Carbohydrate loading or glycogen loading is widely used in endurance sports such as marathons, long-distance swimming, cycling and cross-country skiing. Eating increased amounts of carbohyrate allows the maximum storage of glycogen in the muscles and is usually started during training, several days before the competition. Towards the event training is reduced and often ceases one or two days before. During the reduced training and rest, carbohydrate loading is increased to build up a sufficient store of glycogen in muscles for the event (see below). Carbohydrate loading is not suitable, however, for sports such as weight lifting, football and basketball which rely in large part on an explosive release of energy.

Protein requirements for athletes depend on the sport. In general more is needed during periods of training, but no agreement appears to have been reached on exactly how much. Until recently, a suggestion of 1 g/kg body weight was to be the norm (25 per cent more than the 0.8 g/kg body weight recommended by WHO for an average adult). Now, there are suggestions that the intake of protein for endurance sport could be raised to between 1.2 and 1.4 g/kg of bodyweight.[24] It is believed that without sufficient consumption of protein a loss of

| Carbohydrate intake during training for competition[25] | | | | | | |
|---|---|---|---|---|---|---|
| | Days before event | | | | | |
| | 7 | 6 | 5 | 4 | 3 | 2–1 |
| Training duration (mins) | 90 | 40 | 40 | 20 | 20 | rest |
| calories from carbohydrates (%) | 50 | 50 | 50 | 70 | 70 | 70 |

muscle mass can occur. As the supply of glycogen diminishes muscle proteins begin to be broken down to release energy after some 1–1.5 hours of high intensity endurance activity.

People engaged in body building may need even more protein. Strength development requires a greater consumption of amino acids to replenish and increase the contractile muscle proteins, myosin and actin, and as much as 1.4 to 1.8 g/kg of bodyweight may be needed. With improved strength and training, however, less protein may be required because of the body's increased capacity and efficiency in conserving protein.

Protein intake in excess of the suggested amounts is not necessary, nor, according to the International Olympic Committee, are amino acid supplements. It is more important that the intake of essential amino acids be maintained as these can only be provided through dietary sources. The consumption of saturated fats should be reduced and substituted by unsaturated ones. Although fat is a high energy nutrient, it takes longer to digest and is not a quick source of energy.

The general advice given by dietitians for athletes is:

- Eat larger quantities of carbohydrates during training and before competition
- Eat more protein to compensate for the increased breakdown of muscle protein during training, but adjust the levels according to the activity
- Eat less fat
- Drink carbohydrate-rich liquids during long events
- Drink carbohydrate-rich liquids after the event
- Eat a small meal two hours before an event
- Drink plenty of water

# Essential minerals

About 16 chemical elements, referred to as minerals by nutritionists, are essential to health. Some elements, the macrominerals, are needed in comparatively large amounts compared to the trace elements, or microminerals. A balanced diet should supply all the minerals required.

Knowledge about the effects of deficiencies in these essential minerals often comes from medical conditions that interfere with the body's ability to absorb them or accelerate their loss. But, even in healthy individuals, the uptake or loss of essential minerals and other nutrients in food can be influenced by what we eat. The tannin in tea, and phytic acid in wheat bran and brown rice, for example, can hinder the absorption of calcium, iron and zinc. Vitamin D is needed for the absorption of calcium while Vitamin C helps with the uptake of iron.

Some minerals may be needed in larger amounts at certain times in life. For example women need more calcium and iron during pregnancy, and the loss of magnesium and other minerals during prolonged treatment with diuretic drugs might require supplements. However, self-prescribed mineral supplements should be approached with great caution because, taken in excess, some minerals can be harmful.

| Macro and microminerals[26] | | RDA (mg) | |
|---|---|---|---|
| Macrominerals | Good sources | Male | Female |
| Calcium | milk, cheese, yoghurt, sardines, whitebait, anchovies, soya, watercress | 800 | 800 |
| Chlorine | table salt | 2500 | 2500 |
| Magnesium | wheatgerm, bran, nuts, pulses, spinach, wholegrain cereals, wholemeal bread, cockles, shrimps, whelks | 350 | 300 |
| Phosphorus | meat, fish, eggs, poultry, cereals, nuts and pulses | 800 | 800 |
| Potassium | dried fruits, avocados, bananas, instant coffee, tomatoes, potatoes, nuts | 3500 | 3500 |
| Sodium | table salt, processed foods, cured meats, sausages, pickles, breakfast cereals, bread, margarine, crisps, olives | 1600 | 1600 |
| Microminerals | | | |
| Chromium | liver, meat, brewer's yeast, seafood | trace | trace |
| Copper | shellfish, liver, cocoa, wheatgerm, yeast, brazil nuts | trace | trace |
| Fluorine | fluoridated water, tea | none set | none set |
| Iodine | marine fish and shellfish, seaweed, iodised salt | trace | trace |
| Iron | red meat, offal (especially liver and kidneys), fatty fish such as sardines, egg yolks, dark green leafy vegetables | 10 | 18 |
| Manganese | cereals and wholegrain foods, nuts | trace | trace |
| Molybdenum | wholegrain cereals, yeast, liver | trace | trace |
| Selenium | meat, grains, shellfish, dairy produce | trace | trace |
| Sulphur | animal and vegetable proteins containing amino acids methionine and cysteine | none set | none set |
| Zinc | Shellfish, poultry, meat, eggs, dairy produce | trace | trace |

# Macrominerals

The most important macrominerals are calcium, chlorine, magnesium, potassium, phosphorus and sodium.

## Calcium

Calcium is essential for the formation of bones and teeth, the transmission of nerve impulses, the maintenance of muscle function, for the stimulation of some hormone secretions and for blood clotting. When the intake of calcium is insufficient (or calcium absorption is low because of a lack of Vitamin D), the body draws on bones for its supply. Calcium deficiency, therefore, results in a loss of bone mass or osteoporosis, back pain, brittleness of bones and muscle weakness. For the majority of people a high calcium diet is not harmful because surplus calcium is not absorbed in the body.

Milk and dairy products are among the best sources of calcium; some green leafy vegetables (broccoli, watercress and kale), bean curd (tofu) and the soft bones of fish such as sardines and anchovies are similarly good sources. Be careful though: not all dairy products are rich in calcium. Butter, cream cheese and double cream are poor sources of calcium. Also spinach and spinach beet, or beet greens contain oxalic acid which makes most of the calcium unabsorbable.

The daily recommended intake of calcium for an adult is around 800 milligrams. An additional 400 milligrams is prescribed during the formative years between age 11 and 18 and for pregnant and lactating women. The RDA given here is in accordance with that suggested by the British Medical Association. Other medical bodies offer different daily allowances ranging from 500 mg to 700 mg. Variations also occur because of differences in bodyweight assumptions used in the estimates.

## Chlorine

Chlorine is a poisonous gas, but combined with sodium as sodium chloride (salt), it plays a key role in maintaining the balance of fluids in the body. Combined with hydrogen it produces hydrochloric acid, which is secreted by the stomach lining as a very dilute solution (0.5 per cent) in the gastric juices. The resulting slightly acidic environment helps the enzyme pepsin to begin the breakdown of protein. It also kills many of the bacteria that are taken in with food.

Chlorine is usually consumed and absorbed by the body as a chloride. Table salt is a major source of chloride. These days chlorine deficiencies rarely occur because of the widespread use of salt in processed foods and as a condiment. Any excess chloride is excreted in the urine and sweat.

The recommended daily intake of chloride is about 2500 mg.

## Magnesium

Magnesium is an important component of bones. It is essential for muscle contractions, including those of the heart, and the transmission of nerve impulses.

Magnesium is widely available in a large range of foods including wheat germ, bran, soya, whole-grain cereals, pulses, nuts, dates and figs. Dietary deficiency in magnesium is rare. It can arise, however, as a result of poor absorption by the body or because of excessive loss of fluids. Malfunctioning kidneys or an excessive consumption of alcohol can bring about these two conditions. Symptoms of magnesium deficiency include depression, weakness and cramps and, in severe cases, muscle twitching, heart failure and death. By contrast, excess magnesium is harmless because it is not absorbed.

The recommended daily intake of magnesium is between 350 and 400 mg for men and about 300 mg for women. Children need less. During pregnancy and lactation, larger dosages of magnesium (about 150 mg more per day) are required. The RDAs given here are in accordance with those suggested by the BMA. They are slightly higher than those provided by other organisations such as WHO.

## Phosphorus

Phosphorus, usually in the form of phosphates, is an important component of the body cells and is vital for bone and teeth formation. The process of calcification described earlier (see Chapter 3) involves not only the laying down of calcium but also of phosphates. Phosphorus is essential for energy release and forms part of the high energy phosphate bonds, especially adenosine triphosphate (ATP), essential for muscle contractions. It is also vital for the absorption of other nutrients.

Except for spirits, fats and sugar, all foods contain some phosphorus, with dairy products, meat, fish and eggs being the richest sources. Preservatives containing phosphates are also added to most processed foods and soft drinks. As a result, dietary deficiency of phosphorus is rare. However an excess can occur in the diet and results in poor absorption of calcium and even in the depletion of calcium in bones.

The phosphorus RDA for an adult is 800 mg. An additional 400 mg is recommended between the ages of 11 and 18 years and for women during pregnancy and lactation.

## Potassium

Potassium is essential for maintaining body fluids and their electrical balance in the cells. Together with sodium it maintains muscle and nerve function, regulates blood pressure and maintains a normal heart beat. It is required for the formation of glycogen and is also involved in protein synthesis.

Almost all foods contain potassium. Particularly rich sources include dried fruits, avocados, bananas, instant coffee, tomatoes, potatoes and nuts. Cooking methods can affect the potassium content of food. Boiling reduces it significantly – by as much as half in the case of vegetables. Baking and frying have no effect.

Dietary deficiency in potassium is rare because of its wide availability in foods. It can occur, however, following chronic diarrhoea, sickness and prolonged treatment with diuretics. Any excess in potassium intake is normally expelled from the body in urine. If the body cannot remove the excess, for example in instances of kidney failure, it can inhibit muscle contraction, including that of the heart. Excessively high levels of potassium result in lethargy, slow heartbeat, weakness and confusion.

The RDA of potassium for adults is 3500 mg.

## Sodium

Sodium works with potassium in maintaining the fluid balance in body cells and is vital for the functioning of muscles and nerves. In particular, sodium is important for the absorption of glucose.

A rich source of sodium is table salt (sodium chloride). Dietary deficiency is rare because of the wide availability of salt in processed foods, including cured meats, sausages, pickles, breakfast cereals, bread, margarine and crisps. Eggs, meat, fish and milk also contain small quantities of sodium. Excessive intake of sodium results in fluid retention. It is also associated with hypertension. By contrast, sodium deficiency can bring about cramps, low blood pressure and dehydration.

About 1600 mg of sodium is needed daily per adult. In most cases the problem is an excess rather than a deficiency with most people consuming 4 to 8 g a day.

# Microminerals

Among the microminerals, or trace elements, the most important are: copper, iodine, iron, selenium and zinc. Others include chromium, fluorine, manganese, molybdenum and sulphur. Most trace elements are constituents of enzymes, the catalysts that are vital to the body's metabolism. Because, for the most part, such minute quantities of the minerals are involved, I have not indicated minimum daily requirements. The only exception is iron where the RDA is significant, although still small compared to macrominerals.

## Copper

Copper is needed for blood and bone formation and is especially important during growth. It also aids the absorption of iron. Copper is part of many of the enzymes needed for the formation of proteins in bone, skin and blood vessels and for the production of melanin, the pigment in hair and skin.

Rich sources of copper include shellfish, liver, cocoa, wheatgerm, yeast and brazil nuts. Dietary deficiency of this trace element is rare. As in the case of other trace elements, excess intake of copper is toxic, causing diarrhoea. Prolonged excess intake can result in liver damage.

## Iodine

Iodine is needed by the thyroid gland to produce the thyroid hormones which govern the development and function of the brain and nervous system and regulate body heat and energy.

Rich sources of iodine are marine fish, shellfish, seaweed and iodised table salt. A low level of thyroid hormones can reduce both physical and mental capacity. Although not the only reason, a deficiency in iodine can cause the thyroid gland to enlarge and the neck to swell, a condition known as goitre. In extreme cases it may become so large as to interfere with eating and breathing and part of the gland may have to be removed surgically. Generally, where the swelling is caused by a lack of iodine, it will subside once the diet is corrected and the deficit removed. Iodine deficiency is generally rare in the Western world.

## Iron

Iron is needed for the production of the respiratory pigments haemoglobin in the blood and myoglobin in the muscles. Iron helps to transform beta carotene found in fruits and vegetables such as carrots, papayas and apricots into vitamin A. (Vitamin A is essential, for example, for the development and maintenance of the tissues lining the digestive and respiratory tracts as well as the healthy development of the retina of the eye.) It is also vital for healthy bones and cartilage, gums and teeth.

Good sources of iron are red meat, offal (especially liver and kidneys), fatty fish such as sardines, egg yolks and dark green leafy vegetables such as spinach. However, as mentioned earlier, the phytic acid in green vegetables makes most of the iron content unabsorbable by the body. It is estimated that at least ten times the weight of spinach would have to be eaten to get the same amount of iron as from eating beef. Dietary deficiency in iron results in anaemia with its accompanying symptoms of lethargy, paleness and breathlessness.

The recommended daily intake of iron is 10 mg for an adult male and 18 mg for women, with an additional 30 to 60 mg during pregnancy. Iron is the only nutrient which has a higher RDA for women because of the loss of blood during menstruation, but after the menopause it is the same for both sexes.

## Selenium

Selenium is an essential mineral for maintaining healthy hair, skin and eyesight. It is part of an enzyme that acts as an antioxidant, interacting with vitamin E to protect body tissues against free radicals.

Free radicals are unstable and highly reactive chemicals, often containing oxygen, that are natural by-products of the body's metabolism. They increase dramatically when the body is subject to stress (including air pollution), infection, excessive exertion or damage. If left unchecked by antioxidants, free radicals cause serious damage to cells, particularly the cell membrane, and trigger chain reactions that can interfere with the normal biochemistry of the body. They have been implicated in contributing to a wide range of diseases including cancer, Alzheimer's disease, atherosclerosis and arthritis.

Selenium also helps in the normal functioning of the liver and in the production of important hormones. The best sources of selenium are meat and grains. Shellfish and dairy products are also good sources.

## Zinc

Zinc is needed for the synthesis of protein and nucleic acids (RNA and DNA), the development of the reproductive system and functioning of the prostate gland, and the healing of wounds. It is essential to the functioning of the immune system. Zinc is involved in many enzymes as well as insulin, the hormone that regulates the levels of sugar in the blood.

Zinc is found in shellfish, poultry, meat, eggs and dairy products. Wholegrain cereals and pulses are also good sources, but their phytic acid content inhibits absorption.

Zinc deficiency is comparatively rare and usually associated with eating disorders and malnutrition. It can result in dwarfism, delayed wound repair, night blindness and, when it occurs in childhood, impaired development of the reproductive organs.

## Chromium

Chromium assists the absorption of glucose in cells. This makes it particularly important for those suffering from diabetes because it enhances the action of insulin, the hormone that regulates glucose levels in the body. Chromium is also associated with the control of fat and cholesterol levels in the blood.

Liver, meat, brewer's yeast and seafood are good sources of this mineral.

## Manganese

Manganese is needed for bone formation and the functions of many enzymes including the production of hormones. Cereals and wholegrain foods and nuts are good sources. Natural dietary intake of manganese is normally sufficient.

## Molybdenum

This mineral is also important for the normal functioning of many enzymes. It is vital for enzymes engaged in the release of iron from the body's store, the conversion of fat to energy and the production of genetic material.

Good sources for this mineral are wholegrain cereals, yeast and liver. No cases of deficiency are known.

## Sulphur

Sulphur occurs in all body cells. Adults contain about 120 g of sulphur. It is a constituent of two B vitamins (thiamin and biotin) as well as the essential amino acids methionine and cystine.

Good sources are animal and plant proteins. No cases of deficiency are known.

# Vitamins

Vitamins are organic substances which, though needed in only minute quantities, are essential to our well-being and health. ('Organic' refers here to the carbon content of vitamins – it does not refer to organically grown foods.) Characteristically vitamins are not produced in the body, but *must* be supplied in food. A notable exception is vitamin D, but even here, if the body does not produce enough, as is often the case during childhood growth, it must be supplemented in the diet. Unlike carbohydrate, fat and protein, vitamins do not provide energy or serve as building blocks of the body. Instead, they help drive the metabolism of the body acting as either *co-enzymes*, substances essential for enzymes to work, or precursors to them.

The impact of diets deficient in vitamins can be traced throughout history, most notably in skeletons with the deformities and demineralization commonly caused by a lack of vitamin D. The knowledge that some foods gave protection against particular diseases was undoubtedly built into folk remedies. Probably the best known example of a cure of this nature is the discovery in the eighteenth century that eating limes prevented scurvy, a disease affecting the skin and connective tissues. The expression 'scurvy knave' in early English literature gives some clue as to the prevalence of the disease as does the nickname of 'limey' for British sailors who were among the first to benefit from the remedy.

Despite the knowledge that some foods seemed essential to health, the existence of vitamins was only confirmed in the early twentieth century. The name comes from a contraction of 'vital amine' to 'vitamine' by the chemist Casimir Funk. He discovered that the husk of unpolished rice contained an amine (thiamin) which had anti-Beriberi properties. (Beriberi affects the nerves and skeletal muscles resulting in nerve pains and wasting or it reduces the heart's pumping capacity, leading to blood congestion in the veins and swelling in the legs, and sometimes the trunk and face, caused by an accumulation of fluid.) It was discovered later that other vitamins do not have the same chemical properties or functions and that many do not even contain amines, but the name, now shortened to 'vitamin', came into general usage.

Thirteen vitamins have now been identified. They fall broadly into two groups: fat-soluble vitamins and water-soluble vitamins. Fat-soluble vitamins are vitamins A, D, E and K. They are so called because they are associated with fatty foods and oils. These vitamins have a greater storage capacity than water-soluble ones and, because they are not excreted, can build up to toxic levels in the body. Water-soluble vitamins are vitamins B (combining 8 different B vitamins) and C. Excess quantities of these, by contrast, are excreted in the urine.

## Fat-soluble vitamins

### Vitamin A

Vitamin A, or retinol, is needed for good eyesight (especially night vision), healthy skin, normal cell development and the maintenance of mucous membranes in the respiratory, urinary and digestive tracts.

Fish, particularly fish-liver oils, are rich sources of retinol. Other good sources of vitamin A are animal liver, dairy products, margarine and eggs. Plants do not contain vitamin A, but they do have one or more of the pigments that can be converted to it within the body. Of these, beta-carotene is a particularly good source, although about six times the weight of beta-carotene is needed to produce an equivalent amount of vitamin A. Beta-carotene is also an antioxidant associated with reduced risks of cancer. Good sources of beta-carotene include dark, green, leafy vegetables and roots and fruits that are either red or yellow, such as carrots, red and yellow peppers, mangoes and papayas.

Vitamin A deficiency is rare in the developed world, but still presents a serious problem in developing countries, where over 200 million children are at risk. It can lead to blindness or even death in children. It also hinders growth and lowers resistance to infection. Excessive intake of vitamin A, generally above 150 mg, is harmful because it is fat soluble and is not easily broken down by the body. By contrast, excessive consumption of beta-carotene is not dangerous, but turns the skin yellow. The skin colour returns to normal when the consumption of carotene is reduced.

The recommended daily intake of vitamin A is 1000 micrograms for an adult male and 800 for women. Women need more during pregnancy and lactation. The average Western diet provides more than the recommended daily intake of vitamin A – 5 g of liver or 75 g of butter, margarine or spinach, for example, contain 750 mcg equivalents of vitamin A, which is almost the entire daily requirement for a woman.

## Vitamin D

Vitamin D (ergocalciferol and cholecalciferol) has three important functions in the body. It increases the mineral content of bones, aids the absorption of calcium and helps the kidney to conserve minerals.

Vitamin D can be produced in the skin through exposure to the ultraviolet radiation in sunlight as well as being available in food, for example, margarine, fatty fish and eggs. Dairy foods have only small quantities of vitamin D and other foods practically none. The winter sunshine of northern latitudes or the highly polluted skies above industrial centres can reduce the production of vitamin D, but people generally do not have to rely solely on food for their supply of vitamin D. Exceptions include the sick and elderly who cannot venture out and those individuals who are bound by tradition or religion to be completely covered.

Vitamin D deficiency results in rickets (deformity of the bones, particularly the leg bones and spine) in children and osteomalacia (demineralization and softening of the bones) in adults. Vitamin D deficiency is rare in the developed world, while over consumption causes liver damage as a result of excessive calcium in the blood (hypercalcaemia).

### Vitamin E

Vitamin E is a collective term for substances, the most important of which is alpha-tocopherol, that act as antioxidants, primarily protecting fats from oxidation. Vitamin E is essential for maintaining cell structure, the production of red blood cells and for the functioning of some enzymes. It protects the lungs from harm by pollutants, and red blood corpuscles from damage by poisons in the blood. Vitamin E is believed to lower the risk of disorders connected with free radical damage such as some cancers, stroke, heart disease and atherosclerosis. There is also a possibility that vitamin E may slow down the process of ageing by slowing down the destruction of biological membranes.

Vegetable oils and foods such as nuts and wheatgerm which are high in fats are the richest sources. Meat, eggs, lettuce and other leafy vegetables are often good sources.

Vitamin E deficiency is rare because of its widespread availability in food. It occurs mainly when disorders of the body prevent absorption of the vitamin. When a deficiency does occur it results in anaemia because of the destruction of red blood cells. Prolonged excessive consumption of the vitamin reduces intestinal absorption of vitamins A, D and K. It might also cause vomiting, abdominal pains and diarrhoea.

### Vitamin K

Vitamin K is essential for the synthesis in the liver of substances needed for blood clotting. It is found in green vegetables such as spinach, broccoli and cabbage, vegetable oils, meat, cheese and liver. It is also synthesised by bacteria in the guts.

Vitamin K deficiency is rare and is usually caused by liver disorders that interfere with its absorption from food or by drug treatments that inhibit the growth of the intestinal bacteria which produce the vitamin. The resulting impaired clotting of the blood can lead, for example, to nose bleeds, a failure of wounds to heal and internal bleeding.

## Water soluble vitamins

### Vitamin B

The B vitamins consist of a group of eight different vitamins: $B_1$ (thiamin), $B_2$ (riboflavin), $B_6$ (pyridoxine), $B_{12}$ (a group name for several forms of vitamins), niacin, folic acid, biotin and panthonic acid. Niacin shares with vitamin D the distinction of being capable of synthesis within the body, in this case from tryptophan, an amino acid found in many proteins. Most of the B vitamins act as coenzymes and, apart from vitamin $B_{12}$, they are all involved in the release of energy. Folic acid, together with $B_{12}$, is involved in the synthesis of nucleic acids (DNA and RNA) which carry genetic information. $B_{12}$ is also involved in the synthesis of fatty acids in the myelin sheath that surrounds nerve cells. The myelin sheath insulates nerves and enables the rapid transmission of nerve impulses.

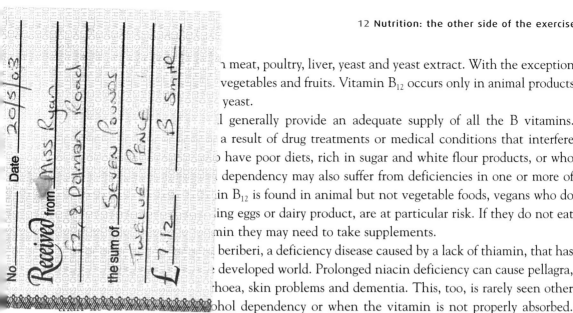

meat, poultry, liver, yeast and yeast extract. With the exception
vegetables and fruits. Vitamin $B_{12}$ occurs only in animal products
yeast.

generally provide an adequate supply of all the B vitamins.
a result of drug treatments or medical conditions that interfere
have poor diets, rich in sugar and white flour products, or who
dependency may also suffer from deficiencies in one or more of
in $B_{12}$ is found in animal but not vegetable foods, vegans who do
ing eggs or dairy product, are at particular risk. If they do not eat
min they may need to take supplements.

beriberi, a deficiency disease caused by a lack of thiamin, that has
developed world. Prolonged niacin deficiency can cause pellagra,
hoea, skin problems and dementia. This, too, is rarely seen other
hol dependency or when the vitamin is not properly absorbed.
More common are conditions associated with a lack of vitamin $B_{12}$ because of an inability to
absorb the vitamin or less frequently because it is lacking in the diet. Shortages as a result of
malabsorption, which may be associated with a lack of folic acid, causes pernicious anaemia,
while a deficient diet results in megaloblastic anaemia. In both instances, the oxygen carrying
capacity of blood is reduced because the bone marrow produces abnormally large and deformed
red blood cells. Left untreated, they can prove fatal. $B_{12}$ deficiency also damages the nerve
tracts in the spinal chord leading to difficulties in walking and even partial paralysis. In vegans
possible damage to the nervous system is hidden because their high consumption of folates,
compounds derived from folic acid and found in abundance in green leafy vegetables, pulses
and nuts, arrests the megaloblastic anaemia and masks the more obvious symptoms of $B_{12}$
deficiency.

With the exception of vitamin $B_6$ and niacin, there are no known harmful effects from
excessive consumption of B vitamins because they are normally excreted in the urine.
Excessively high doses of vitamin $B_6$, often prescribed to relieve premenstrual syndrome, mood
swings and bloatedness, can result in nerve damage causing the ends of fingers and toes to lose
any sense of feeling. Large doses of niacin over extended periods can cause skin flushes and
lead to liver damage.

## Vitamin C

Vitamin C, or ascorbic acid, is vital for the formation of collagen, a key protein for healthy
skin, bones and supporting tissues as well as the healing of wounds. Vitamin C increases the
absorption of iron and helps avoid iron deficiency anaemia, strengthens the body's immune
system and helps guard against infection. Vitamin C also assists with the synthesis of serotonin,
a substance which influences mood and levels of consciousness, and noradrenaline, a hormone
which regulates blood flow.

Relatively large amounts of vitamin C are needed. Vegetables and fruits are the best sources, and citrus fruits are particularly rich in vitamin C. Blackcurrants, guava, kiwi, strawberries and rosehips are also good sources, as are green peppers, Brussels sprouts, watercress and dark green vegetables. Vitamin C is difficult to preserve in foods because it is easily destroyed by oxidation and heat. Long exposure to air after peeling or preparing fresh fruits and vegetables or damage such as wilting will seriously reduce the vitamin C content. Over-cooked vegetables contain little or none.

Dietary deficiency of vitamin C is rare, but there is a widespread belief, still a matter of scientific debate, that large doses offer extra protection from virus attack and other dangers. Vitamin C cannot be stored in the body, but large doses are retained until the body cells are saturated. The excess is excreted in the urine. Although not normally considered harmful, regular  large doses of more than a gram per day can cause stomach upsets, cramps, diarrhoea and even kidney stones in susceptible people.

### Vitamins: sources and recommended daily allowances[27]

| | | RDA | |
|---|---|---|---|
| Fat soluble vitamins | Good sources | Male | Female |
| Vitamin A (retinol) | liver, dairy products, margarine, eggs, carrots, red and yellow peppers, mangoes, papayas | 1000 mcg | 800 mcg |
| Vitamin D | margarine, fatty fish, eggs | 5 mcg | 5 mcg |
| Vitamin E | vegetable oils, nuts, meat, cereals, wheatgerm, egg yolks | 10 mg | 8 mg |
| Vitamin K | spinach, broccoli, cabbage, vegetable oils, pork, cheese, liver | 70 mcg | 65 mcg |
| Water soluble vitamins | | | |
| Vitamin $B_1$ (thiamin) | pork, liver, offal, wholemeal bread, wheatgerm, bran nuts, pulses | 1.2 mg | 1.1 mg |
| Vitamin $B_2$ (riboflavin) | brewer's yeast, meat, wheatgerm, poultry, fish, eggs | 1.3 mg | 1.1 mg |
| Vitamin $B_6$ (pyridoxine) | meat, poultry, fish, brewer's yeast, cereals, nuts, soya beans | 1.3 mg | 1.3 mg |
| Niacin (nicotinic acid) | meat, poultry, pulses, nuts, potatoes, wheatgerm | 16 mg | 14 mg |
| Pantothenic acid | meat, vegetables, cereals | 5 mg | 5 mg |
| Biotin | all foods, especially liver, peanuts, egg yolks, brewer's yeast | 30 mg | 30 mg |
| Folic acid | leafy green vegetables, pulses, wheatgerm | 400 mg | 400 mg |
| Vitamin $B_{12}$ | virtually all animal protein: meat, poultry, fish, eggs, dairy products | 3 mg | 3 mg |
| Vitamin C (ascorbic acid) | fruits and vegetables, especially citrus fruits, black-currants, rosehips, kiwis, strawberries, green peppers | 60 mg | 60 mg |

Note: mcg = microgram, a millionth of a gram.      mg = milligram, a thousandth of a gram.

# Water

We cannot exist without water. Some 60 per cent of the body weight of an adult consists of it. Water is essential to bodily processes and functions. The interface between the air and our lungs is kept continually moist to allow the exchange of carbon dioxide and water for life-giving oxygen. Digestive juices break down the nutrients required for nourishment. The nutrients are transported around the body in the blood, an aqueous solution. About half the volume of blood consists of blood cells and the remainder is a plasma of which 95 per cent is water. Water helps in the regulation of body temperatures. It acts as a protective cushion, from acting as a barrier for our joints, to supporting the foetus within the amniotic sac.

Life is thought to have originated in or around shallow seas and we carry the badge of our origins to this day. The skin protects the body from dehydration. Certainly, the transition to the land meant that creatures had to conserve water. Removal of the waste products in urine and faeces requires water, but the body retrieves as much of it as possible before they are finally expelled. Even so, water is lost and must be replaced, both directly and through the breakdown of food.

An inadequate intake of water can cause headaches, poor concentration, constipation, poor complexion and over a longer period, kidney stones. We require about three litres of water per day. Typically drinks such as milk, tea, coffee, squash, fruit juices and plain water provide the bulk of needs, followed by solid foods such as dairy products, bread, cereals, meat, fish, eggs, fruits and vegetables. Overall, if eight glasses of water are drunk each day and a wide range of vegetables and fruits are eaten, the daily water requirement will be met. If, however, the level of physical activity is high or the weather hot, more is needed to replace an increased loss through perspiration.

# Alcohol

Alcohol is not essential to a healthy diet. It is, however, part of the social lifestyle in many societies, especially in the West. Taken in moderation and alongside food, as in the Mediterranean, alcohol may help reduce the risk of coronary heart diseases in men and women. The problem lies with the definition of moderation. According to WHO, alcohol should not be consumed, or at least not exceed 4 per cent of our total daily calorie intake. Even in the case of the latter, incorporating one or two alcohol-free days each week is advisable to enable the body to detoxify itself.

In the UK, on average, about 5 per cent of the total calorie intake per person is alcohol. In some reports, the figure is as high as 8 per cent. To keep individual consumption to a moderate level means keeping to just 1 or 1½ units of alcohol per day and never exceeding a maximum of 21 units per week (3 units per day) for men or 14 units per week (2 units per day) for women. One unit is equivalent to half a pint of beer, a small glass of wine (maximum 125 ml), an even smaller glass of sherry (50 ml) and still smaller glass of spirits (25 ml).

Alcoholic drinks consist mainly of 'empty' calories, in that they tend to have little nutritional content. A small glass of wine contains 85 Calories and half a pint of beer 175 Calories. Worse is the impact that they have on bodily functions. Heavy consumption of alcohol reduces coordination and control, inhibits speech, results in dehydration and impairs decision-making and response patterns. Taken in excess over time, alcohol enlarges the liver, causes cirrhosis, fibrosis and scarring, and a propensity to liver cancer. It increases the risks of cancer in other parts of the alimentary system (mouth, throat, oesophagus and stomach). In others, it results in personality changes and dependence.

Poor health and nutritional inadequacies are often associated with excessive alcohol consumption because of its diuretic effect, which results in the depletion of vitamins, especially water-soluble ones such as vitamins B and C. It also interferes with the body's ability to absorb some vitamins (vitamin $B_6$, foliate and thiamin) and minerals (zinc). Broadly speaking, the consumption of alcohol is incompatible with fitness and health.

# Exercise and eating for the over-fifties

# 13

While ageing is inevitable, the symptoms are not necessarily insurmountable. With good care, the process of ageing can be much more manageable than you might first think. These days, people are less inclined to take the fatalistic view of 'what will be, will be'. They want instead to take charge of their destiny. To do so, however, it is important to understand the physical and functional changes that take place in the body with age, their implications and any special needs arising from them. I have touched upon some of these points elsewhere, but I want to develop them further here. My over-fifties class is among the most satisfying that I take because of the changes I see in the participants, not just in terms of mobility and body shape, but in the broadening of attitudes in terms of what is possible as one grows older.

Ageing is not a disease. But life-long stress and hard work take their toll on the human body. Gradually, muscles and other soft tissues lose their strength. The heart becomes less efficient and, as a result, cardiac output is reduced, and with it the oxygen delivered to body cells. The lungs also weaken, adding to the problem. The energy available for activities diminishes. Muscle coordination declines because of a decrease in nerve cells. Lean body mass is reduced and, as a consequence, the basal metabolic rate falls. The digestive juices are reduced and the smooth muscle declines in activity and strength. This, in turn, can interfere with the absorption of nutrients and cause constipation. The kidneys function less efficiently. Bones and teeth become demineralised. Eyesight and hearing deteriorate.

For women, ageing brings a fundamental change – the menopause. This loss of reproductive capacity and the cessation of menstruation, following the 'emptying' of the ovaries, results from a decline in the reproductive hormone, oestrogen. Symptoms associated with it include hot flushes, tingling sensations in fingers and toes, night sweats, mood swings and depression, a loss of bone mass and threat of osteoporosis and an increased risk of cardiovascular heart disease. Some women fear they are unattractive and less feminine, caused in part by socio-cultural attitudes to this phase in life.

All this may seem daunting, but good eating habits and exercise can help stem the tide and prolong active life and improve the quality of life in general. Just as important, by offering a positive outlook at a time of profound change, they can raise the spirit by providing benefits that we all agree, whether man or woman, are worth working for.

# Aerobics: keep on moving!

Muscles are never completely lost: they atrophy mainly because they are not used. Insufficient exercise reduces the work load on the heart, and the cardiac muscles, like any muscle in the body, lose strength. As a result the cardiac output declines, oxygen uptake falls and the capacity of the lungs diminishes. But these conditions are not confined to the old; the young are similarly affected if they are sedentary, although the full impact may well not come to light until later in life.

You must not regard age, any age, as a barrier to exercise. Reaching 50 years of age, for example, does not mean that you have become old overnight. You have just added another year to your life. You have certainly not raised a barrier to activity or started on the fast-track to a life of reminiscence from an armchair. It is vital to remain active. Make exercise part of your daily routine even if this was not so before. Set aside time for daily brisk walks of not less than thirty minutes. Take time off, two or three times a week, to attend low impact aerobic or dance classes for the over-fifties. Take up t'ai chi or aqua-aerobics.

Pursuits like these will provide the cardio-vascular stimulation vital to the health and strength of heart, lungs and muscles. Regular attendance at exercise classes and routine daily activity will improve blood circulation and provide a healthy injection of endorphins that keep at bay feelings of depression. With the exception of aqua-aerobics which is not weight bearing, these activities will help maintain bone mass. These benefits are vital for women in the menopausal phase. Classes also offer another positive feature: they bring together people in the same age group and the sharing of achievements and indeed problems can become an enriching experience.

In pursuing aerobic exercise care must be taken to build up to activities, especially if you are new to them. Unless you have always jogged before, it would be preferable to walk briskly. Reduce or avoid activities, such as jumping or similar bouncy movements, that jar the hips, knees and ankles. Keep joints mobile with a good warm-up before the activity and stretch out at the end of it. It is more important to maintain the continuity, intensity and rhythm of the movements using big muscle groups, such as the quadriceps and calves, to achieve an effective cardio-vascular work-out than to carry out vigorous moves.

# Strength, endurance and stretching

Maintaining muscle tone and strength means devoting time specifically to strength building exercises. Most aerobic classes incorporate some form of strength building routines, but if you are not attending classes and your aerobic activities consist primarily of, say, walking, then set aside 15 to 20 minutes, two or three times a week for strengthening muscles. Alternatively, 10 minutes daily might be a better option. It depends on your lifestyle.

It is important to maintain the strength of all our muscles, but some muscles merit special consideration as you grow older. They include:

- the back muscles, specifically the erector spinae and the latissimus dorsi
- the abdominal muscles
- the pelvic floor
- the quadriceps

These muscles are especially important for the over-fifties because their weakness often gives rise to commonly experienced problems such as back pain, incontinence and knee and pelvic/hip pains.

## Back problems

The causes of back pain are as diverse as the people you consult. Everyone has a different explanation ranging from strained ligaments to psychological stress. The treatments proffered are just as diverse. One thing is clear, physical fitness programmes can both reduce back pain and create a sense of well-being. They tackle the problem from both ends of the spectrum – the physical and emotional. Personally I have little doubt that most back problems can be traced to poor posture and incorrect body alignment.

Long hours spent sitting at a desk or working looking down create future problems for the body's framework. Other contributing factors which add to pressure on the back are the increased weight and greater girth associated with age and caused by the reduction in basal metabolic rate and lean body mass. When abdominal muscles are strong they help support the stress borne by the back. A strong transverse abdominus, for example, acts like a corset to keep the body aligned. When this is weak the lower back has to support the weight of the body creating great stress in the lumbar region.

The back has yet another constraint. When we stand the entire weight of the body bears down on the spinal column, compressing the intervertebral discs that lie between the vertebrae. The spinal column is longer, and the height of a person greater, in the morning than in the evening because lying down to rest reduces the pressure on the intervertebral discs, allowing them to return to their normal thickness. As muscles shorten and tighten with age this problem of compression worsens and can become permanent. The back rounds and the head moves forward, giving rise to the stereotypical bent frame of the elderly. These problems do not arise overnight. They can affect the young as well, but the elderly have inevitably spent considerably more time with poor body alignment and experiencing gravitational pull than a 20 year old.

To provide relief for the spinal column and tackle the problem it is important to improve body posture, strengthen the abdominal muscles, mobilise the back and stretch the back muscles. The exercises below are designed especially to meet the specific problems associated with ageing, but they can also be used by younger people who want to improve abdominal muscle control but wish to have some support for their back while exercising.

# Strengthening abdominal muscles

The abdominal exercise that I suggest here involves techniques which, as far as I know, are not used elsewhere. From experience with my classes it works really well. You might like to use music with the routine which helps to make it more interesting. Choose music with a regular but slow tempo. I have repeated the sequence for getting into correct body alignment in each exercise to stress its importance and also for easy reference. Regard it as a blueprint that, once mastered, you should not need to refer to again. My hope is that eventually you will automatically position your body correctly before starting the work-out.

### Scaling the wall (abdominal muscles)

- Lie in front of a wall and place both feet, hip distance apart, flat against it. Make sure that the knees are aligned above the hips and the thighs are vertical from the floor. You should be comfortable in this position.

- Place the palms on each side of the head, ensuring that both shoulders are on the floor. This avoid the tendency to attempt to reach forward or press down on the floor, passing stress to the hands rather than working the abdominal muscles.

A

- Take a deep breath and exhale, sending the navel toward the spine; the lower back moves toward the floor and the lower abdomen deflates and tightens, tilting the pubic bone up slightly, the bottom comes slightly off the floor and your feet push harder onto the wall. If this is uncomfortable, because the small of the back remains off the floor, place a towel folded flat under this area.

A

- Hold and then release.

- Repeat the above six to eight times to start with and then in subsequent sessions build up the number of repeats. Vary the contractions, say, two contractions up and release for two.

- You exhale to come out of the position and, if you can, bring your knees towards the chest. Then return to even breathing.

- Hold, to stretch out the lower back and release the tension in the abdominal muscles.

These floor exercises might not suit those who suffer from dizziness and/or have difficulties getting down on the floor. If so perform the exercises standing up: inhale and exhale sending the navel toward the spine and allowing the lower abdominal muscles to contract and flatten. Do a 'pelvic floor', tilting the pubis slightly up. Release and return the pelvis to its normal position. Repeat as many times as is comfortable.

The floor version of the exercise can be done without the wall, but it is safer with it and more effective for those with weaker muscles because it provides support and helps to focus better on the abdominal muscles. The exercise is also a good starter for those not acquainted with the transverse abdominal muscles. To progress even further the next stage is to 'walk up the wall', contracting the lower abdominal muscles with each step. It is not as complicated as it sounds but does require practice.

## Wall walk (lower abdominal muscles)

- Lie in front of a wall and place both feet, hip distance apart, flat on it. Make sure that the knees are aligned above the hips and the thighs are vertical from the floor. This time, make sure that the lower leg, from the knee down to the foot, is parallel to the floor. You should be comfortable in this position (see A, opposite).

- Place the palms on each side of the head, keeping your shoulders on the floor.

- Take a deep breath and exhale, sending the navel toward the spine; the lower back moves toward the floor and the lower abdomen deflates, tilting the pubic bone up slightly. This is the starting position.

A | - Breathe in and move your right foot one step up (about 10 inches), then as you place the foot on the wall exhale, sending the navel towards the back of the spine and contract the lower abdominal muscles.

A

- Breathe in and move the left foot a similar step up and breathe out as before.

- Breathe in and step down with the right foot and breathe out to contract the lower abdominal muscles.

- Breathe in and step down with the left foot, breathing out.

This is one set.

- Repeat three further sets of these steps. Build up the number of repetitions in future sessions.

- Exhale and bring the knees to the chest. Hold, stretching out the lower back and releasing the tension in the abdominal muscles.

### The pelvic floor

For women, to strengthen the pelvic floor, build on the two positions above. When you contract the lower abdominal muscles focus also on the pelvic floor by tightening the muscles around the vagina as though you are drawing them inward and upwards towards your navel. In the following steps *the pelvic floor component is added in italics.*

- Lie in front of a wall and place both feet, hip distance apart, flat on it. Make sure that the knees are aligned above the hips and the thighs are vertical from the floor. Ensure that the lower leg, from the knee down to the foot, is parallel to the floor.

- Take a deep breath and exhale, sending the navel toward the spine; the lower back moves towards the floor and the lower abdomen deflate tilting the pubic bone up.

- *In the next out-breath, contract the muscles around the vagina and the muscle sphincter surrounding the bladder neck of the urethra; the bottom comes slightly off the floor and your feet will be pushing harder onto the wall.*

- Release, breathing in.

- Repeat as before.

Men have similar pelvic floor muscles and can face the same problem of weak bladder control. This occurs, for example, after treatment for an enlarged prostate. They can also benefit from the pelvic floor exercises described above, with some adjustments, of course, for differences in anatomy. Men should tighten and pull up the muscles of the pelvic floor, imagining they are passing water and attempting to stop it.

Pelvic floor exercises should be done daily to avoid problems of incontinence. For those uncomfortable doing the exercise lying down, an alternative is to stand with the feet slightly apart and follow the sequence above starting with the breathing. Obviously, the reference to the floor does not apply. This is equally effective for the pelvic floor, but is less so for the abdominal muscles.

## Maintaining the back

The postural muscles in the back are almost continuously contracted in order to hold the body up. These muscles have to be stretched to release the stress exerted on them and to maintain their flexibility. Maintaining the flexibility of the muscles essentially involves retaining their natural length. To keep the back flexible requires more than muscle flexibility, it also needs the 'joints', the junctions between the vertebrae, to be mobile. If they are not mobile the movement of the spinal column will be severely restricted.

## Feline stretch (erector spinae)

A
- Kneel with the knees hip distance apart. Place both palms on the floor, aligning the palms (fingers pointed forward) directly below the shoulders. Make sure that the weight of the body is evenly distributed.

B
- Exhale, and tuck your chin in towards the chest, tuck the base (coccyx) of your spine and sitting bones under and tuck your tummy in, sending the navel towards the spine. The body is now curved like an angry cat.

- Hold and release, breathing in as you do. You should feel the muscles in your back lengthening from the head down to the tail end, giving space between the vertebrae. The trapezius muscles which lie between the shoulder blades lengthen from shoulder to shoulder.

- Repeat three times at least. Each movement should be slow and controlled.

## Standing feline stretch (erector spinae)

For those who have knee problems and find it difficult to kneel, a modified back stretch can be performed standing up.

A
- Stand with feet hip distance apart, cross arms and place hands on opposite knee or upper thigh.

B
- Take a deep breath and exhale. As you exhale tuck your chin in towards the chest, tuck the tail end (coccyx) and sitting bones under and tuck the tummy in sending the navel toward the spine. The body is now curved like an exaggerated question mark.

- Hold the stretch, breathing normally, and then release. Return to the normal position, but do not arch your back.

- Repeat three times.

# Maintaining the quadriceps

Strong quadriceps help support the knees and assist movements such as climbing steps, walking uphill, sitting down and getting up, especially from a deep armchair, and getting out of cars. The easiest way to strengthen quadriceps is to climb up the stairs. However, you might still find it useful to set aside two to three minutes per day to do the following:

### Squats with support (quadriceps)

**A** • Hold on to a support such as the back of a chair or a wall. If using a chair make sure it will not topple over. Stand with your feet hip distance apart and your body upright.

**B** • Gently bend the knees as though you are going into a sitting position, breathing out as you do so. Go down, if possible, some 45 degrees, but not lower than the level of your bottom. In bending the knees, make sure that they are aligned above the toes but not beyond them.

• Gently return the body to an upright position. The movements should be slow and controlled. You should feel the upper part of the thigh, the quadriceps, working.

• Repeat. The number of repeats depends on the individual. Start with a comfortable six or eight squats and build up to as many as you can sustain. You might try for 12 to 15 a day, but, if this is too ambitious, do a set of six, rest and do another six.

The slower the squat, the more difficult it is. When you have mastered the exercise you can vary it by going down in two stages and coming up in two stages, pausing at each one. If you are strong and have good balance, do the squats without a chair, balancing the body with arms stretched forward.

### Thigh stretch with support (quadriceps)

This is an exercise for stretching out the quadriceps after the squats.

- Hold on to a wall or chair for support.
- **A** Keeping the knee of the supporting leg soft, bring the heel of the other leg towards the bottom. Keep the knees together and tilt the pelvis forward to give a better stretch of the quadriceps.
- Hold and release. Breathe evenly throughout.
- Repeat the stretch on the other side.

## Extras for the brave

The package of strengthening and stretching exercises is above is geared toward the special needs associated with ageing. Many individuals, however, may wish to do more. How much will depend on your level of fitness. It is difficult to generalise. The example of Helen Klein in Chapter 4 gives heart to all of us. I have included in the following exercises the use of a wall. A little support to start with does no harm and can help in maintaining correct body alignment because by using a wall you can judge if you are standing straight or not. If these exercises are too easy for you there is nothing to stop any one from using the exercises given in Chapters 9 and 10. Well executed with correct body alignment, the following exercises which look deceptively easy may prove more difficult than you think. This is why they are also suitable for younger people.

Remember, you can always adjust the intensity of the exercise according to your needs. Now turn on the music!

### Back leg lift (gluteals)

- Stand facing the wall with your feet no more than hip distance apart.
- Place both hands on the wall for support.
- **A** Take a deep breath and then, as you exhale, let the navel subside and tilt the hips slightly forward, and extend the right leg to the back. This helps to keep the hips stable and prevents you from lifting the leg too far behind, causing the small of the back to sag. Keep the supporting leg soft, with a slight bend to the knee.

**B** • Lift and lower the extended right leg in a slow and controlled manner, pausing at the end of the lift to work harder. Breathe out as you lift and in as you lower.

• Repeat 6–8 times or as many times as is comfortable.

• Change leg.

You can vary the contraction. If you find that the supporting leg tires easily, then reduce the number of repeats and perhaps increase the number of sets instead. In this way you will find that there is less stress on the supporting leg. When you become stronger the stress will eventually disappear.

### Leg curls (gluteals and hamstring)

• Stand facing the wall with your feet no more than hip distance apart.

• Place both hands on the wall for support.

• Take a deep breath and then, as you exhale, let the navel subside, tilt the hips slightly forward and extend the right leg to the back. This is again to help keep the hips stable and prevent you from lifting the leg too far behind causing the small of the back to sag. Keep the supporting leg soft with a slight bend to the knee.

**A** • In the next out-breath, lift the extended leg off the floor and bend it to bring the heel towards the buttocks and then straighten. The movements should be slow and controlled, and the breathing even.

• Repeat 6–8 times or as many times as is comfortable.

• Change leg.

## Side leg lift (tensor fascia latae and gluteals)

- Stand next to a wall or a strong, firm chair (one that will not topple over) and place one hand on the wall/chair for support.

- Take a deep breath and then, as you exhale, let the navel subside and tilt the hips slightly forward. This gives the stability you need and stops the following movement from being a hip movement.

- Bring the leg furthest from the wall slightly out to the side and bend the body slightly towards the extended leg. This is the starting position. By bending towards the leg that you are going to work, you will relieve the supporting leg from carrying the full weight of the body.

**A** |
- Lift and lower the extended leg in a slow and controlled manner. This 'working leg' should be straight, but keep the knee slightly bent. Breathe out as you lift and in as you lower.

- Repeat 6–8 times or as many times as is comfortable.

- Change leg.

You should feel a tightening of the buttocks and the outer thigh muscle. Beginners who find that the supporting leg tires easily should re-examine their body alignment. One of the most common problems is keeping the supporting leg rigid and leaning towards it. This brings the whole weight of the body onto the supporting leg, resulting in the stress – keep the supporting leg soft.

Another mistake is to lift the 'working' leg using the hip, so do check your body alignment. It may also be necessary to do fewer lifts per set and incorporate lots of rests in between. When you gain strength you will find that the stress on the supporting leg goes and all the work-out is on the leg desired! Take heart, even those in their early twenties can have difficulties initially in getting into the right position.

As you gain strength you can increase the number of repeats or sets of these exercises. Vary also the speed in the lifting and lowering of the leg, but take it easy to start with; give top priority to perfecting the technique. Then build up to more repeats and sets.

It is important to stretch out the leg muscles after the exercise. In particular, the calves and the hamstrings have to be lengthened to maintain their flexibility. Any of the stretches outlined in Chapter 6 on warm-ups can be used if it is difficult to stretch out on the floor, but hold them marginally longer (12 to 15 seconds) and use support such as a wall or chair if necessary. The main aim is to return the muscles to their original length rather than develop their length.

Since the positions of these stretches have already been covered earlier, I have provided only two illustrations in this chapter to show how a wall (or chair) might be used for support in stretching out the calves and hamstring at the end of the work-out. For those with no difficulties in going onto the floor and who are supple, some of the floor stretches illustrated in Chapter 10 on flexibility training may be used. However, these are advanced and I would suggest using only the static position for stretching the hamstring, at least to start with (see p. 122).

### Calf stretch using wall (gastrocnemius)

- Stand facing a wall, about one foot away with enough space to lean forward towards it.
- Lean forward and place both hands on the wall for support.

A
- Take a deep breath and exhale, tucking in the tummy and placing one leg behind you, bending the front leg in the process.

- The knee of the bent leg should be aligned above the ankle to avoid any stress on the knee.
- The heel of the extended leg should be on the floor with toes pointed forward for proper alignment.
- The upper trunk of the body is inclined slightly forward because a vertical position would stress the lower back.
- Hold the stretch on the calf of the extended leg for 12 to 15 seconds and release.
- Repeat on the other side.

You will find that, supported by the wall, the hold can be held for more than 12 to 15 seconds without discomfort. You can also stretch the calves out more by bringing the leg further out behind.

### Hamstring stretch using wall

- Stand with your side to the wall and place one hand on the wall for support.

A
- Take a deep breath and, as you exhale bend the leg nearest the wall (the supporting leg) and extend the other leg in front. You should be absolutely stable and comfortable.

**B** • Bend the body slightly, placing the free hand on the thigh of the supporting leg for greater stability, and gently move the upper trunk forward until you feel a stretch in the hamstring of the extended leg. Hold for 12 to 15 seconds and release. Be careful not to 'slump' the body when moving forward.

• Gently come back to the upright position.

• Repeat on the other side.

Appendix 4, Programme 5 (p. 208) provides suggestions on how to structure exercise programmes for the over-50s.

I lead an over-fifties class in a local hall. Such classes offer a social occasion as well as an opportunity to improve or maintain fitness and health. Attention to general well-being is an important aspect of fusion fitness.

# Nutrition for changing needs

Nutritional needs do change with age. The decline in lean body mass and basal metabolic rate together with reduced physical activity mean that the body's energy requirement diminishes. If the same calories are consumed as in earlier years, the result will be increased weight and even obesity. Energy requirements can fall by as much as 5 per cent for each decade after 40 years of age (see Chapter 4, p. 45 on the recommended daily calorie allowance).

Although the total energy requirement is less, other nutritional needs increase because of the greater need for regeneration and repair. While the amounts of vitamins and minerals required by those over 50 years of age are about the same as those of a younger adult, the need for protein increases. In the US, for example, a consumption of 60–75 g of protein a day, depending on body weight, is recommended for those over 50 by the American Association of Dietitians. In the UK no additional quantities of protein are suggested, but the recommendation for the elderly to have foods that are concentrated sources of proteins, vitamins and minerals reflects a similar view. This emphasis on the need for a more nutritious diet is seen also in the guidelines on eating habits for the elderly in Japan. They are encouraged to 'eat side dishes first', rather than the main staple rice, and to 'eat every kind of food'.

The increased requirement for nutrients combined with a decreased ability of the digestive system to absorb them, makes it vital to choose foods of high nutrient density that are easy to absorb. Elderly people have difficulties in digesting and absorbing calcium, vitamin $B_{12}$, vitamin C and iron. Older people often develop difficulties in digesting milk because the body no longer produces enough lactase, the enzyme that digests lactose in milk. In some cases the medication taken to combat illnesses associated with ageing interfere with the absorption of calcium. Corticosteroids prescribed for rheumatoid arthritis, for example, decrease calcium absorption and increase its excretion in the urine. It is important, therefore, to include in the diet foods that are good sources of these nutrients to ensure an adequate supply of them. Eating hard cheeses that are low in lactose, yoghurt with active cultures or drinking lactose-reduced milk or buttermilk are some suggestions for those with problems digesting milk.

Replenishing vitamin $B_{12}$ is thought to help reverse lapses of memory and improve coordination and balance because of the role it plays in protecting nerve cells. Incorporating a wide range of animal protein in the diet should meet the requirements of both the amino acid lysine and vitamin $B_{12}$. Although a balanced diet should provide an adequate supply of vitamin $B_{12}$, supplements might be needed by individuals undergoing treatment with antibiotics.

Ensure a balanced intake of all vitamins and minerals (see boxes on pp. 164 and 174). These are as important for the elderly as they are for the young. In the US, people over 50 are encouraged to boost their consumption of antioxidants. Vitamins C and E are important antioxidants that can help mop up harmful free radicals that can damage health. They also help repair the damage to body cells caused by them. Supplements are not really needed if plenty of fruits and vegetables are eaten. A good rule of thumb is to have at least five servings of fruits and vegetables a day. Medical advice should be sought before taking any supplements.

Foods high in sugar should be avoided because they only contribute calories. An easy step is to stop drinking sweetened beverages. The same is true of fatty foods, although essential fatty acids (see Chapter 12) must be eaten because of their roles in hormone production and the nervous system. It is important, therefore, to be selective with fat consumption. The consumption of saturated fats such as hard animal fats should be reduced in favour of unsaturated fats of the kind found in fish oils, and vegetable oils such as sunflower and olive oil. Sodium consumption should be moderated because of its association with hypertension. One effective way is to gradually reduce the salt used in cooking. Saltiness is an acquired taste that can be reversed with time. Salt with reduced sodium is also available.

The weakening of the smooth muscles of the gastrointestinal tract that comes with age often results in constipation. To offset this elderly people should ensure that they have sufficient fibre in their diet. Soluble fibre helps lower cholesterol and manage blood glucose levels while insoluble fibre alleviates digestive disorders and may help prevent colon cancer. Adequate fluid must also be consumed to maintain the water balance of the body and to contribute to regular bowel habits. The requirement to drink at least eight glasses of water a day remains unchanged with age. Unfortunately many older people do not drink enough because of the discomfort associated with a full bladder and weak bladder control.

The following simple guidelines should prove useful to help you arrive at a suitable diet and sensible pattern of food consumption.

## To help digestion and the absorption of nutrients

- Eat regularly and often
- Do not miss meals
- Eat small quantities at each meal
- Eat and chew slowly

## To avoid constipation and improve the efficiency of the kidneys and gastrointestinal tract

- Drink plenty of water, but in small quantities. The excess gas in the digestive system which causes feelings of discomfort and bloatedness is frequently a result of swallowing air when eating and drinking
- Moderate the consumption of tea and coffee
- Reduce the intake of refined carbohydrates such as sugar
- Incorporate lots of fibre in the diet
- Avoid excess consumption of salt
- Moderate the consumption of alcohol

## To avoid unnecessary weight gain

- Avoid foods and drinks high in sugar
- Avoid foods high in saturated fat

## To ensure adequate nutrition intake

- Eat small quantities of a wide variety of foods
- Include in the daily diet:
  - carbohydrates and starches
  - lean meat, poultry, fish (especially oily fish) or eggs
  - dairy produce
  - vegetables and fruits
  - pulses and beans

| Some beneficial foods for older people* | |
|---|---|
| Beansprouts | Economical, good source of vitamin C (single helping provides ¾ of adult RDA), B complex, easily digestible protein, produces less intestinal wind than unsprouted beans, low in calories |
| Chicken (without skin) | Economical, low fat, easily digestible protein, rich in vitamin B |
| Dried fruits | Good source of fibre, vitamin A, iron, calcium and energy |
| Fish, especially oily (sardines, mackerel, salmon) | Excellent source of vitamin A and D, omega-3 fatty acids, protein, iron |
| Beans, peas and lentils | Eaten with food grains provide a good source of easily digestible protein, B vitamins and fibre |
| Strawberries | Soft and easily eaten, rich in vitamin C and beta-carotene, help to encourage the excretion of uric acid associated with gout and arthritis |
| Garlic | Lowers cholesterol, reduces blood pressure, protects the heart, helps fight infections and is believed to neutralise cancer causing chemicals |
| Turnips | Eliminate uric acid |

*This is not a complete or exhaustive list. It highlights just a few selected foods that meet the requirements and problems generally associated with ageing.

To ensure that the nutrients in foods can be absorbed, special attention needs to be paid to preparation. Soups, for example, are a good medium because they are easy to consume and digest and they also provide fluid. Mincing lean meat or poultry is ideal for those with problems with chewing. Steaming and grilling reduces the need for fat and the high temperatures help seal in the nutritional goodness of the food.

Some people prepare food with a weighing machine and a list of calorie contents, but there is really no need for this. With experience and a little common sense it will soon be easy to strike a happy balance in your daily diet. Do not be afraid to experiment with new dishes that offer or increase the variety of your diet. Above all else enjoy your food!

## APPENDIX

# Body Mass Index (BMI) in imperial measurements

To determine the BMI when weight and height are given in pounds and inches, divide the weight in pounds by the square of the height in inches and multiply by 703.

For example, if the weight of a person is 130 lb and his/her height is 64 in., then the BMI of this person would be 22.

$$\frac{130}{64 \times 64} \times 703 = 22.3$$

The calculation is already undertaken in the following table which provides BMI for body weights in pounds and heights in inches. To read your BMI, find your height in the left column, and move across the row to the weight corresponding to yours. As mentioned previously (see p. 11), for middle-aged adults, BMIs ranging from between 20 to 27 are normal. BMIs over 27 indicate overweight, and those over 29 indicate obesity. WHO's classification of what represents normal, overweight and obese is marginally different. A normal BMI is between 18.5 and 24.9, overweight is between 25 and 29.9 and those over 30 would be classified as obese.

## Determining your body mass index (BMI) – (imperial measurements)[28]

| BMI (kg/m²) | 19 | 20 | 21 | 22 | 23 | 24 | 25 | 26 | 27 | 28 | 29 | 30 | 35 | 40 |
|---|---|---|---|---|---|---|---|---|---|---|---|---|---|---|
| Height (in) | Body Weight (lb) | | | | | | | | | | | | | |
| 58 | 91 | 96 | 100 | 105 | 110 | 115 | 119 | 124 | 129 | 134 | 138 | 143 | 167 | 191 |
| 59 | 94 | 99 | 104 | 109 | 114 | 119 | 124 | 128 | 133 | 138 | 143 | 148 | 173 | 198 |
| 60 | 97 | 102 | 107 | 112 | 118 | 123 | 128 | 133 | 138 | 143 | 148 | 153 | 179 | 204 |
| 61 | 100 | 106 | 111 | 116 | 122 | 127 | 132 | 137 | 143 | 148 | 153 | 158 | 185 | 211 |
| 62 | 104 | 109 | 115 | 120 | 126 | 131 | 136 | 142 | 147 | 153 | 158 | 164 | 191 | 218 |
| 63 | 107 | 113 | 118 | 124 | 130 | 135 | 141 | 146 | 152 | 158 | 163 | 169 | 197 | 225 |
| 64 | 110 | 116 | 122 | 128 | 134 | 140 | 145 | 151 | 157 | 163 | 169 | 174 | 204 | 232 |
| 65 | 114 | 120 | 126 | 132 | 138 | 144 | 150 | 156 | 162 | 168 | 174 | 180 | 210 | 240 |
| 66 | 118 | 124 | 130 | 136 | 142 | 148 | 155 | 161 | 167 | 173 | 179 | 186 | 216 | 247 |
| 67 | 121 | 127 | 134 | 140 | 146 | 153 | 159 | 166 | 172 | 178 | 185 | 191 | 223 | 255 |
| 68 | 125 | 131 | 138 | 144 | 151 | 158 | 164 | 171 | 177 | 184 | 190 | 197 | 230 | 262 |
| 69 | 128 | 135 | 142 | 149 | 155 | 162 | 169 | 176 | 182 | 189 | 196 | 203 | 236 | 270 |
| 70 | 132 | 139 | 146 | 153 | 160 | 167 | 174 | 181 | 188 | 195 | 202 | 207 | 243 | 278 |
| 71 | 136 | 143 | 150 | 157 | 165 | 172 | 179 | 186 | 193 | 200 | 208 | 215 | 250 | 286 |
| 72 | 140 | 147 | 154 | 162 | 169 | 177 | 184 | 191 | 199 | 206 | 213 | 221 | 258 | 294 |
| 73 | 144 | 151 | 159 | 166 | 174 | 182 | 189 | 197 | 204 | 212 | 219 | 227 | 265 | 302 |
| 74 | 148 | 155 | 163 | 171 | 179 | 186 | 194 | 202 | 210 | 218 | 225 | 233 | 272 | 311 |
| 75 | 152 | 160 | 168 | 176 | 184 | 192 | 200 | 208 | 216 | 224 | 232 | 240 | 279 | 319 |
| 76 | 156 | 164 | 172 | 180 | 189 | 197 | 205 | 213 | 221 | 230 | 238 | 246 | 287 | 328 |

## APPENDIX

# Calculating the Basal Metabolic Rate (BMR)

The simplest way to calculate BMR is to multiply 0.9 (women) or 1.0 (men) by the weight of the individual in kilograms and 24, the total number of hours in a day. This was the formula used as an example in Chapter 4. The lower factor for women is because their energy expenditure is generally smaller than men because of differences in body composition.

In the example given in Chapter 4 of a woman weighing 63 kg, the estimated BMR is:

$$63 \times 0.9 \times 24 = 1361 \text{ Calories}$$

More elaborate formulae exist for the calculation of BMR. The *Harris-Benedict Equation*, which is based on a biometric study of basal metabolism in the US, takes into account sex, age, weight and height as follows:

*Males*      $66 + (13.7 \times W) + (5 \times H) - (6.8 \times A)$

*Females*    $655 + (9.6 \times W) + (1.9 \times H) - (4.7 \times A)$

where     W = body weight in kg
          H = height in cm
          A = age in years

Thus, a 40 year old woman, weighing 63 kg and 163 cm tall (about 5' 4") has an estimated BMR of:

$$655 + (9.6 \times 63) + (1.9 \times 163) - (4.7 \times 40) = 1382 \text{ Calories}$$

In the UK, BMR calculations applied by the Department of Environment, Food and Rural Affairs (DEFRA, previously MAFF), take into account sex, age group and weight and use the following formulae:

| Age group (years) | Formulae for BMR |
|---|---|
| *Males* | |
| 10–17 | 17.7 W + 657 |
| 18–29 | 15.1 W + 692 |
| 30–59 | 11.5 W + 873 |
| *Females* | |
| 10–17 | 13.4 W + 692 |
| 18–29 | 14.8 W + 487 |
| 30–59 | 8.3 W + 846 |

where

$$W = \text{body weight in kilograms}$$

Using the same example of a woman of 40 year old woman weighing 63 kg, the estimated BMR is:

$$(8.3 \times 63) + 846 = 1369 \text{ Calories}$$

As you can see, differences in BMR occur according to which formula is used to make the calculation.

# APPENDIX

# 3

# Measures and conversion factors

The book uses the calorie as a measure of food energy rather than the international standard unit, the Joule, because of the widespread use of the calorie in the food industry and in popular literature related to food and diet. The Joule was adopted as a measure of energy because the value of the calorie varies slightly according to the temperature of the water at which measurements are made. For ease of calculation, however, one calorie is taken as being equivalent to 4.2 Joules. Because the calorie is a small unit of measurement, the kilocalorie (kcal) or Calorie, which is 1000 times larger, is generally used (in some books, authors have dropped the capital letter used to denote the larger unit which may lead to some confusion). Mass is generally given in kilograms (kg) or grams (g). Other measurements of mass used in the book are the microgram (mcg), which is a millionth of a gram, and the milligram (mg), which is thousandth of a gram. Height is given in metres.

The following are the conversion factors for the metric measures on length/height/mass/weight/liquid volume used in the book. To convert from the previous imperial system used in the UK to metric, multiply by the factor provided. To convert from metric to the imperial system, divide by the factor.

| Length and height | |
|---|---|
| yard: metre | 0.9144 |
| feet: metre | 0.3048 |
| inch: centimetre | 2.54 |

| Mass/weight | |
|---|---|
| stone: kilograms | 6.3503 |
| pounds: kilograms | 0.4536 |
| ounces: grams | 28.3495 |

| Liquid volume | |
|---|---|
| pint: litre | 0.568 |

where
microgram = one millionth of a gram
milligram = one thousandth of a gram

# APPENDIX

# Training programmes

How you structure your own training programme depends on what you seek from the exercise. Numerous variations and combinations can be made of the different exercises illustrated in the book. The following are only suggestions and you may wish to modify the combination as well as the number of sets or reps of the different exercises you perform. A suggestion of 1 x 8 means 1 set of 8 reps; sometimes a range of reps, for example 8–10, is suggested. You should listen to your own body to know what is right for you.

The exercises are structured to provide training to all the major muscle groups, targeting common problem areas. They are sequenced in a way that minimises the need to change position. For example, there are instances where it is more convenient to perform different exercises on different muscle groups on both legs while lying on the same side before changing positions.

You will need a mat, preferably non-slip, for the floor exercises.

# Programme 1 (1 hour)

*All round fitness – cardio-vascular improvements, motor skill, muscle strength and endurance flexibility training*

This programme is divided into three components consisting of a warm up/aerobic section (25 mins), toning (25 mins) and stretch/relaxation (10 mins).

### 1. Warm-up/Aerobic training (lively motivating music)

If you are doing this on your own and at home, you might find it easier to combine the warm-up with the aerobic training. Start, say with a gentle/brisk march to music, and progress to a gentle dance, adapting the various moves such as side steps, heel digs, grapevine and box step to a simple routine. One simple way forward is to choose dance steps that add up to counts of eight. A rumba, mambo or foxtrot are examples. Repeat the moves until you feel warm and pliable.

Alternatively, you could go for a walk; start out slowly to raise your pulse gradually, and after about 5 minutes increase the speed of the walk until you are walking briskly. Continue for a further, say 10 minutes, and then head for home, still keeping to a brisk pace. Slow down as you approach home. The very fit participant, however, might wish to warm-up with a brisk walk for 5 minutes and slow jog for say 15 minutes, before slowing down to a walk. Others might find it easier to alternate between brisk walks and slow jog every one to two minutes. At the end of the aerobic activity do the following:

- static (standing still) mobilising moves i.e. rotate hips, circle shoulders, bend sideways, turn the upper trunk, bend the knees, flex and point the feet (p. 60).

- mobilise the neck, turn the head from side to side in a slow and controlled manner, then bend the head forward and, supporting the back of the head with your palms, tilt the head back to stretch the front of the neck gently.

- short stretches to prepare (pp. 61–2).

## 2. Toning: beginners (slow music with strong beat)

| | | |
|---|---|---|
| Squats | 8–10 | p. 106 |
| Triceps extension | 1 x 8 | p. 117 |
| Chest press | 10–12 | p. 113 |
| or | | |
| Box press-ups | 1 x 6 | pp. 112–13 |
| Back leg lift | 12–16 | p. 99 |
| Hamstring leg curl | 12–16 each side | p. 110 |
| Toning the inner thigh | 12–16 | pp. 104–5 |
| Transverse abdominal squeeze incorporating pelvic floor component | 1 x 8, rest and repeat | p. 90 |
| Conventional crunch with fusion modification | 1 x 8 | p. 88 |
| Shoulder to knee | 1 x 8 each side | p. 95 |

### 3. Stretching/relaxation

The time shown indicates the length of hold.

| | | |
|---|---|---|
| The Yawn | 8–10 secs | p. 128 |
| Z-stretch | 10–12 secs | p. 128 |
| Hamstring | 30 secs each side | p. 122 |
| Thigh and shin | 30 secs each side | p. 134 |
| Feline stretch | 3 x 15 secs | p. 125 |
| Groin stretch | 30 secs | p. 133 |
| Roll back for the chest muscles | 8–10 secs | p. 129 |
| Roll-forward, upper back | 8–10 secs | p. 129 |
| Relaxation/quiet breathing | | |

# Programme 2 (1 hour)

*Strength and endurance (toning) training*

This is for intermediate to fairly advanced participants. Also divided into three components, it has a short warm-up (10 mins), 40 mins of toning and 10 mins of stretch and relaxation.

### 1. Warm-up (lively motivating music)

Brisk march, brisk knee bends, side steps; repeat until you feel warm. Then perform:

- static (standing still) mobilising moves i.e. rotate hips, circle shoulders, bend sideways, turn the upper trunk, bend the knees, and flex the feet (p. 60).
- mobilise the neck, turn the head from side to side in a slow and controlled manner, then bend the head forward and, supporting the back of the head with your palms, tilt the head back to stretch the front of the neck gently.
- short stretches to prepare (pp. 61–2).

### 2. Toning: intermediate–advanced (slow music with strong beat)

| | | |
|---|---|---|
| Back arm lifts | 8 | p. 118 |
| Scissoring the arm | 8 | p. 118 |
| | Repeat both exercises | |
| Pedal and stride resting on elbows | 2 x 8 single lifts, up for one and down for one<br>1 x 8 double lifts, up for two and down for two | pp. 107–8 |
| | Change sides and repeat | |

The following three exercises for the buttocks can be performed separately with rests in between for the intermediate participant or they could be performed without any breaks by the stronger participant.

| | | |
|---|---|---|
| Modified buttock lift, feet apart | 1 x 8 single lifts + 1 x 8 double lifts + 1 x 8 small pulsing single lifts | p. 103 |
| Modified buttock lift, knees in-and-out | 1 x 8 single + 1 x 8 double lifts | p. 103 |
| Modified buttock lift, knees and feet together | 1 x 8 single lifts + 1 x 4 double lifts + 1 x 8 small pulsing single lifts | p. 103 |
| Toning the inner thigh | 1 x 8 single lifts + 1 x 8 double lifts + 1 x 8 small pulsing single lifts | p. 104 |
| Toning the inner thigh, adding the crunch | 1 x 8 single lifts + 1 x 8 double lifts | p. 105 |
| | Change sides and repeat the two inner thigh exercises | |
| Floor press-ups half extension | 10 singles + 6 doubles (optional) | p. 113 |
| Conventional crunch with the fusion modification | 1 x 8 singles + 1 x 8 double lifts + 1 x 8 small pulsing lifts | pp. 88–9 |
| Transverse abdominal squeeze/ incorporate pelvic floor component | 1 x 12 | p. 90 |
| Reverse abdominal squeeze/ incorporate pelvic floor component | 1 x 8 singles + 1 x 8 doubles + 1 x 8 small pulsing movements | p. 91 |
| Reverse abdominal squeeze with extended legs | 1 x 8 singles + 1 x 8 doubles + 1 x 8 small pulsing movements | p. 92 |
| Side reach | 1 x 8 singles + 1 x 8 doubles + 1 x 8 small pulsing movements | pp. 94–5 |
| Back extension | 1 x 10 | p. 97 |

## 3. Stretching/relaxation

| | | |
|---|---|---|
| The yawn | 8–10 secs | p. 128 |
| Z-stretch | 10–12 secs | p. 128 |
| Thigh and shin | 30 seconds each side | p. 134 |
| Feline stretch | 1 x 15 secs | p. 125 |
| Prayer position | 1 x 15 secs | p. 126 |
| Forward bend hamstring and calf | 30 secs | pp. 134–5 |
| Wide angle stretch | 30 seconds | p. 133 |

| Roll-back for the chest muscles | 8–10 secs | p. 129 |
| Roll-forward, upper back | 8–10 secs | p. 129 |
| Relaxation/quiet breathing | | pp. 138–9 |

# Programme 3 (1 hour)

*Advanced strength and endurance (toning) training*

This is geared towards advanced participants with strong abdominal muscles. Its three components consist of a short warm-up (10 mins), 40 mins of toning and 10 mins of stretch and relaxation.

### 1. Warm-up (lively motivating music)

Brisk march, brisk knee bends, side steps; repeat the sequence until you feel warm. Then perform:

- static (standing still) mobilising moves i.e. rotate hips, circle shoulders, bend sideways, turn the upper trunk, bend the knees, and flex the feet (pp. 60–1).

- mobilise the neck, turning the head from side to side in a slow and controlled manner, then bend the head forward and, supporting the back of the head with your palms, tilt the head back to stretch the front of the neck gently.

- short stretches to prepare (pp. 61–2).

### 2. Toning: advanced (slow music with strong beat)

| The barre: lift, bend and stretch | 1 x 8, pause and repeat, 1 x 8<br>Change sides | pp. 108–9 |
| or | | |
| Pedal and stride resting on elbows | 1 x 8 single lifts, up for one and down for one<br>1 x 4 double lifts, up for two and down for two | pp. 107–8 |
| Pedal and stride, full sitting position | 1 x 8 single lifts, up for one and down for one<br>1 x 8 double lifts, up for two and down for two | p. 108 |

The following five exercises should be done in sequence first on one and then the other side:

| Straight back leg extension | 1 x 8 single lifts + 1 x 8 double lifts + 1 x 8 small pulsing single lifts | p. 101 |
|---|---|---|
| Right angle lift | 1 x 8 single lifts + 1 x 8 double lifts + 1 x 8 small pulsing single lifts | p. 102 |
| Acute angle moving in | 1 x 8 single lifts + 1 x 8 double lifts + 1 x 8 small pulsing single lifts | p. 102 |
| Toning the inner thigh | 1 x 8 single lifts + 1 x 8 double lifts + 1 x 8 small pulsing single lifts | p. 104 |
| Toning the inner thigh, adding the crunch | 1 x 8 single lifts + 1 x 8 double lifts | p. 105 |

After completing the sequence on both sides, continue with:

| Floor press-ups half extension or full extension | 10 singles + 6 doubles | p. 113 |
|---|---|---|
| Transverse abdominal squeeze/pelvic floor | 1 x 12 | p. 90 |
| Reverse abdominal squeeze/pelvic floor | 1 x 8 singles + 1 x 8 doubles + 1 x 8 small pulsing movements | p. 91 |
| Reverse abdominal squeeze extended legs | 1 x 8 singles + 1 x 8 doubles + 1 x 8 small pulsing movements | p. 92 |
| Moon walk I | 2 x 8 singles | p. 93 |
| Moon walk II | 2 x 8 singles | p. 93 |
| Z-position | 2 x 8 singles | p. 96 |
| Back extension | 1 x 12 | p. 97 |
| Triceps extension/buttocks off the floor | 2 x 8 singles | p. 117 |

### 3.Stretching /relaxation

| The yawn | 8–10 secs | p. 128 |
|---|---|---|
| Z-stretch | 10–12 secs | p. 128 |
| Thigh and shin | 30 secs | p. 134 |
| Feline stretch | 1 x 15 secs | p. 125 |
| Prayer position | 1 x 15 secs | p. 126 |
| Forward bend hamstring and calf | 30 sec | pp. 134–5 |
| Wide angle stretch | 30 secs | p. 133 |
| Roll back for the chest muscles | 8–10 secs | p. 129 |
| Roll-forward, upper back | 8–10 secs | p. 129 |
| Relaxation | | p. 138 |

# Programme 4 (1 hour)

*Stretch and tone: intermediate*

This is for participants who are familiar with the static stretch positions and are seeking greater strength and flexibility. Its three components consist of a short warm-up (5 minutes), 30 minutes of toning and 25 minutes of stretch and relaxation. The stretch exercises are organised in a way that allows you to proceed easily from one position to another giving a sequence of smooth flowing movements.

### 1. Warm-up (lively motivating music)

Brisk march, brisk knee bends, side steps; repeat the sequence until you feel warm. Then perform:

- static (standing still) mobilising moves i.e. rotate hips, circle shoulders, bend sideways, turn the upper trunk, bend the knees, and flex the feet (p. 60).
- mobilise the neck, turn the head from side to side in a slow and controlled manner, then bend the head forward and, supporting the head with your palms, tilt the head back to stretch the front of the neck gently.
- short stretches to prepare (pp. 61–2).

## 2. Toning (slow music with strong beat)

| Squats | 1 x 8 singles + 1 x 8 doubles + 1 x 8 pulsing movements | p. 106 |
|---|---|---|
| Back arm lift | 1 x 8 | p. 118 |
| Scissoring the arm | 1 x 8 | p. 118 |
| Repeat arm exercises | | |
| Chest press | 10–12 | p. 113 |
| Pedal and stride resting on elbows | 1 x 8 single lifts – up for one and down for one<br>1 x 4 double lifts – up for two and down for two | p. 107 |

The following five exercises should be done in sequence first on one and then the other side:

| Straight back leg extension | 1 x 8 single lifts + 1 x 8 double lifts + 1 x 8 small pulsing single lifts | p. 101 |
|---|---|---|
| Right angle lift | 1 x 8 single lifts + 1 x 8 double lifts + 1 x 8 small pulsing single lifts | p. 102 |
| Acute angle moving in | 1 x 8 single lifts + 1 x 8 double lifts + 1 x 8 small pulsing single lifts | p. 102 |
| Toning the inner thigh | 1 x 8 single lifts + 1 x 8 double lifts + 1 x 8 small pulsing single lifts | p. 104 |
| Toning the inner thigh, adding the crunch | 1 x 8 single lifts + 1 x 8 double lifts | p. 105 |

After completing the sequence on both sides, continue with:

| Transverse abdominal squeeze/pelvic floor | 1 x 12 | p. 90 |
|---|---|---|
| Reverse abdominal squeeze/pelvic floor | 1 x 8 singles lifts + 1 x 8 double lifts + 1 x 8 small pulsing lifts | p. 91 |
| Reverse abdominal squeeze with extended legs | 1 x 8 single lifts + 1 x 8 doubles lifts + 1 x 8 small pulsing movements | p. 92 |
| Moon walk I | 2 x 8 singles | p. 93 |
| Side reach | 1 x 8 singles + 1 x 8 double | p. 94 |

### 3. Stretching/relaxation (calm quiet music)

Lie on your back:

| The yawn | 8–10 secs | p. 128 |
|---|---|---|
| Z-stretch | 15 secs each side | p. 128 |
| Static and active hamstring stretch | 25–30 secs. Release, and repeat on the same leg. Stretch each side | p. 122 |
| Bum stretch | 15–20 secs. Repeat on other side | p. 131 |

Between each of the above stretches, bring both knees to the chest exhaling as you do so, and rock *gently* from side to side to release the stretches. Breathe evenly as you rock.

Turn over to lie on your front.

| Thigh and shin | 30 secs each side | p. 134 |
|---|---|---|
| Feline stretch | 15 secs | p. 125 |
| Prayer position | 15 secs | p. 126 |
| Half serpent | 15 secs | p. 126 |

Repeat the feline stretch, prayer and half serpent, three times in a smooth fluid manner. Then, if you wish, go into:

| Full serpent/half cobra | 15 secs + 15 secs | p. 127 |
|---|---|---|
| Prayer position | 15 secs | p. 126 |

Sit up tall.

| Wide angle stretch | 20 secs, release and repeat for 30 secs | p. 133 |
|---|---|---|
| Stretching in flight | 30 secs, release and repeat Change leg | p. 136 |
| Roll-back for the chest muscles | 10–12 secs | p. 129 |
| Roll-forward, upper back | 10–12 secs | p. 129 |
| Forearm twist | 12–15 secs, release and repeat | p. 130 |
| Relaxation | 5–7 mins | p. 138 |

# Programme 5 (20 minutes)

*50 Plus gentle toning and stretching*

This is for beginners. For those who are used to exercise and have stronger muscles, the following exercise programme is still applicable, support might not be necessary in some of the positions which I have indicated. You should listen to your body. The exercises focus on strengthening and maintaining the flexibility of those major muscle groups that generally pose the most problems as you get older. The duration of the programme is just 20 minutes, but I suggest that you do follow it at least three times a week, combined with a heart/lung activity, such as walking, swimming or dancing. If you do the programme immediately on returning from a walk, the effect is optimised. If you do not, then you should start with a short warm-up.

### Warm-up (slow music with strong beat)

Start with a march, followed by side steps and box steps. Repeat the sequence until you feel quite warm. Then mobilise the neck (turn from side to side, tilt from side to side), circle the shoulders, turn the torso, first to one side then the other, rotate the hips, bend and straighten the knees gently, flex and point the feet take each one in turn. See p. 60.

### Tone and stretch (slow music with a good beat or light soothing music)

| | | |
|---|---|---|
| Squat with support | 1 x 6, rest, 1 x 6. More advanced students should squat without support and increase reps slightly. | p. 184 |
| Thigh stretch with support | Hold for 10–12 sec, change leg | p. 185 |
| Back leg lift | 1 x 6, rest, 1 x 6. More advanced students increase reps (2 x 8) without rest in between. | pp. 185–6 |
| Leg curls | 1 x 6, rest, 1 x 6. More advanced students increase reps (2 x 8) without rest in between. | p. 186 |
| Side leg lifts | 1 x 6, rest, 1 x 6, More advanced students increase reps (2 x 8) without rest in between. | p. 187 |
| Hamstring stretch | 10–12 secs, release. Repeat for 20 secs. Change leg | pp. 188–9 |
| Calf stretch | 10–12 secs, release. Repeat 20 secs. Change leg | p. 188 |
| Standing feline stretch | 10–12 secs x 3 | p. 183 |

On the floor:

| Scaling wall with pelvic floor | 1 x 6, rest, 1 x 6 | p. 180 |
| --- | --- | --- |
| Advanced: Wall walk | 2 x 4, rest, 2 x 4 | p. 181 |

To end the session:

Stand with your feet hip distance apart, making sure that the body is aligned and balanced. Inhale and as you exhale, slowly turn the torso to the right, hold for 6 seconds then come back to the centre. Repeat on left. Bring both arms above the head and stretch up to the ceiling. Then go into another standing feline stretch, release and repeat (see p. 183). Gently unfold and straighten the body, roll the shoulders, turn the head from side to side, gentle even breathing.

# Further reading

Aaberg, Everett, 'Full range movement, fact or fallacy', in *Fitpro* Oct/Nov 2000

American Council on Exercise, *Group Fitness Instructor Manual*, ACE, 2000

Barlow, Wilfred, *The Alexander Principle*, Victor Gollancz Ltd, 1990

Bean, Anita, 'Protein the powerhouse', in *Fitpro*, Feb/March 2001

Berk, Lotte, and Prince, Jean, *The Lotte Berk Method of Exercise*, Quartet Books, 1978

Bingham, Sheila, *Dictionary of Nutrition: A Consumer's Guide to the Facts of Food*, Barrie and Jenkins, 1977

Bird, Steve, 'Is exercise really good for us?', in *Biologist* Vol 44:5, Nov 1997

Blakey, Paul, *The Muscle Book*, Bibliotek Books, 1992

Brennan, Richard, *The Alexander Technique Workbook*, Element Books Ltd, 1998

British Medical Association, *Complete Guide to Family Health Encyclopaedia*, Dorling Kindersley, 1995

Cook, Simon, and Toms, Tony, *Royal Marine Commando Exercises*, Sphere Books Ltd, 1990

Cullum, Rodney, and Mowbray, Lesley, *The English YMCA Guide to Exercise to Music*, Pelham Books, 1992

Donovan, Grant, McNamara, Jane and Gianoli, Peter, *Exercise Danger*, Wellness Australia Pty Ltd, 1988

Egger, Gary, and Champion, Nigel, (eds), *The Fitness Leader's Handbook*, 3rd edn, Kangaroo Press, 1997

FAO, *Joint FAO/WHO Expert Consultation on Human Vitamin and Mineral Requirements, 21–30 September, 1998* (Rev. July 2000), FAO

Fox, Stuart Ira, *Human Physiology*, 5th edn, Wm. C. Brown Publishers, 1996

Garn, Stanley M., 'Human Evolution', New Encyclopedia Britannica, Macropaedia (Indepth Knowledge) 18, 1997, 803–54

Gray, John, *Your Guide to the Alexander Technique*, Victor Gollancz Ltd, 1990

Hegarty, Vincent, *Nutrition, Food and the Environment*, Eagan Press, 1995

Hewett, James, *Yoga*, Hodder Headline, 1997

Hicks, Andrew, McGill, Stuart, and Hughson, Richard, 'Tissue oxygenation by near-infrared spectorscopy and muscle blood flow during isometric contractions of the forearm', *Canadian Journal of Applied Physiology*, 24(3) 1999

Hughes, Joyce (ed), *Your Greatest Guide to Calories*, John Starr, 1980

*Journal of Sports History* (Spring) 20(1):1–24, 1993

Kosich, Daniel, 'Functional kinesiology movement analysis', in *Fitpro*, Oct/Nov 2000

McFarlane, Stewart, *The Complete Book of T'ai Chi*, Dorling Kindersley, 1997

Marchall, Janette, and Heughan, Anne, *Eat for Life Diet*, Vermillion, 1992

Mehta, Mira, *How to Use Yoga*, Lorenz Book, 1994

Menezes, Allan, *Complete Guide to Joseph H. Pilates' Techniques of Physical Conditioning*, Hunter House, 2000

Ministry of Agriculture, Fisheries and Food, *Manual of Nutrition*, 10th edn, The Stationary Office Books, London, 1995

Newsholme, Eric, Leech, Tony, and Duester, Glenda, *Keep on Running, The Science of Training and Performance*, John Wiley & Sons, 1994

Pawlett, Raymond, *T'ai Chi: A Practical Introduction*, An Oceana Book, 1999

Peeke, Pamela, 'When stress makes you fat', *Fitpro*, Aug/Sept 2000

Pinckney, Callan, *Callanetics Countdown*, Ebury Press, London, 1990

Reader's Digest, *Good Health Fact Book*, Reader's Digest Association, 1999

——*Foods that Harm, Foods that Heal*, Reader's Digest Association, 1997

Robinson, Lynne, and Thomson, Gordon, *Pilates*, Pan Books, 1999

——Fisher, Helge, Knox, Jacqueline and Thomson, Gordon, *The Official Body Control Pilates Manual*, Macmillan Publishers Ltd, 2000

Rosser, Mo, *Body Fitness and Exercise: Basic Theory and Practice for Therapists*, Hodder & Stoughton, 1999

Schulze, Sonja, 'Managing patello-femoral pain', in *Fitness Network*, June/July 2000

Shave, Robert, and Whyte, Greg, 'Can the heart fatigue?', in *Fitpro*, Aug/Sept 2000

Smith, Tony (ed), *The Human Body*, Dorling Kindersley, 1995

Stewart, Mary, *Yoga*, Headway Lifeguides, 1998

——*Yoga Over 50*, Little Brown, 1998

Stroud, Mike, *Survival of the Fittest: Understanding Health and Peak Physical Performance*, Random House, 1998

Troop, Nick, and Seato, Steven, *The Handbook of Running*, Pelham Books, 1997

Williams, Peter L. *et al* (eds), *Gray's Anatomy*, 37th edn, Churchill Livingston, 1989

# Selected useful websites

www.bmb.leeds.ac.uk/illingworth/muscle
This website of the School of Biochemistry and Molecular Biology, University of Leeds, has detailed and well-illustrated explanations of the structure of muscles and their function.

www.eatright.org
The American Dietetic Association website provides good and extensive coverage of the nutritional contents of different foods and includes information on the special requirements for the elderly, albeit relating principally to the US.

www.mayoclinic.com
The Mayo Clinic website includes concise information on sports injuries, their cause and treatment.

www.meddean.luc.edu/lumen/MedEd/GrossAnatomy/dissector/mml/index.html
This website of the Loyola University Medical Education Network gives concise information on muscles, including their origin, insertion, nerve supply and action.

www.nismat.org/index.html
Created by the Nicholas Institute of Sports Medicine and Athletic Trauma (NISMAT) at Lenox Hill Hospital, New York, this website has an excellent coverage of exercise physiology, nutrition, athletic training as well as muscle contraction and energy supply.

www.nutrition.org.uk
The British Nutrition Foundation website provides useful data on nutrition in the UK.

www.pueblo.gsa.gov/press/nfcpubs/
The website of the Federal Communication Information Center has a wide range of articles including several on health, nutrition and related topics.

www.runnersworld.co.uk/injury/injury2.html
This website is a good information source for sports injuries, especially those associated with running.

# Sources and References

[1] Newsholme, E., Leech, T., Duester, G., *Keep on Running*, John Wiley & Sons, Inc., 1994

[2] Allied Dunbar National Fitness Survey, 1992

[3] British Heart Foundation Survey, 2002

[4] Adapted from the data in the Statistical Bulletin, Metropolitan Life Insurance Company, 1983

[5] Peeke, P., 'When stress makes you fat', *Fitpro* Aug/Sept 2000

[6] MAFF, *Manual of Nutrition*, HMSO, 1992; data on sports activities from First DataBank data, The Hearst Corporation, 1994

[7] *Recommended Dietary Allowance*, NAP, 1989; *Dietary Reference Values for Food Energy and Nutrients for the United Kingdom*, HMSO, 1991

[8] Stroud, M., *Survival of the Fittest: Understanding Health and Peak Physical Performance*, Random House, 1998

[9] *Journal of Sports History* 1993 (Spring) 20(1) 1–24

[10] See also Egger, G., Champion, N., Bolton, A., *The Fitness Leader's Handbook* 3rd ed, Kangaroo Press, 1997; Rosser, M., *Body Fitness: Basic Theory and Practice for Therapists*, Hodder and Stoughton, 1999; Donovan, G., McNamara, J., Gignoli, P., *Exercise Danger*, Wellness Australia, 1988

[11] Stewart, Mary, *Yoga*, Headway Lifeguides, 1998

[12] Hewett, James, *Yoga*, Hodder Headline, 1990

[13] Hicks, A., McGill, S., Hughson, R., 'Tissue oxygenation by near-infrared spectroscopy and muscle blood flow during isometric contractions of the forearm', *Canadian Journal of Applied Physiology* 1999 24 (3)

[14] The British Medical Association, *Complete Family Health Encyclopaedia*, Dorling Kindersley, 1996; Troop, N., Seato, S., *Handbook of Running*, Pelham Books, 1997

[15] *Trim the Fat from Your Diet*, British Heart Foundation, 2000

[16] DHSS Report, 'Public Health and Medicine', Sub 120 1969

[17] British Nutrition Foundation (1998) and WHO

[18] British Nutrition Foundation (1998) and WHO

[19] British Nutrition Foundation (1998)

[20] British Nutrition Foundation

[21] British Nutrition Foundation (1998) and COMA

[22] *Encyclopedia of Sports Science and Medicine*, American College of Sports Medicine

[23] Hegarty, V., *Nutrition, Food and the Environment*, Eagan Press, 1995; American Council on Exercise, *Group Fitness Instructor's Manual*, ACE, 2000

[24] Bean, A., 'Protein the Powerhouse', *Fitpro* Feb/March 2001

[25] Adapted from Gatorade Sports Science Institute

26 Joint FAO/WHO Expert Consultation on Human Vitamin and Mineral Requirements, 21–30 Sept. 1998 (rev. July 2000), FAO; Bingham, S., *Dictionary of Nutrition*, Barrie and Jenkins, 1977; British Medical Association, *Complete Family Health Encyclopedia*, Dorling Kindersley, 1996; Reader's Digest, *Foods that Harm, Foods that Heal*, Reader's Digest Association Ltd., 1997

27 Joint FAO/WHO Expert Consultation on Human Vitamin and Mineral Requirements, 21–30 Sept. 1998 (rev. July 2000), FAO; Bingham, S., *Dictionary of Nutrition*, Barrie and Jenkins, 1977; British Medical Association, *Complete Family Health Encyclopedia*, Dorling Kindersley, 1996; Reader's Digest, *Foods that Harm, Foods that Heal*, Reader's Digest Association, Ltd., 1997

28 www.consumer.gov/weightloss/bmi.htm

# Index

Note: page numbers in italic refer to tables and boxes, those in bold to figures. Initial capitals indicate exercises.